IMAGES
of America

TOMALES BAY

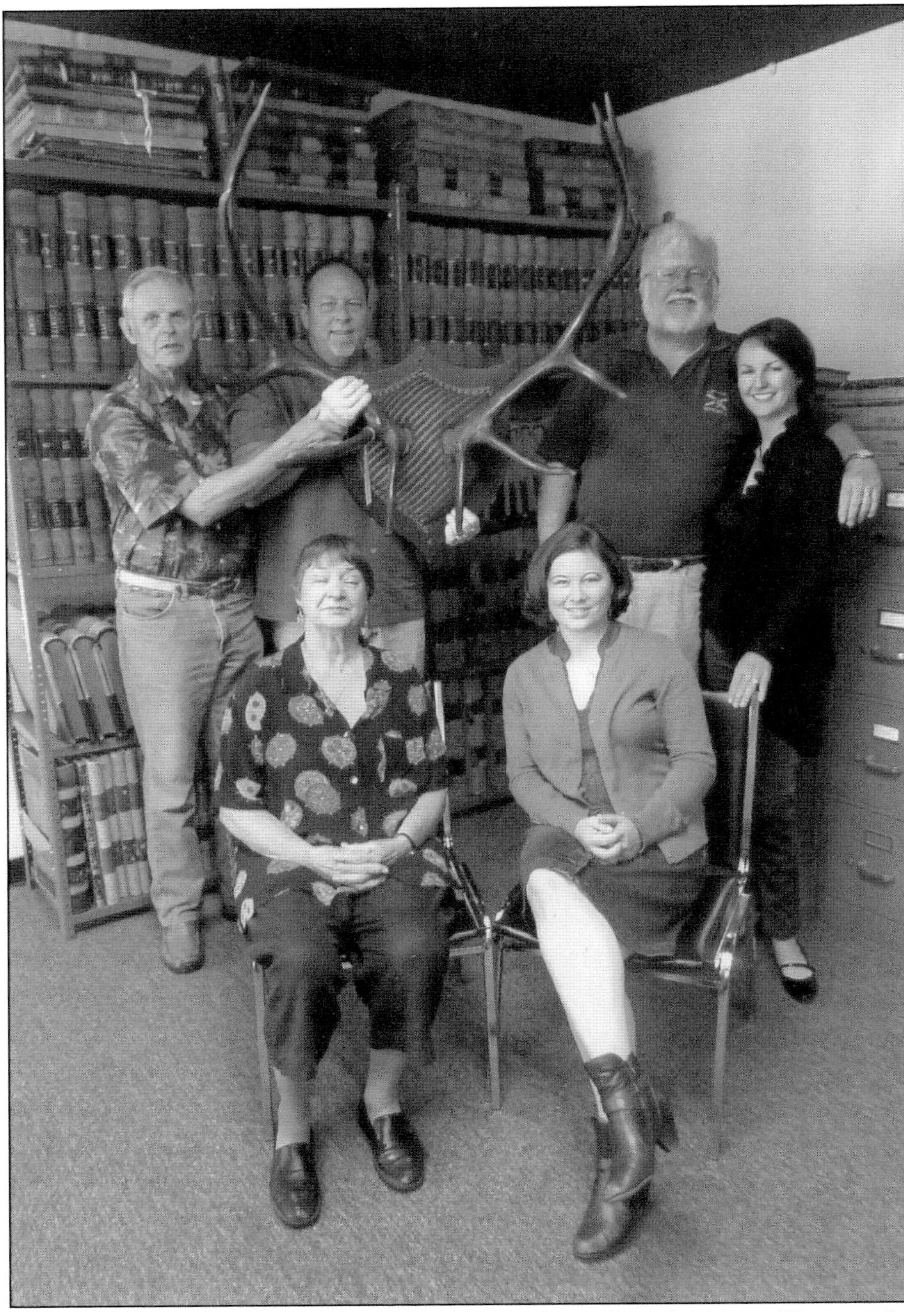

Supporting a three-foot-wide 12-point antler rack is the staff of the Marin History Museum. Pictured are, from left to right, (first row) research librarian Jocelyn Moss and curator Holly Gallagher; (second row) volunteer Ray Lorber, collections manager Doug Defors, volunteer Bill Kaufman, and director Michelle Sarjeant Kaufman. Tule elk are still indigenous to West Marin. Twenty-six-year-old John Keys shot this one in 1850. Keys emigrated from Fermanagh, Ireland, to become one of the earliest settlers of Tomales Bay. (Courtesy of Marin History Museum.)

ON THE COVER: Blake's Landing is named for Jeremiah Ladd Blake, who, at age 20, first came to Tomales Bay in March 1853. (Courtesy of Marin History Museum.)

IMAGES
of America

TOMALES BAY

Anthony Raymond Kilgallin

ARCADIA
PUBLISHING

ISBN 978-0-7385-9641-9

Published by Arcadia Publishing
Charleston, South Carolina

Printed in the United States of America

Library of Congress Control Number: 2012945081

For all general information, please contact Arcadia Publishing:
Telephone 843-853-2070
Fax 843-853-0044
E-mail sales@arcadiapublishing.com
For customer service and orders:
Toll-Free 1-888-313-2665

Visit us on the Internet at www.arcadiapublishing.com

To the ever increasingly grateful descendants of Alexander Stitt Marshall, who, like their progenitor, embody the pioneering ambition to successfully achieve their own California dreams.

CONTENTS

Acknowledgments

To each of the following, I extend my gratitude for contributing selflessly to this volume's mosaic nature: Carol Acquaviva, Justin Bernard, Nancy Blue, Henry Bridges, Nicole Cerini, Patricia Nikolina Clark, George Clyde, Gayle and Jim Crayne, Paul Elmore, Branwell Fanning, Frankie Frankeney, Dena Grunt, Diana Haven, Marsha Haydel, Dan Horan, Kiki, Amy and Jim Kilgallin, Patricia Kilgallin, Patricia Martini, Larry Massolo, Rob Mazzei, Eileen McLeran, Kelsey Meagher, Gwendolyn Meyer, Kate Monahan, Christopher Nichols, Carl Nolte, P.J. Norlander, Amy Perryman, Brett Poirier, John Poultney, Tom Riley, Terry Sawyer, Herb Seidel, Janet Short, Barbara Shurtz, and Erin Wrightsman.

To Ginny Mackenzie Magan, curator of the Tomales Regional History Center; Carola DeRooy, archivist of the Point Reyes National Seashore Library and Research Center; and Daniel S. Brown, historical exhibit specialist of Point Reyes National Seashore, National Parks Service, I give my ever ongoing thanks for sharing your historical acumen.

Without the assistance of the staff of the Marin History Museum Library and Research Center at 70 Galli Drive, Novato, California, this book could not have been completed. Unless otherwise noted, all images appear courtesy of the Marin History Museum. I cannot overstate the unique scholarly camaraderie, bonhomie, dedication, and fellowship I have shared with Michelle, Jocelyn, Holly, Bill, Doug, and Ray. They epitomize truly the total worthiness of sharing history with every interested citizen. To my editor Jared Nelson, proofreader Jim Kempert, and publisher Jeff Ruetsche at Arcadia Publishing, I give the highest of praises for finding a way to win in 2013.

Introduction

Among the 500 Indian tribes that once inhabited California, the tribe that inhabited Tomales Bay was the Olamentko or Western-Bodega Miwok. They used a distinct dialect of the Penutian language. As part of the larger Coast Miwok family, their economy was based on fishing, hunting, and the gathering of acorns. Salmon, steelhead, and shellfish were abundant, while acorns, buckeye, and pepperwood fruits could be ground down to make mush or bread. Located on the east side of Tomales Bay were three of their settlements, including Echakolum, also known as Fishermen's, located two miles south of the present town of Marshall; Utumnia, just north of the present town of Tomales; and Sakloki shotomko-wi, present-day Tom's Point. Sir Francis Drake encountered Miwoks in 1579, and Sebastian Cermeno met them in 1595. Tomales Bay was featured on Spanish charts as early as 1603. According to the historian George Emanuels, "Captain James Vancouver, charged with mapping the entire Pacific coastline, returned to England with a complete chart which, to the exclusion of all other inlets, showed soundings only in Tomales Bay."

Between 1931 and 1932, Isabel Kelly interviewed Maria Capa Frias, a Miwok who lived at Fishermen's. At this time, fewer than five Miwok remained. In her biography of Chief Marin, Betty Goerke cites the following quotation taken from ethnographer Kelly's recorded notes: "Before the Spanish came, the Nicasio people fought with the Healdsburg people. I never heard of a fight with the Tomales people, but the Tomales people didn't like the Nicasio people. The Nicasio people didn't like the Healdsburg (Southern Pomo) or the Petaluma people. The Marshall people didn't like the Bodega people, and nobody liked anybody else."

About 3,000 miles east of Tomales Bay, in an 1832 speech to Congress, Daniel Webster uttered: "What can we ever hope to do with the western coast, a coast of 3,000 miles, rockbound, cheerless, uninviting, and not a harbor on it? What use have we for such a country? Mr. President, I will never vote 1¢ from the public treasury to place the Pacific coast one inch nearer to Boston than it now is." Fortunately, John Bidwell was not listening. At age 21, he had just lost his Missouri land to a claim jumper and decided to enlist members for his newly formed Western Emigration Society, which made the first wagon train journey to California. It arrived without wagons, which were abandoned in the desert.

John Bidwell's journal *A Journey to California: Bodega, Port of the Russians, Upper California, March 30, 1842*, is about his trip accomplished a year earlier. To write his journal, he sat at a Russian table with the Pacific Ocean behind him at Rumyantsev Bay where Ivan Kuskov had founded a base in 1809. He had promised his Missouri friends an account of the journey with an eye to future prospects for ambitious settlers. The following three observations would change the course of commerce in Tomales Bay for the rest of the 19th century: "Potatoes—Irish potatoes grow well and are of a good quality—should be planted in April;" "Cattle—of all places in the world, it appears to me, that none can be better adapted to the raising of cattle, than California. The cattle here are very large, and a person who has not a thousand is scarcely noticed as regards stock;" and "Butter and Cheese—but little butter and cheese made in this country; pains not being taken to milk the cows; butter is worth 50¢ per lb. What a chance there is in this line of business for industrious Americans."

In April 1851, a 27-year-old Irish immigrant, also coming from Missouri, planted a crop of potatoes in the sandy soil of Bodega Point. This was a new potato later known as the Bodega Red. When the crop matured in the autumn, he loaded the potatoes on his barge and took them to San Francisco, where they sold for unheard-of prices.

Future Irish-born pioneers in Tomales Bay had watched Ireland live and die by the potato from 1800–1850. At the turn of the 19th century, an adult Irish laborer would consume 10 to 12 pounds of potatoes a day washed down with a pint of whole milk. By the early 1840s, roughly three quarters of rural Irish citizens were largely or fully dependent on potatoes, lacking other supplemental foodstuffs. When the potato blight persisted from 1845 to 1850, 30 percent of Ireland emigrated. A million perished at home. Another million had already left Ireland after Napoleon's defeat at Waterloo rather than continue to suffer under British tyranny.

John Keys was the second settler in Tomales County. The first was George Thomas Wood, a native of the state of New York, who, at 19, deserted the whaling ship *Warren* in San Francisco Bay in 1844. Known as Tom "Vaquero" Wood for his horsemanship, he erected the first wooden building on Tomales Bay and became headman at the aforementioned Miwok settlement Shotomko-wi. As a "squaw man," he taught his Indians to cultivate potatoes and harvest grain.

Other settlers soon realized that Tomales Bay was the Pacific frontier, a new world for second-chancers, and truly the rainbow's end with pots of gold for many industrious newcomers, such as George W. Burbank, William Vanderbilt, Warren Dutton, and John Keys, but only if their land grants were granted legal validity. It took almost a decade of legal maneuvering before the US Supreme Court ruled in their favor. William Paton Vanderbilt and Jeremiah Clark had saved for the day, and a huge celebration was promised with the following advertisement in the *Marin Journal*: "All through the evening of April 1st and the morning of the party a 1,000 pound ox carcass was slowly roasting in anticipation of the 1,500 dinner guests. There were many speeches introduced musically by the Bloomfield Brass Band and the citizens of Petaluma presented a silk banner to the victorious settlers. An evening ball concluded the festivities."

One

Pioneers and Prominent Settlers

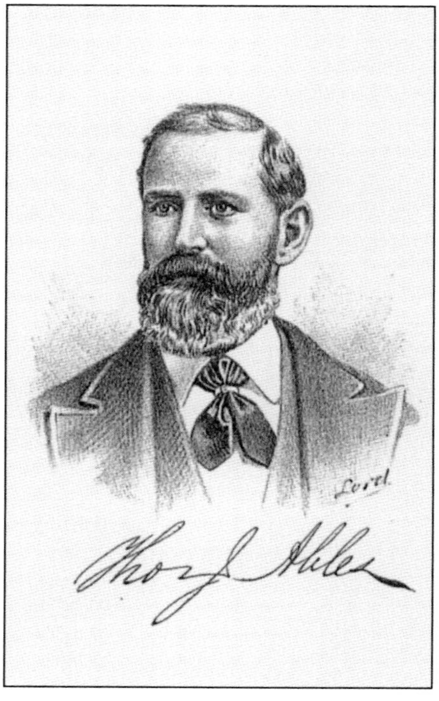

Thomas J Ables (1855–1917) was the oldest pioneer banker of Marin County, a former superintendent of schools, and a former member of the assembly. Born and raised in Guernsey County, Ohio, he became a schoolteacher at 17. Accompanied by his brother Benjamin and two uncles, he collected baggage and horses at Booneville, Missouri, on May 8, 1857, and drove cattle west, reaching Bloomfield, Sonoma County, on October 10. Here, he resumed his teaching career, saving his earnings for a year until he and his brother purchased 200 acres in Tomales Township. Benjamin conducted the dairy farm while Thomas remained teaching. In 1860, he was elected school superintendent for Marin County, being the only successful Republican candidate that year and the first Republican official in Marin County. He represented Marin County twice, from 1867 to 1888 and 1873 to 1874, in the California assembly. He helped incorporate the Bank of Tomales in 1875 as a stockholder, receiving the appointments of director and cashier, positions he held until his retirement in 1907. He was justly called the first Progressive in Marin County.

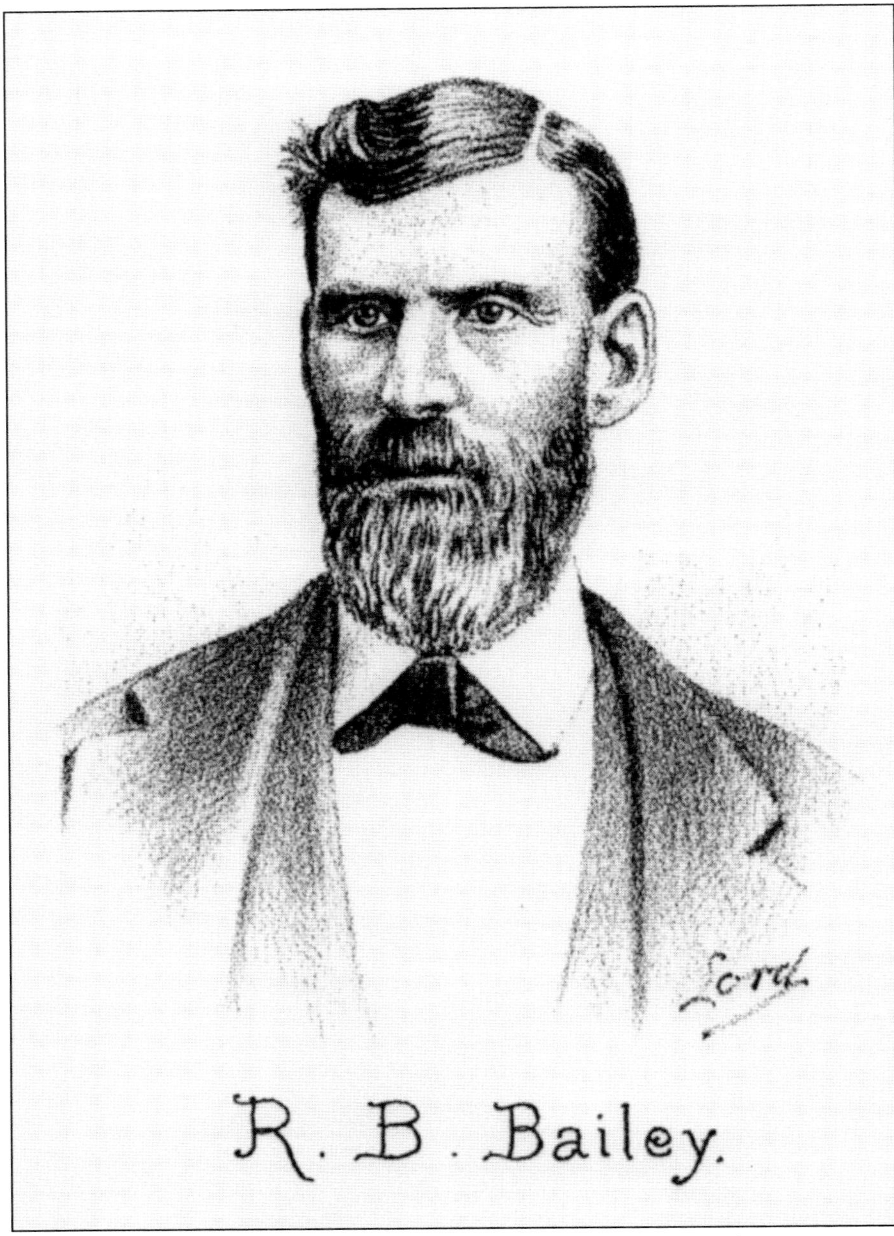

Born in Kentucky on December 26, 1827, Robert Bailey (1827–1891) moved at age seven with his parents to Illinois. In 1848, he moved to Iowa until the spring of 1850, when he crossed the Plains with ox teams, reaching the mines in Placer County in October. In November 1851, he married Mary Hickman, a native of Massachusetts. He worked in Placer County until the spring of 1852 and then moved to Bloomfield, Sonoma County. In 1856, he drove another herd of cattle from Missouri to California. By 1880, he was rich enough to build a splendid two-story mansion in Tomales for his wife and seven children. Despite a highly successful ranching career and a happy family life, tragedy struck in 1888 when his second son, William Hendricks Bailey, committed suicide in San Francisco by shooting himself in the head behind the right ear. He had hoped to be cured of inflammatory rheumatism in the city, but to no avail. His remains were returned to Tomales by train, and from the train station, a mile-long procession followed him to his grave.

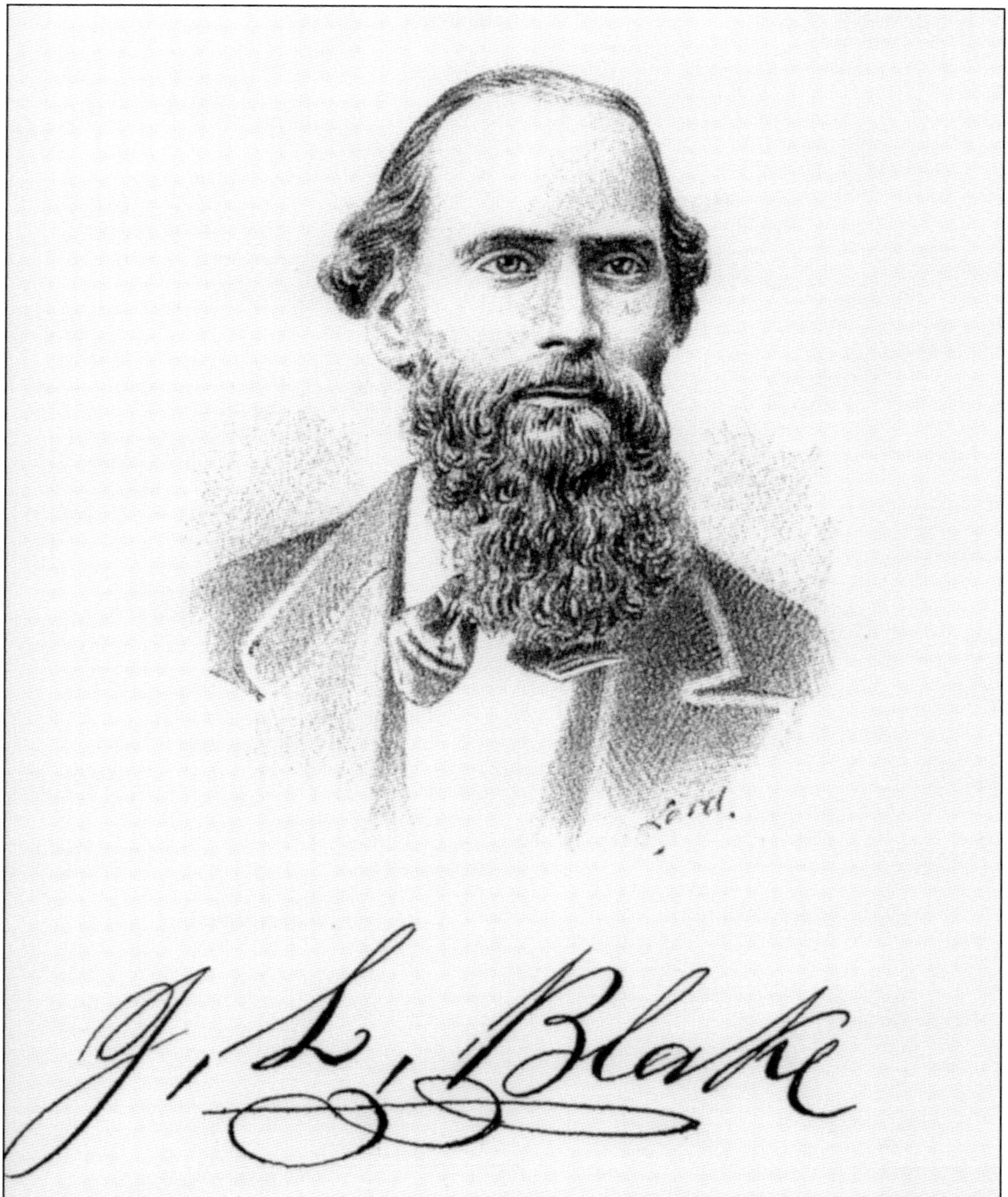

Jeremiah Ladd Blake (1833–1908) was a descendant of Jaspar Blake, who emigrated from England in 1650. Jeremiah was born in Orange, New Hampshire, but grew up in Pittsfield, New Hampshire, where he took up the trade of saddlery. He voyaged by steamers to San Francisco via Nicaragua in 1852. Finding no work there, he moved to Petaluma and thence to Tomales Bay in March 1853. In Tomales Bay, he got a tract of land and built a 16-by-20-foot house by splitting the timber from logs washed up on the Pacific shores of Point Reyes. Blake's Landing became a destination for all horse lovers. He became the pioneer saddle manufacturer in Marin County but also farmed and cultivated fruit trees, eucalyptus, pine, and cypress. Peacefully dying in his sleep from heart failure, he was survived by nine children, three brothers, and a sister. His obituary honored a half-century of philanthropy, and said: "his whole life has been an open book and no man in Marin County who has passed over the great divide leaves behind him a cleaner or more honorable record."

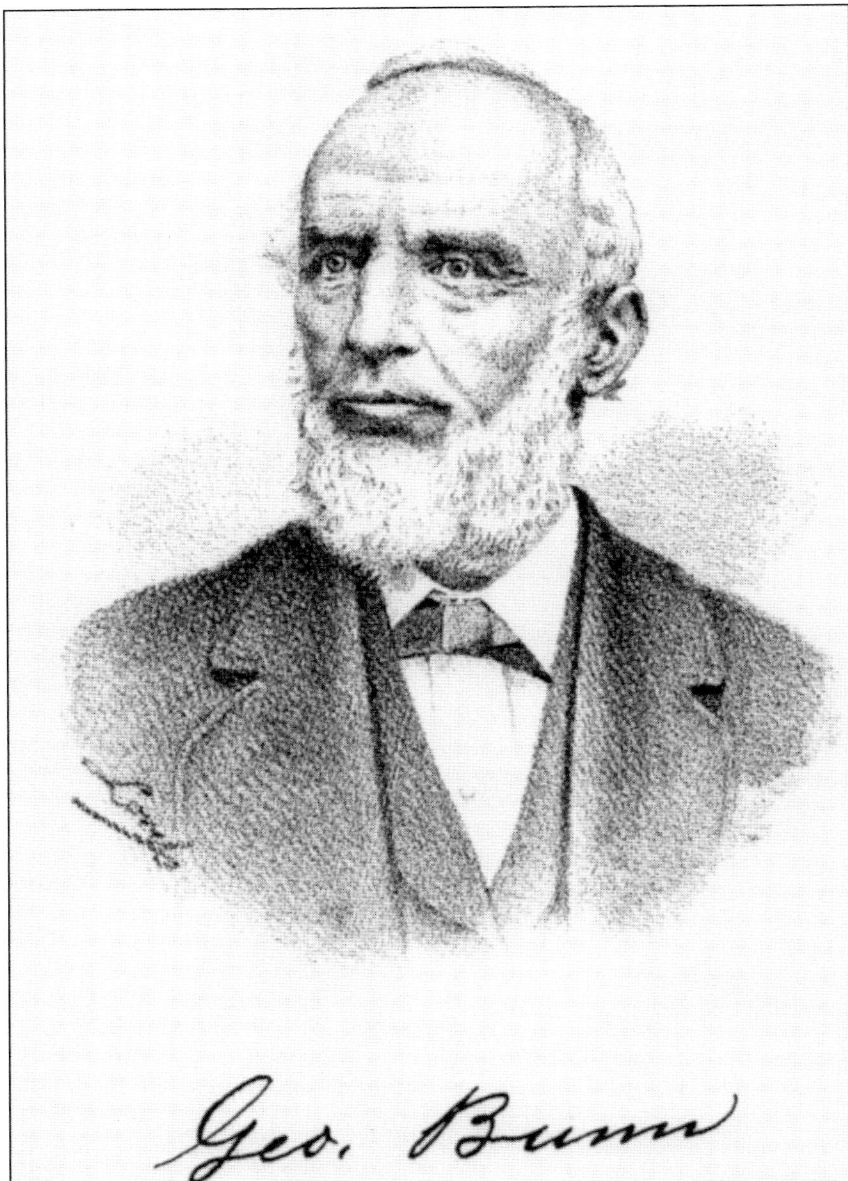

Born and raised in Hunterdon County, New Jersey, George Bunn (1820–1894) embarked on the steamer *Northern Light* on May 5, 1852, heading to the Pacific via Nicaragua. He landed in San Francisco on July 7, 1852, and then proceeded to Sacramento and hence to Spring Valley, Butte County, as the superintendent of the construction of a quartz mill. Finding quartz mining on the decline, he became a farmer in Cotati and, finally, in Valley Ford in 1857. He was one of the founders of the Bank of Tomales, becoming a stockholder and director. In 1884, he sold his very handsome ranch property in Tomales and moved to a new residence on Fifth Street in San Rafael. Never one to sit still or resist a good investment, he bought a large cattle ranch in Hembrie, Crockett County, Texas. Traveling there in late winter of 1894, he contracted a severe cold, which settled into a case of acute pneumonia. He managed to get back to San Rafael before dying shortly thereafter. An obituary cited him as "a man of sterling character and blameless life, and though not one given to social relaxations, had many friends who sincerely mourn his death."

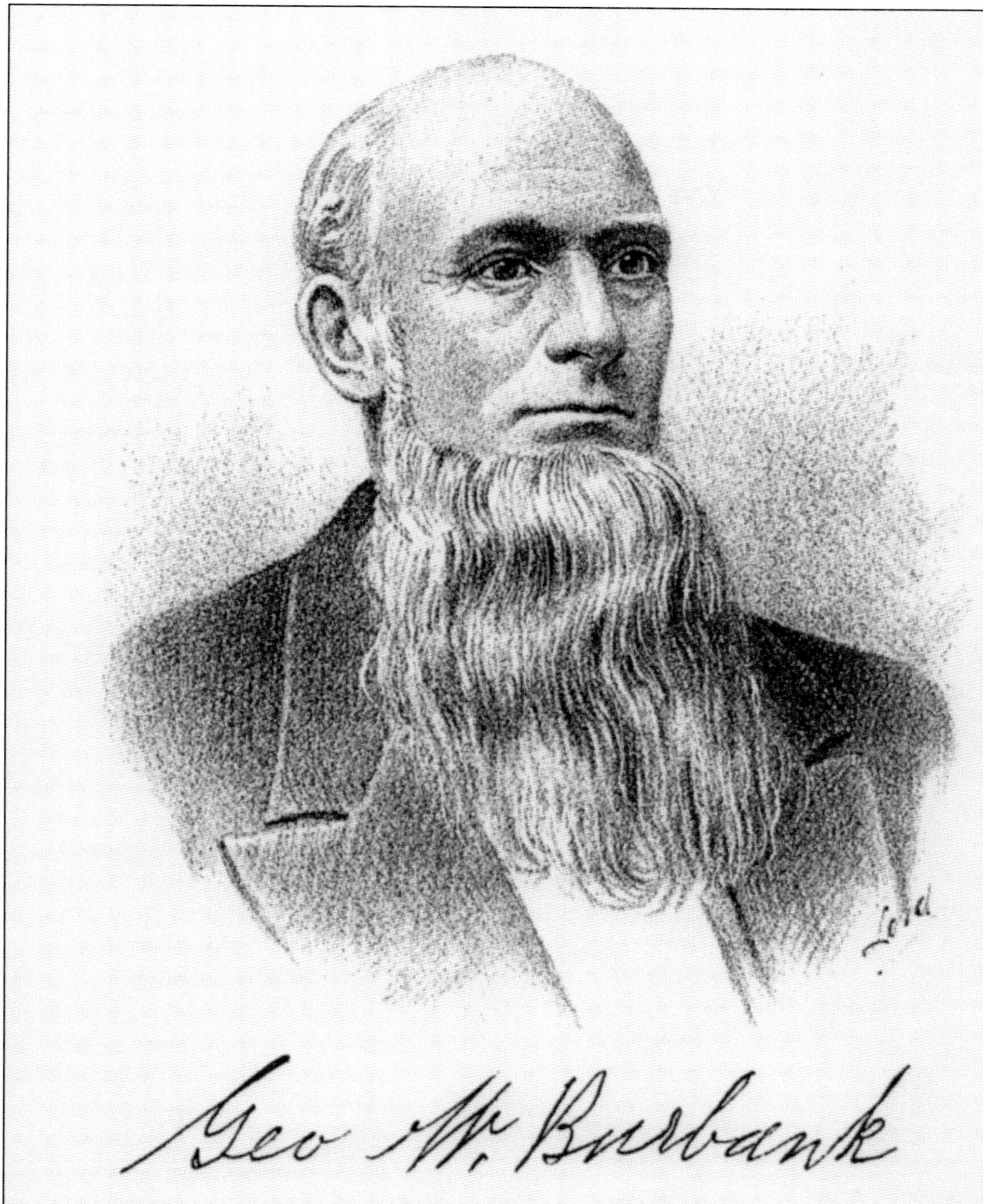

A native of Lancaster, Worcester County, Massachusetts, George Wilton Burbank (1829–1901) was born in 1829 and was educated in his native state. Later, he set out for California by steamer via Nicaragua, arriving in San Francisco on the *Sierra Nevada* on May 19, 1854. He came to Tomales Township in 1855 and chose a lifetime residence on a farm along the banks of the Estero San Antonio Laguna. He was one of the eight men who formed into a league to resist the claimants of the Balsa de Tomales land grant. In 1864, he was elected one of the supervisors of Marin County, and in 1875, he represented Marin County in the lower house of the state legislature. He married Apphie Blake of Paris, Maine, in 1862 and became a widower in 1896. Together, they created a conservatory and flower garden that contemporaries acknowledged could not be equaled by any in Marin County.

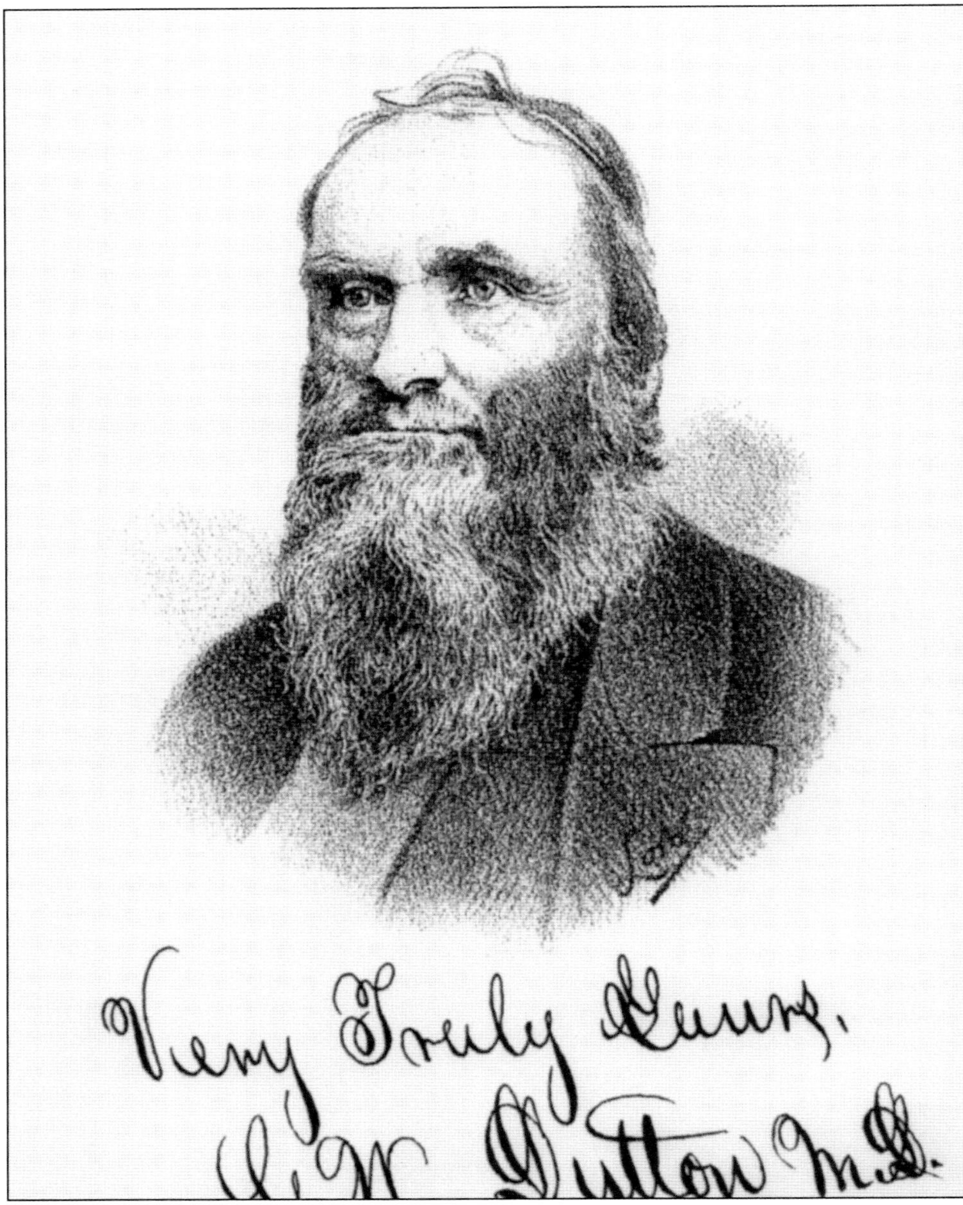

A grandson of Captain Dutton, a soldier in the Continental Army during the Revolutionary War, George Washington Dutton, MD, was born in Sheldon, Franklin County, Vermont, in 1826. At the commencement of the Mexican War in 1846, he enlisted as a private soldier but was detailed from the ranks to do duty in the medical department. After taking many courses over the next decade, he commenced the practice of medicine and surgery in the spring of 1856, four years before coming to Tomales. Over the next quarter century, he was devoted to the citizens of Tomales Bay. Peter Mattei's young son, whose leg was crushed almost to powder but was restored by the good doctor nearly as good as ever, attended his funeral in 1885. Long distances, tempests, dark nights, or poor patients made no difference to him. Many times he crossed Tomales Bay at imminent peril of his life. At the funeral, a former patient commented, "I feel toward him just as I would to a man who had saved me from drowning, for I know that I was raised up from a fearful sickness only by his skill and care."

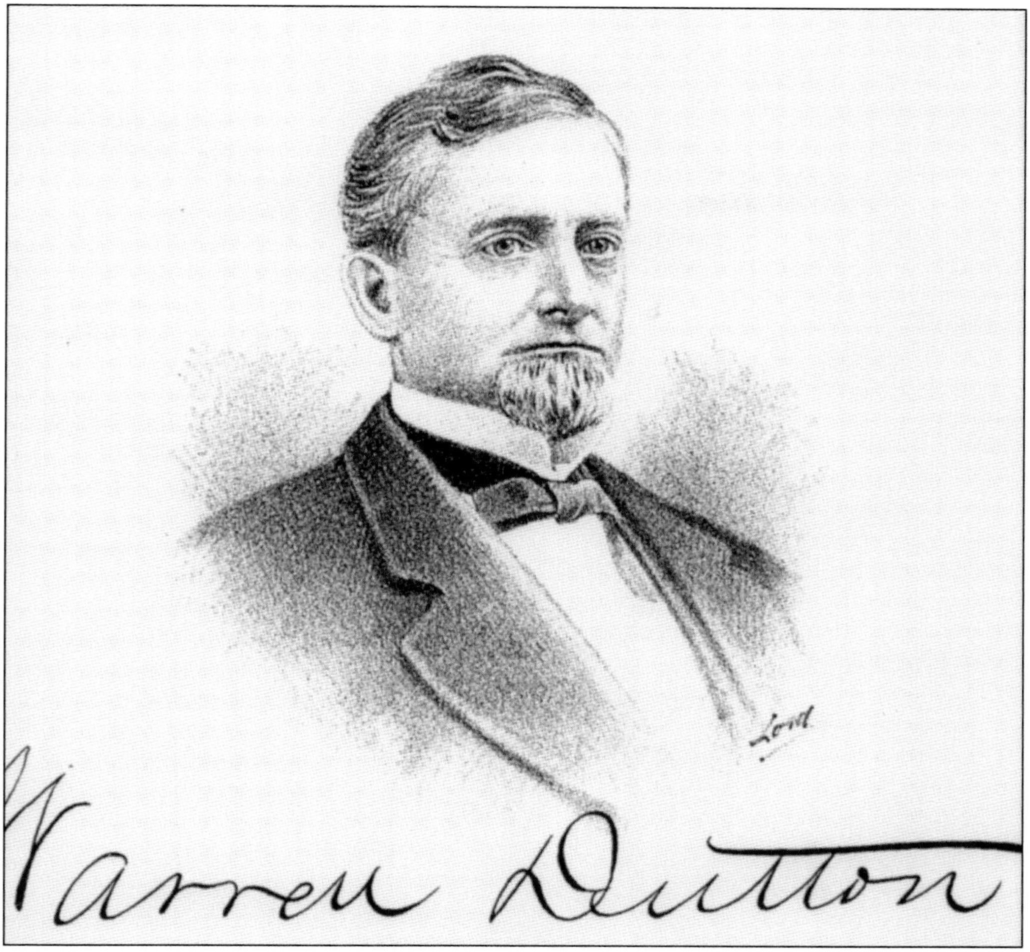

Canadian born but of English and American ancestry, Warren Dutton (1823–1903) left home at 14 "to try his fortune among strangers, without the assistance of money or friends." He prospered so much that, in 1849, he purchased the brig *Sarah Mcfarland* in New York City and, in the company of 41 others, sailed pleasantly around Cape Horn, arriving in San Francisco on August 1, 1849. A true 49er, he arrived in Tomales three years later to try his fortune again, this time with potatoes. He purchased some Spanish oxen, and after a hard year's toil, living on the flesh of elk, deer, and antelope, an initial crop was produced. When the cash account for that year was balanced, a deficit of $2,000 was found, which, afterwards, was balanced by a charge of $2,000 in experience. Potatoes became the principal crop for shipping to San Francisco. Returning southbound from his funeral in Tomales, a train chartered by his family for 28 passengers jumped the tracks, killing Anton Roman, the founder of *Overland Magazine*, and Michael Kirk, a retired farmer.

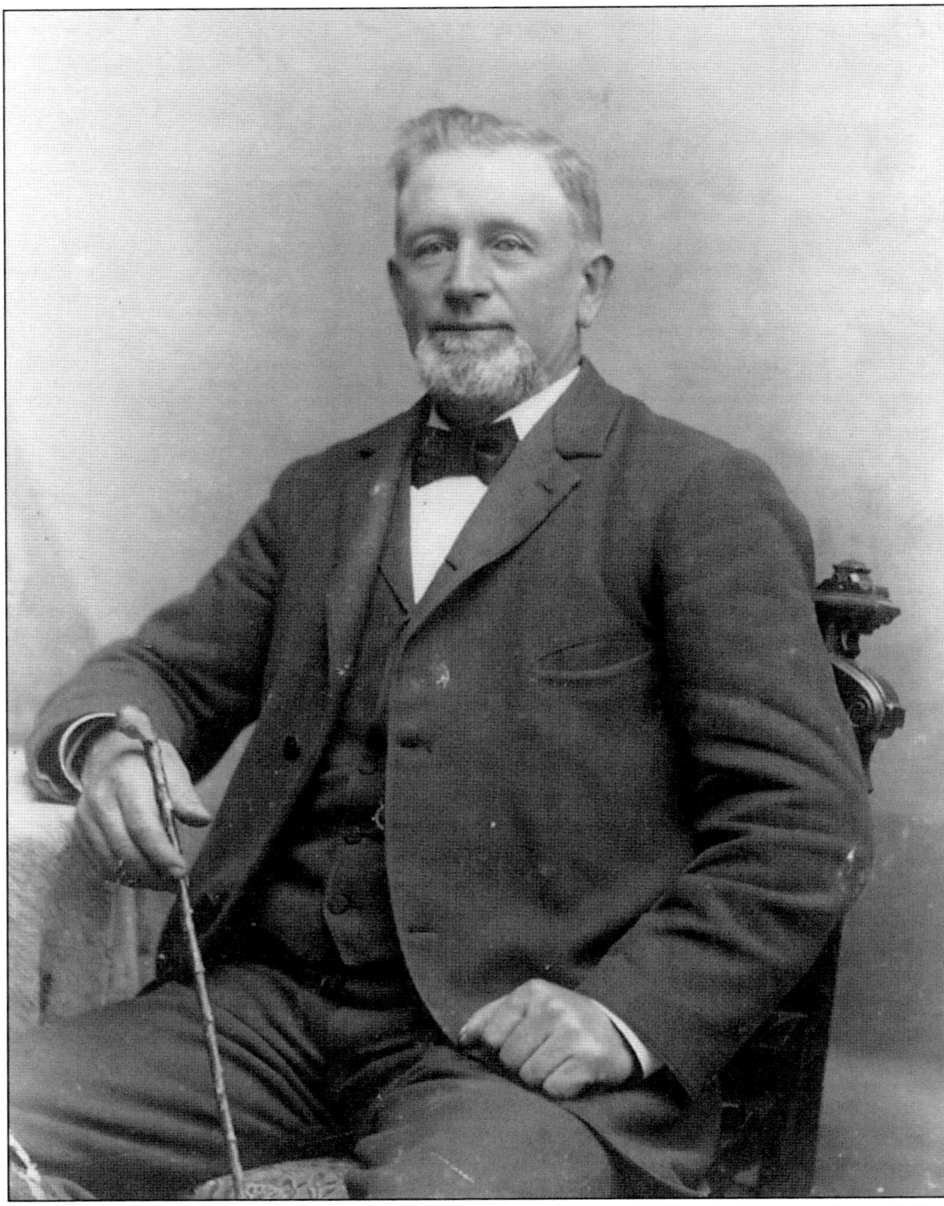

Andrew Ludwig Fisher (1826–1908) was born July 1826 in Holbaek, Denmark, and died in 1908. He married the Irish-born Lucinda Salmon April 10, 1867, in Tomales and was one of two contractors for the Catholic church rectory. In the mid-1860s, he moved the old Keys and Noble cedar-shake shanty, built around 1850, to its present location at 26650 Highway 1, directly across from the Catholic church. In Ginny Magan's opinion, "The original, side-gabled section of this dwelling is probably the earliest residential building in town." Andrew served as an elected Justice of the Peace from 1869 to 1875. Andrew and Lucinda raised six children: Elizabeth Theresa, Mary May, Charles James, Lucinda Rose, Ellen Jane, and Joseph Andrew. Elizabeth Theresa was born August 11, 1876, in Tomales and married Peter Yokum Petersen December 11, 1902, in Petaluma. Their four sons, Kenneth Ludwig, Andrew Earle, Clifford Carl, and Norman, were all born at Two Rock, Sonoma. Kenneth Ludwig Peterson married Alyce Marie Chicorp on April 28, 1937, in San Juan Bautista, California.

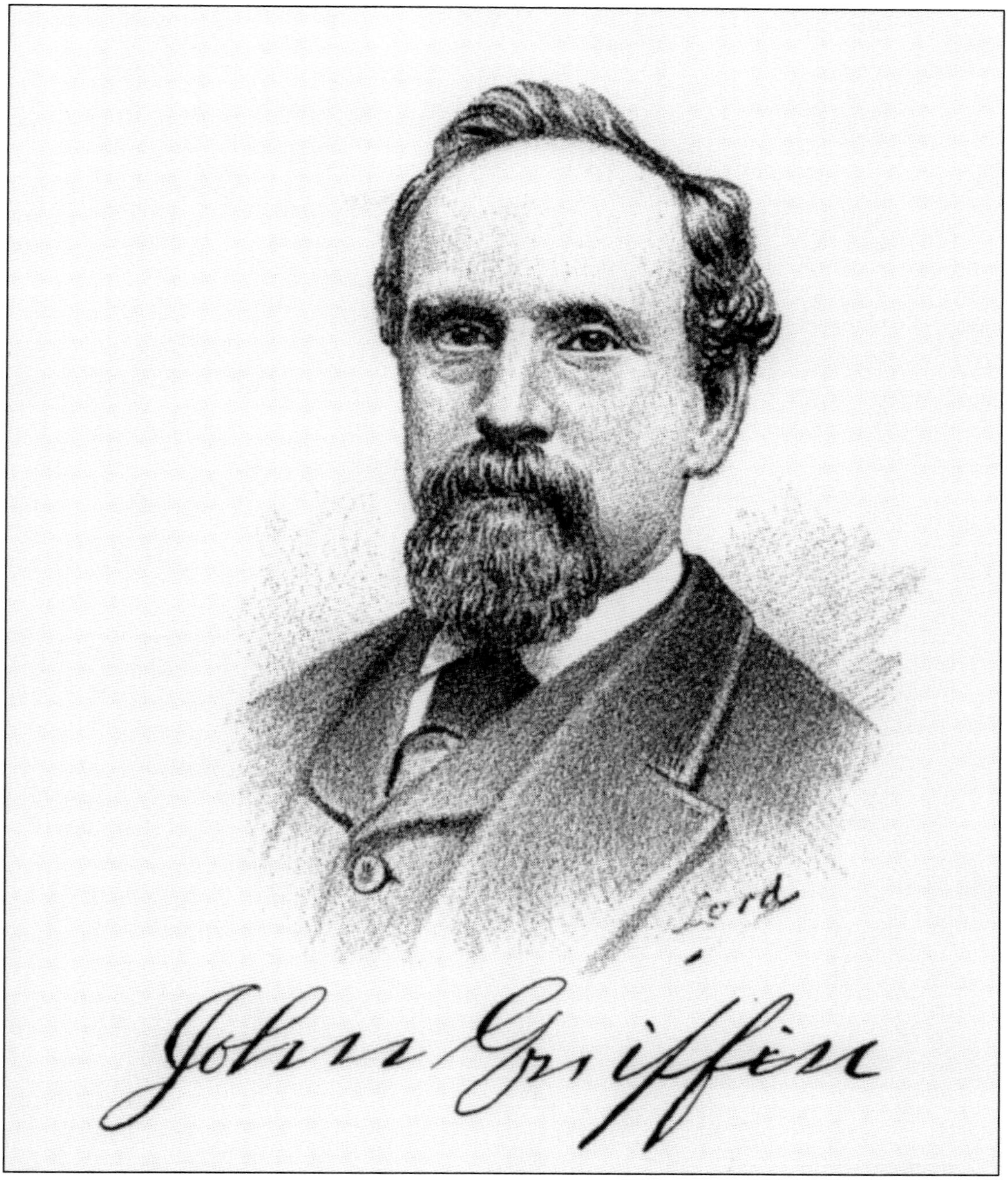

Born in County Limerick, Ireland, John Griffin (1830–1888) immigrated to the United States where a brother and sister awaited him. He had escaped "Black 47," the worst year of Ireland's potato famine. He arrived in San Francisco on November 20, 1852, to spend three years in the Mariposa mines, saving enough to buy 320 acres in the Fallon District north of Tomales. By 1880, he owned 1,000 acres in Griffin Valley. He was elected one of the directors of the Bank of Tomales in 1877, to be reelected annually. He married a blue-eyed colleen named Ellen Malone on New Year's Day 1856, the mother-to-be of six children. One writer recounts that Griffin was not always lucky: "Unfortunately for Griffin, his chance at immortality was swept away when the narrow-gauge railroad was built up the coast in the mid-1870s. Since Luke Fallon was generous enough to allow a right-of-way through his property for the tracks, a grateful railroad officially called the Griffin Valley whistle-stop 'Fallon,' thus forever memorializing the Fallons at the expense of the Griffins."

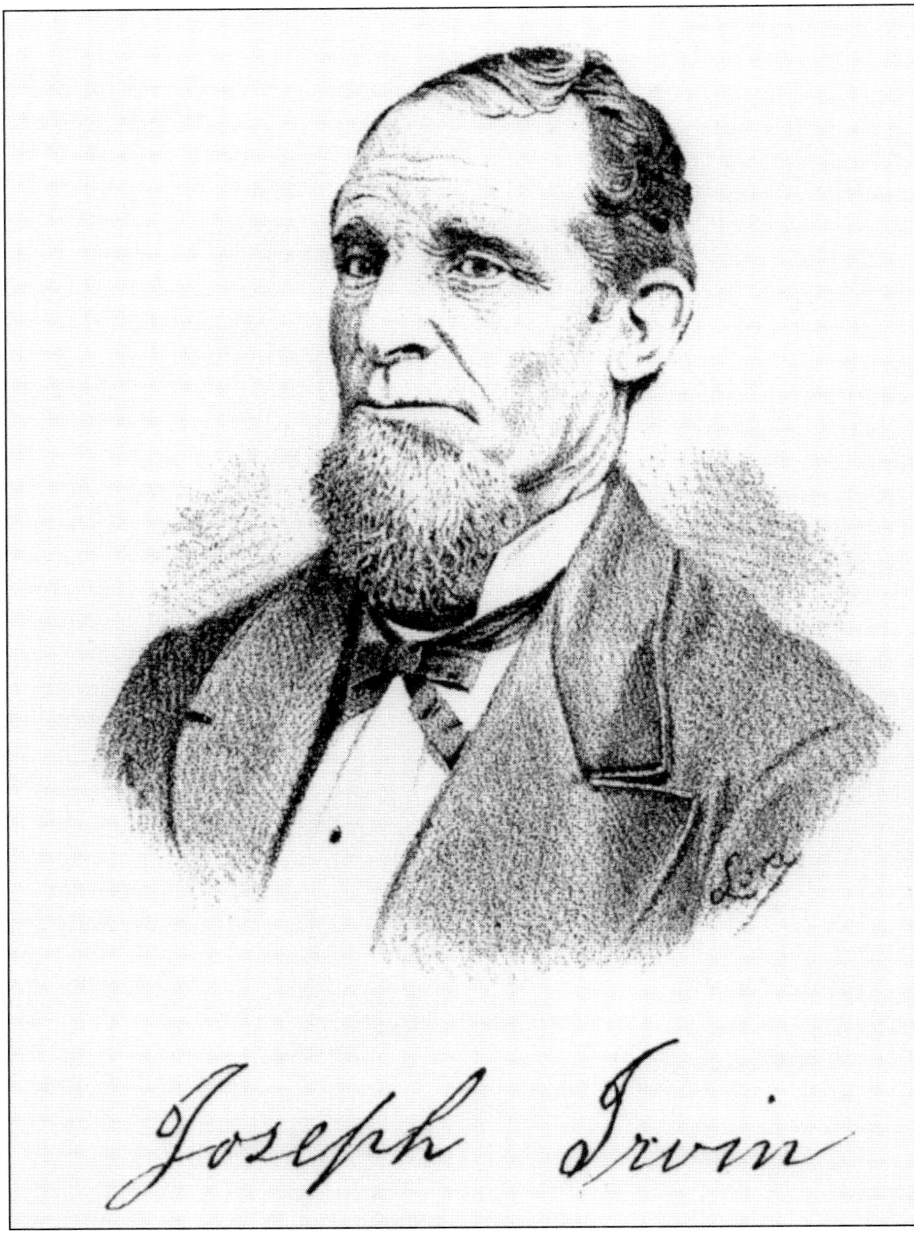

Born in Belfast, Ireland, Joseph Irvin (1832–1898) immigrated first to Baltimore, Maryland, and then to San Francisco via the Isthmus of Panama, arriving April 1853. He obtained employment at once in the government mill at Corte Madera. In 1856, he moved to Tomales and bought a 240-acre farm east of town. Tomales was becoming a microcosm of Ireland by this time. In 1868, Irvin married 20-year-old Annie Granlees, Philadelphia born, who had traveled to San Francisco via Panama 11 years earlier. She had moved to Tomales only the year before. Parenting five children, Joseph and Annie were instrumental in organizing the First Presbyterian Church of Tomales, under the care of the Presbytery of Benicia and Synod of the Pacific. Joseph and Annie were elected ruling elders. Joseph was also elected as a Trustee. He had come far from the troubles that had begun with Ireland's potato famine. How ironic is it that the potato created riches for transplanted Irish settlers in Tomales whereas it had caused untold misery in the old sod?

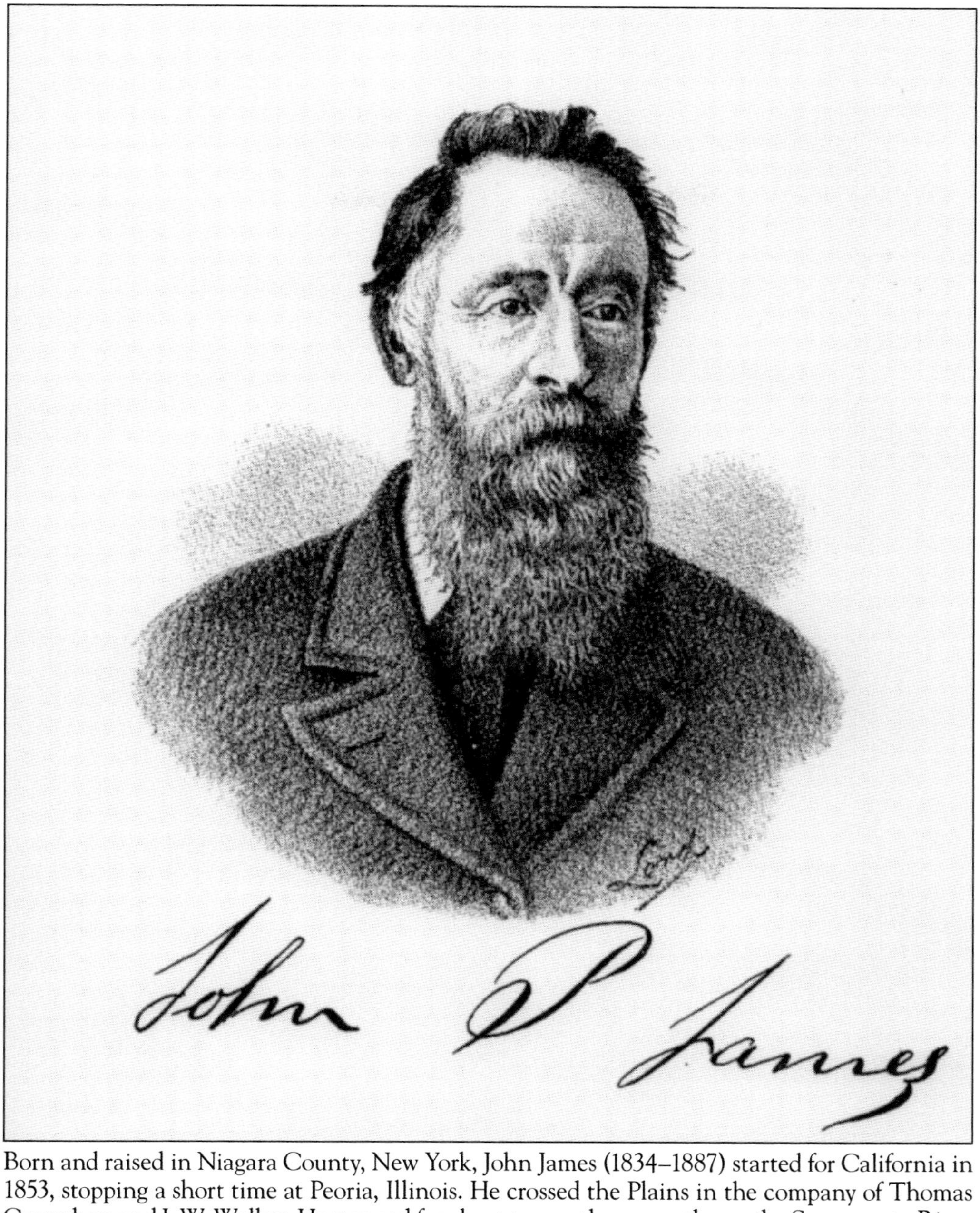

Born and raised in Niagara County, New York, John James (1834–1887) started for California in 1853, stopping a short time at Peoria, Illinois. He crossed the Plains in the company of Thomas Carruthers and L.W. Walker. He stopped for about two or three months on the Sacramento River and then came to Tomales Township to settle on the Woodworth Ranch, which borders the Marshall's home ranch on the west. Walker's name was given to the stream on which they settled. James later moved to San Antonio Township on lands bordering the county line at Spanish Town and south of the lagoon. Carruthers rejoined James in 1854, taking up the land in Rocky Canyon that bordered the Marshall brothers on the north and east. James and Carruthers were well known to all old settlers by their firm name "Tom and Jack." According to the reputable historian A. Bray Dickinson, "Carruthers committed suicide by hanging himself in his barn October 17, 1879. The act was due to worry over an incurable disease." James moved south of Tomales to the bluffs overlooking the town with his wife, Frances, and seven daughters.

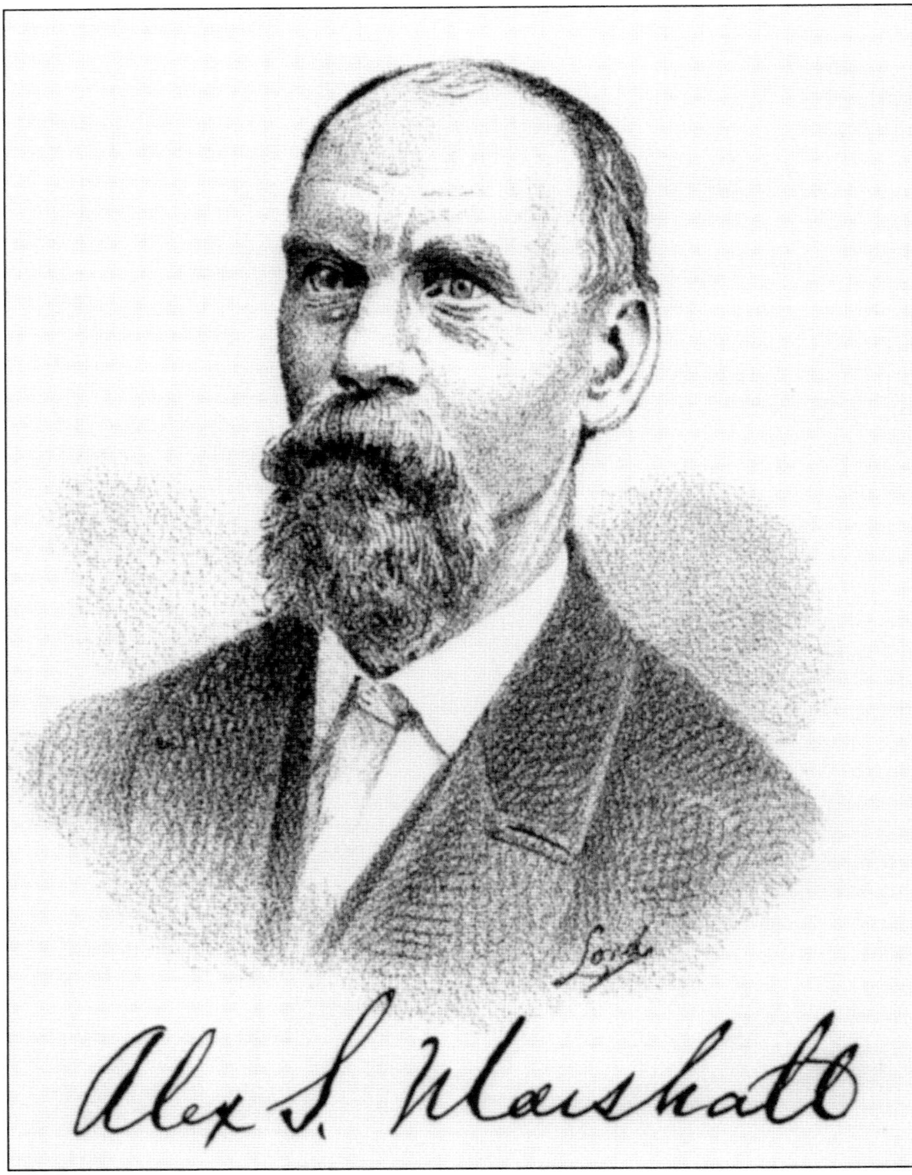

Born in Markethill, Armagh, Ireland, December 27, 1829, Alexander Stitt Marshall (1829–1903) remained there until 1849 when his father died. The consequent disposition of the family home to the eldest brother William through primogeniture inspired him and brothers Hugh, David, Samuel, and James to leave Ireland with the blessings of William. With James and Hugh, he immigrated to Indianapolis, Indiana. On March 4, 1854, he married Fannie Brown, a young Kentucky native whose parents had strongly disapproved of this marriage due to three factors: Alexander was Irish, unemployed, and intended to relocate their daughter thousands of miles west. Alexander initially moved to the West with cattle and horses while Fannie went on a hunger strike until her parents relented, sent out a rider to recall Alexander, and reluctantly agreed to the wedding. They settled in Tomales after a seven-month-long, extremely difficult journey full of hardships, culminating in a bitter lawsuit between Alexander and Hugh and Samuel primarily as to who owned the cooking stove that Fannie utilized every day of the expedition. Alexander contended that Fannie deserved it, and the court agreed.

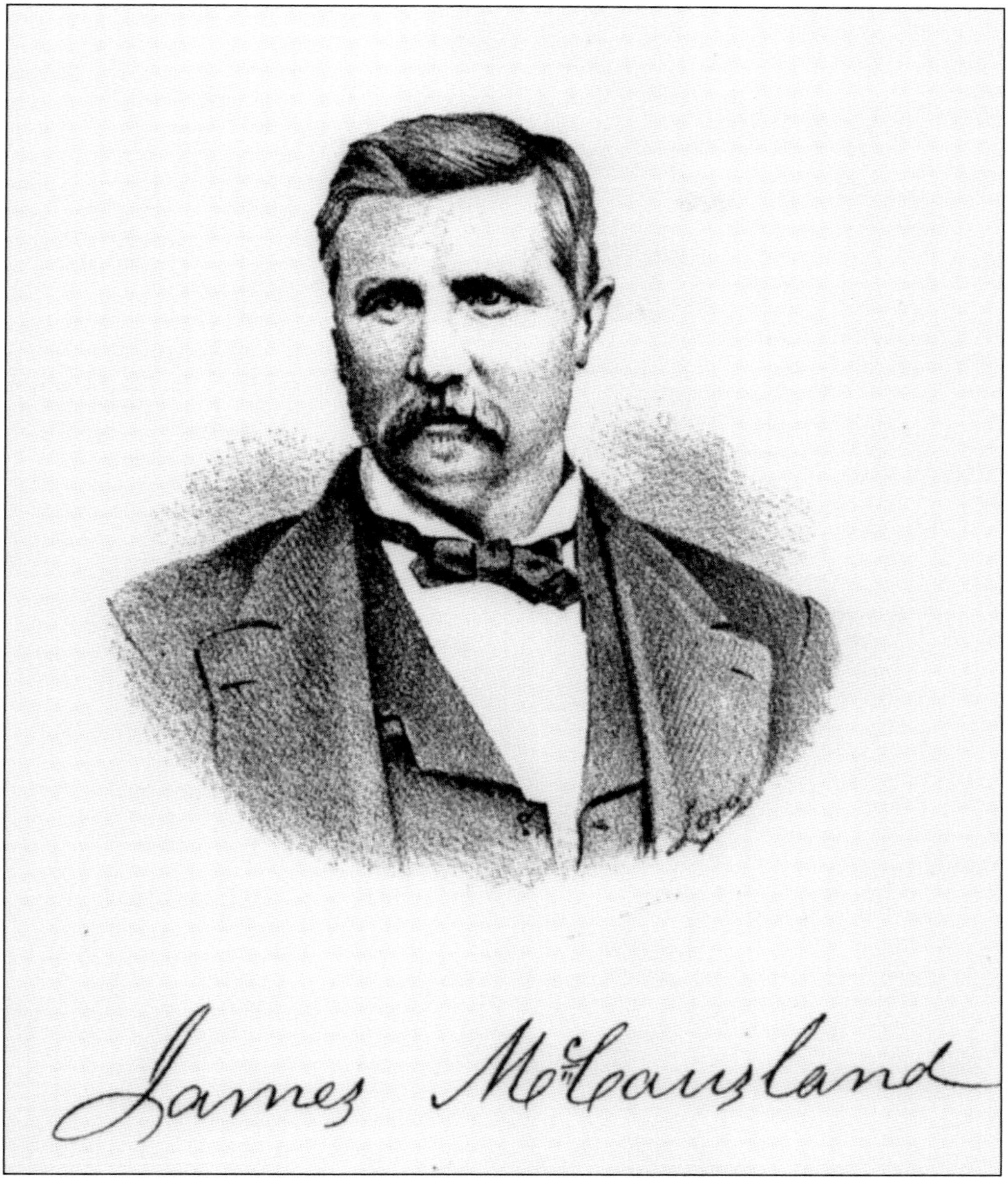

James McCausland (1830–1896) and his brother William were both born in Lancaster County, Pennsylvania, in 1830 and 1828, respectively. Together they started for California in 1853, most likely by steamer through Nicaragua or the Isthmus of Panama, arrived in San Francisco on March 5, and headed straight to the mines in Calaveras and Tuolumne Counties, working there for three years and saving enough money to buy a Tomales ranch and put in potatoes together. A biographer wrote: "No man . . . has done more to forward the interests of the county. He is just in his dealings, true to his instincts, honest in his convictions and genial in his manners; taking him all in all, no truer Friend exists than the ever popular Jim McCausland." At his death, his estate amounted to $26,000. The chief subdivisions were a 1,300-acre tract of timberland in Mendocino County valued at $6,500, a 640-acre ranch known as "the Hermitage" valued at $2,500, 45 shares in the Bank of Tomales amounting to $10,575, and property in San Francisco with the value of $6,000. The property was left equally to his wife and daughter.

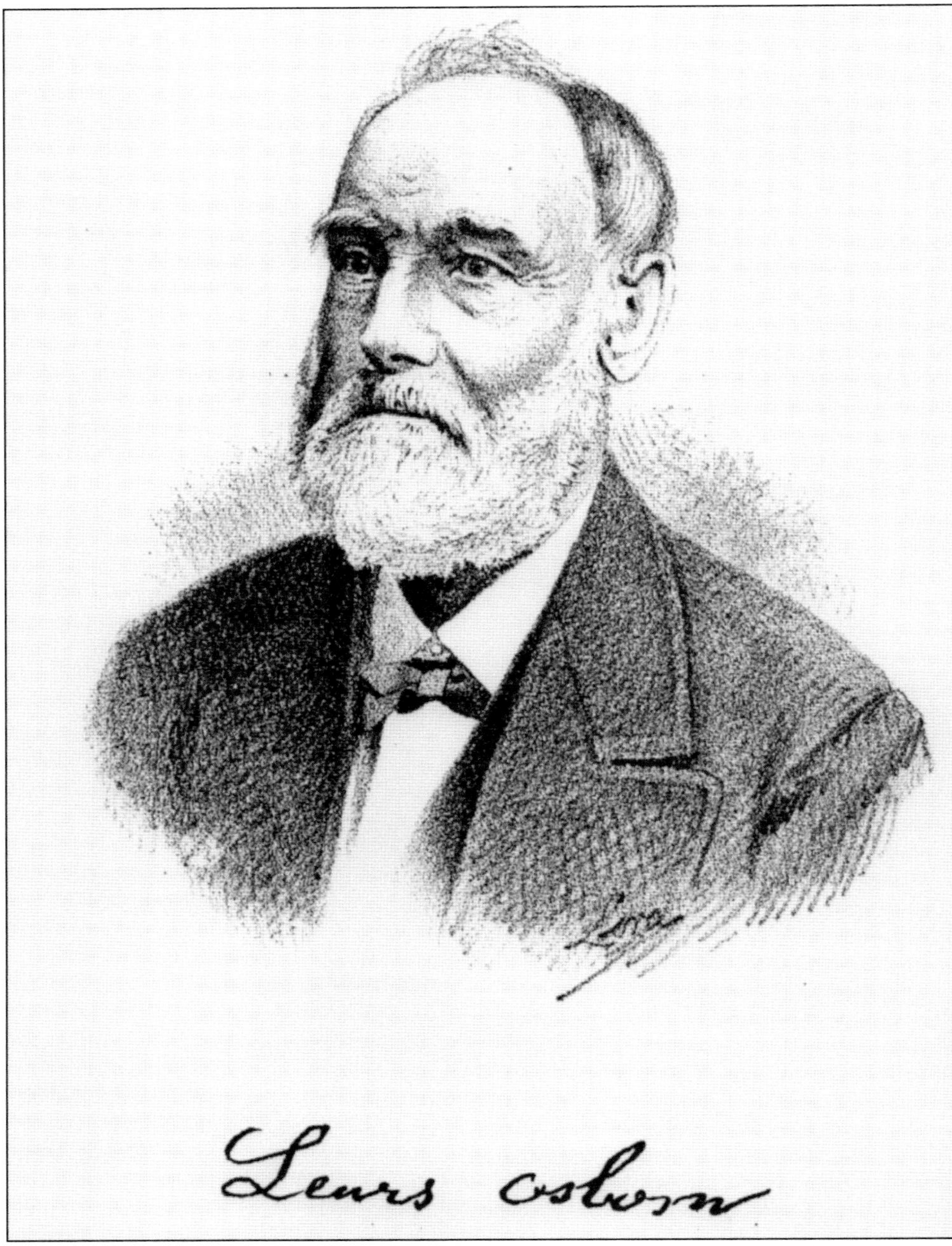

Lewis Osborn (1824–1889) was born in Hamlin County, Massachusetts, educated in Connecticut, and then moved to Iowa. From there, he started across the Plains with teams and arrived in Nevada City in 1850. He worked in the mines until the fall of 1853, when he settled at the foot of the hills east of Aurora Corners on a farm of 185 acres, which abutted Fallon–Two Rock Road. He was killed August 29, 1889, while on the road with a team in Tomales. One of the span of horses he was driving was balky. When he started the team, this horse balked, and the wheel went into a ditch. He jumped toward the bank, but his foot got caught in a halter; he fell short of the bank when a rack on the wagon struck him on the neck and pinioned him tight. He died due to either a broken neck or strangulation, for his feet did not touch a rest and he was truly hanged by the neck. He was an old and highly-esteemed citizen of Tomales.

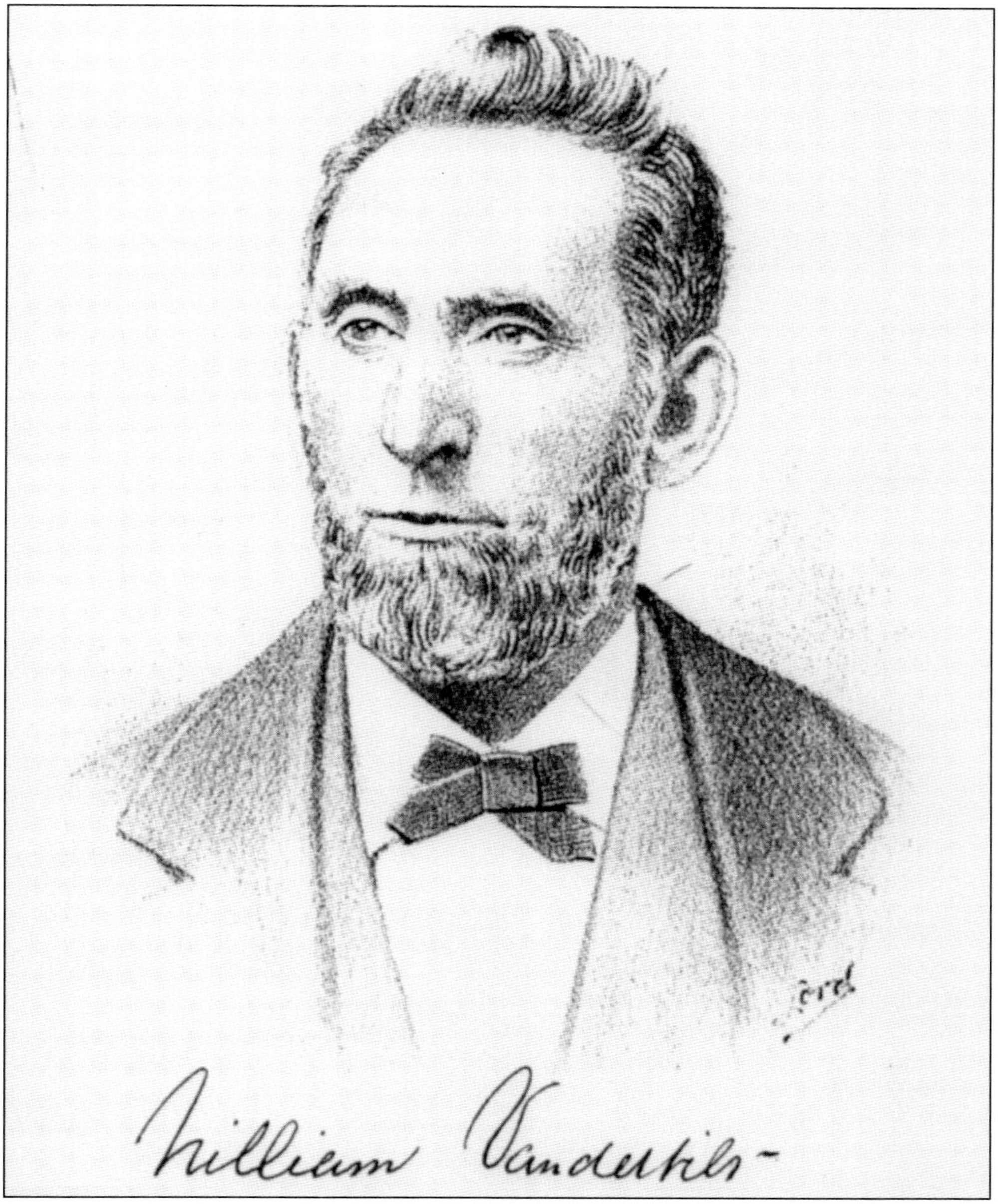

William Paton Vanderbilt (1831–1905) was born in Lyons, Wayne County, New York. Arriving in California via the Isthmus of Panama in 1850, he worked in the mines of Placer and El Dorado Counties until 1857, when he embarked on farming and dairying for wages on the Woodworth Ranch. Then he took up government land on the north slope of Clark's summit west of the county road and worked at Warren Dutton's store in Tomales. Managing the store was Franklin Holland, grandfather of Florence Donnelly. Vanderbilt was appointed assessor for Marin County in 1859, gaining the trust of older settlers such as Warren Dutton, John Keys, and G.W. Burbank. They sent him to Sacramento to learn the law on their behalf to save their lands. While crossing the Plains on his way back to Tomales from a visit to the Supreme Court in Washington, a poisoned Indian arrow struck deep into the calf of his right leg. He excised it with a jack knife and then deeply cauterized the wound with the red-hot end of the wagon's kingbolt; an axle-grease dressing was applied to the wound.

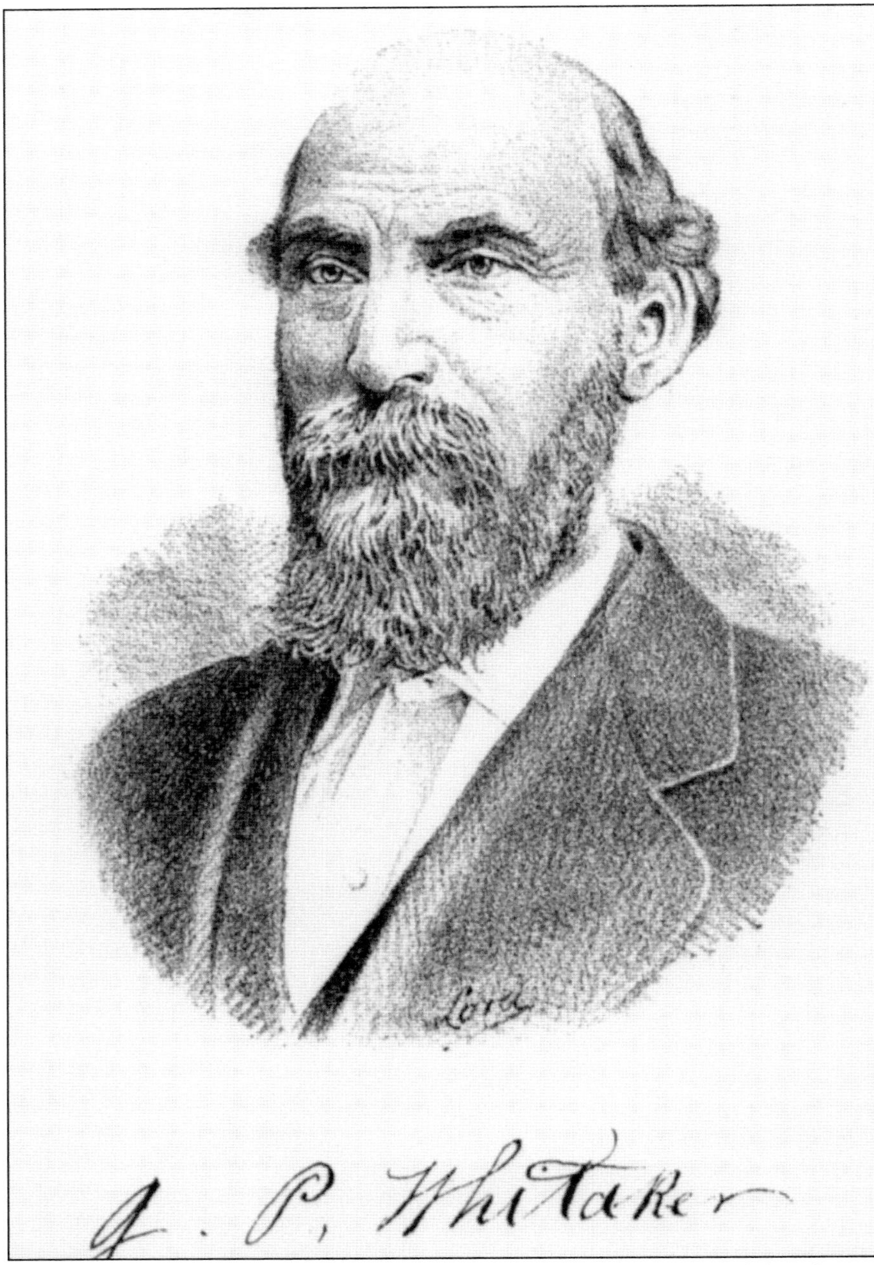

J.P. Whitaker (1824–1891) was born in Hamilton County, Ohio, and crossed the Plains with an ox team in 1849, a very difficult journey of five months to reach Sacramento and the mines. He worked hard but saved enough to buy a farm on the north side of Estero San Antonio in 1853. He married Irish-born Jane Carroll in 1858, the first teacher hired by the nearby American Valley Schoolhouse in 1855. In the year of their marriage, total expenditures for the school were $705. Jane Carroll's salary was $50 per month for six months. The school housed 54 pupils and was built at a cost of $405. J.P. Whitaker ignored public life, preferring to stay at home and devote his time and energies to the education of his four children. He was a strong and lifelong advocate of total abstinence, believing that the greater portion of crime and misery in this world is caused by intemperance. He maintained this vow to the grave.

Two

Marconi, McClure, and Mazzei

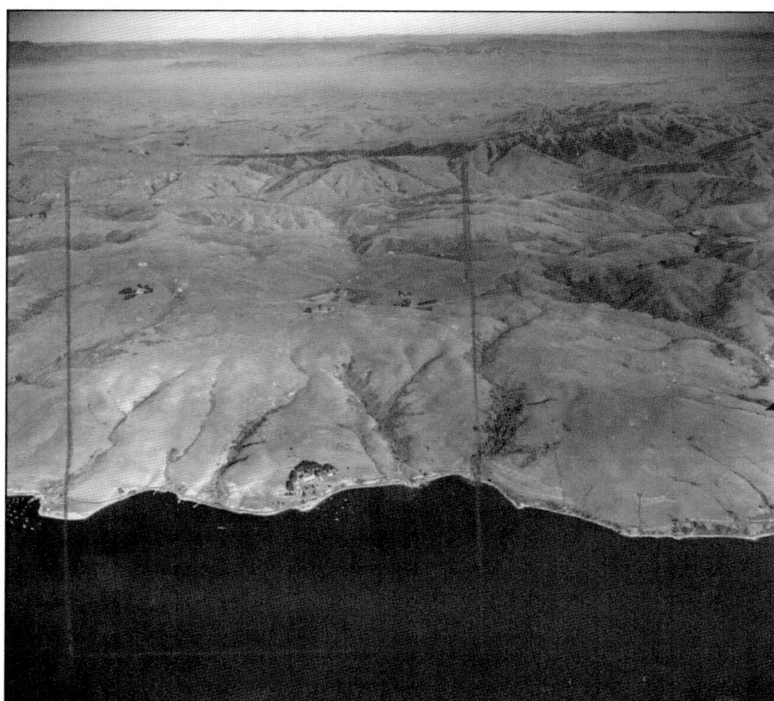

On August 31, 1912, the Marconi Wireless Company bought a total of 1,127 acres, including bay frontage of the village called Fishermen's, from Silvio Maggetti. The purchaser was middle-aged half-Italian, half-Irish Guglielmo Marconi, who, in his youth, was fascinated by the inventions of Benjamin Franklin. (Courtesy of Ed Brady.)

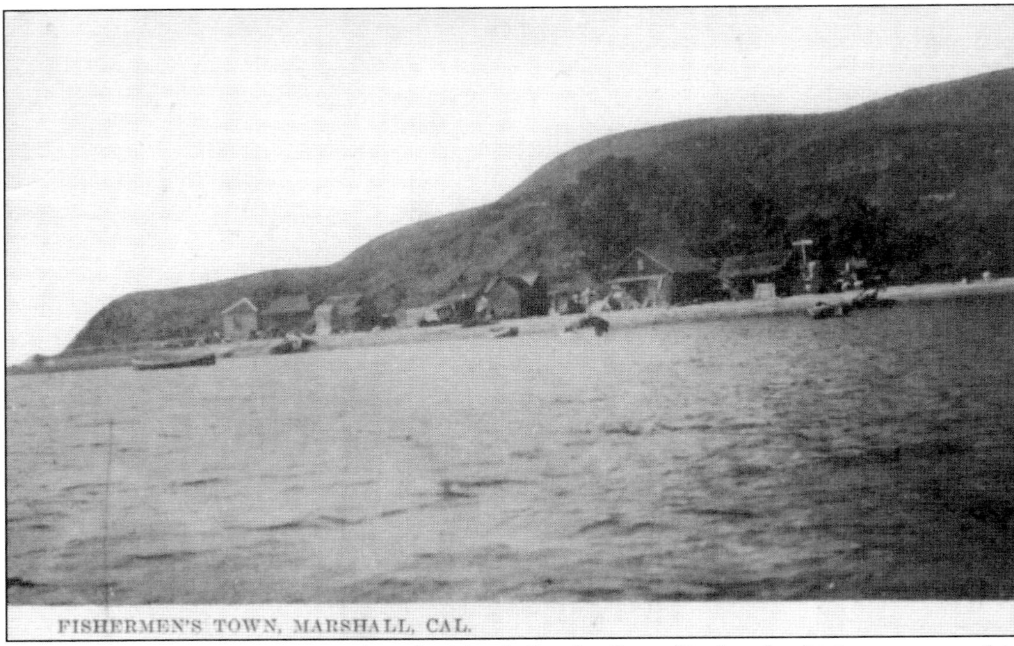

A. Bray Dickinson has written that the North Pacific Coast Railroad, which commenced in 1876, would stop at Fishermen's to load clams and fish. He also noted, "Surviving members of the Tamallos Indian tribe resided here. Their dwellings rested on piling over the tidewaters. Sailing boats usually were anchored in a nearby cove while nets dried on its sandy beach. Smiling Indian women in bright calicoes waved to passengers from doorways and windows." (Courtesy of Dan Brown.)

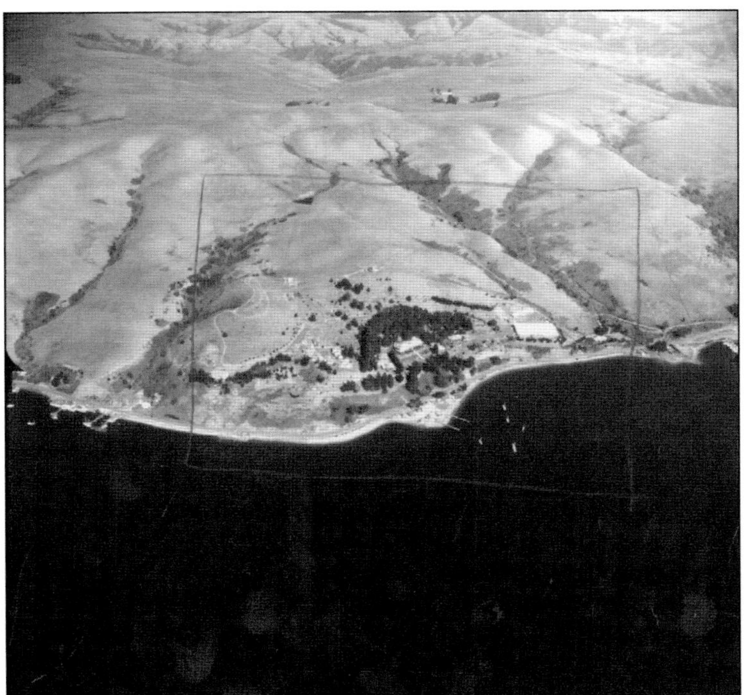

To accommodate and house male wireless station employees at the first trans-Pacific communication center, the Marshall Receiving Station was built in 1914 at a cost of $226,000 by the J.G. White Engineering Company. The Marconi Hotel was dedicated September 24, 1914. In addition to its 35 rooms, 10 complete with private baths, were two single-story bungalows for the chief and assistant engineers.

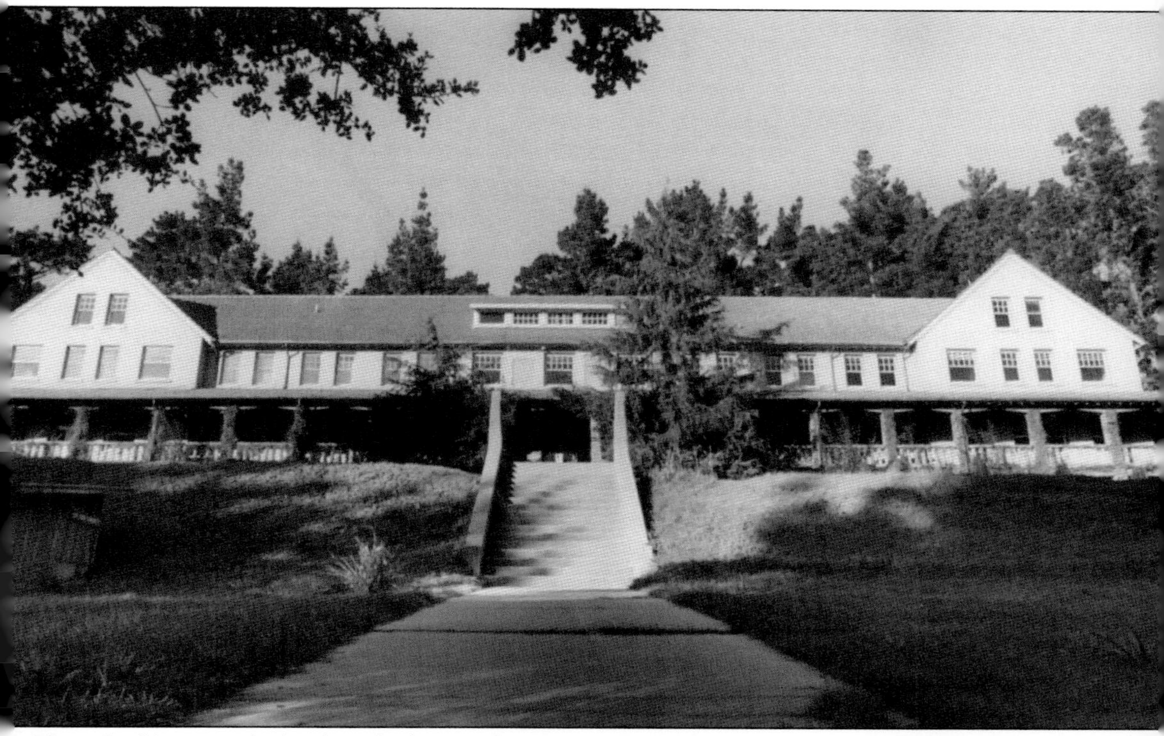

These buildings might be described as Mediterranean Revival with Craftsman allusions. Every steel, concrete, and tile material was selected to ensure minimum maintenance and maximum fire protection. The Mediterranean and Italian stylistic elements included the extensive use of tile, verandas, the symmetrical treatment of window fenestration, and an overall formal approach. The Craftsman style, popular at the time, can be seen in the decorative treatment of the eaves, the use of dormers, and multi panel upper sash windows. The hotel's interior featured restrained, rectilinear millwork, natural wood finishes, and five cross-panel doors with transoms. There were two massive first-story masonry fireplaces with rustic half-log mantels. The American Marconi Company also constructed small wooden cottages for married employees and their families. On the hills above the operations building stood the 270-foot towers that held aloft the mile-long antenna. Guy-wires attached to four concrete anchors supported the masts.

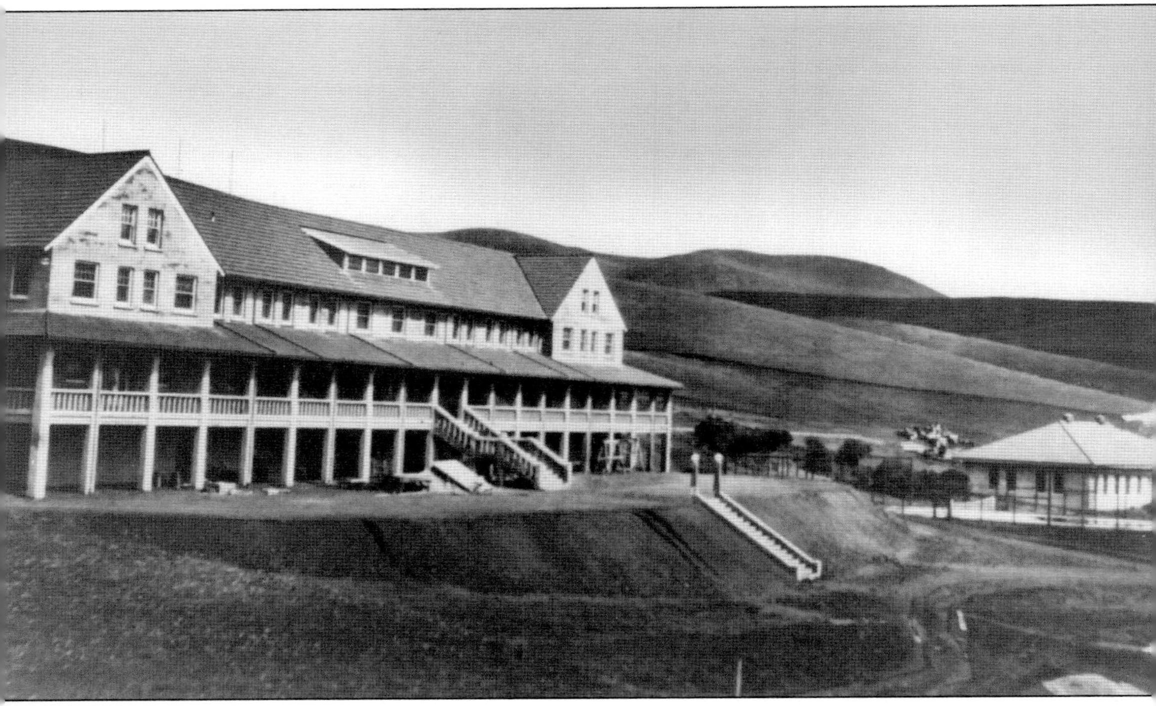

Samuel Newsom was a 19-year-old radio electrician assigned to the Marconi Receiving Station in 1918 for instruction in the new field of wireless telegraphy. Upon entering World War I in 1917, the US Navy had taken control of the station. Newsom remembered "seven tubular masts 300 feet tall that ran up the hill for over a mile, oriented for the best receiving angle from Hawaii . . . we could hear pretty much of everything even from Europe. Finally the Armistice came with a message from the Eiffel Tower, 'fermez la porte,' referring to the legend of Janus whose temple gates were opened in times of war and closed in times of peace." It is fitting to add that Frank Geisel at Marconi Receiving Station was the first person on the US mainland to receive word of Japan's attack on Pearl Harbor.

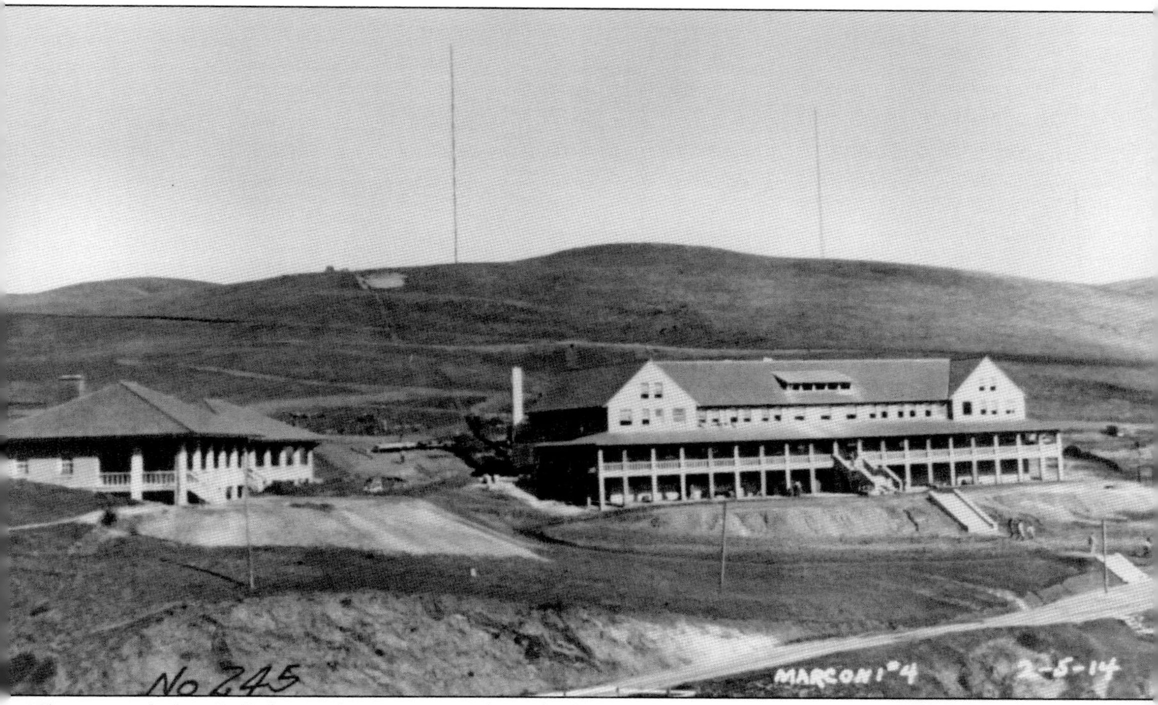

The genius behind all this architecture was described by his biographer Calvin Durand Trowbridge Jr.: "Marconi was a giant in his time, akin to Bill Gates and Steve Jobs of today. As a technological inventor/entrepreneur/businessman, he foreshadowed the booming era of Silicon Valley 100 years later, paving the way for the communications revolution of today's Wi-Fi, smart phones and ultraportable computers." He may never have seen the Marconi Station itself, but he visited San Francisco in October 1933 and spoke to the Italian businessmen's group Il Cenacolo, signing the guest book on October 24. Ten thousand people welcomed him to San Francisco, where, in several speeches, he proclaimed: "In this day of stress and depression it is science that will bring man relief. It is not the aim of science to take work from man, which is, after all, his greatest joy, but to provide him with sufficient devices by which his brain may be sharpened so he may enjoy the leisure which is his birthright." He would die in Rome less than four years later. The 100th anniversary of the Marconi Station, now transformed into the Marconi Conference Center, is in 2013–2014.

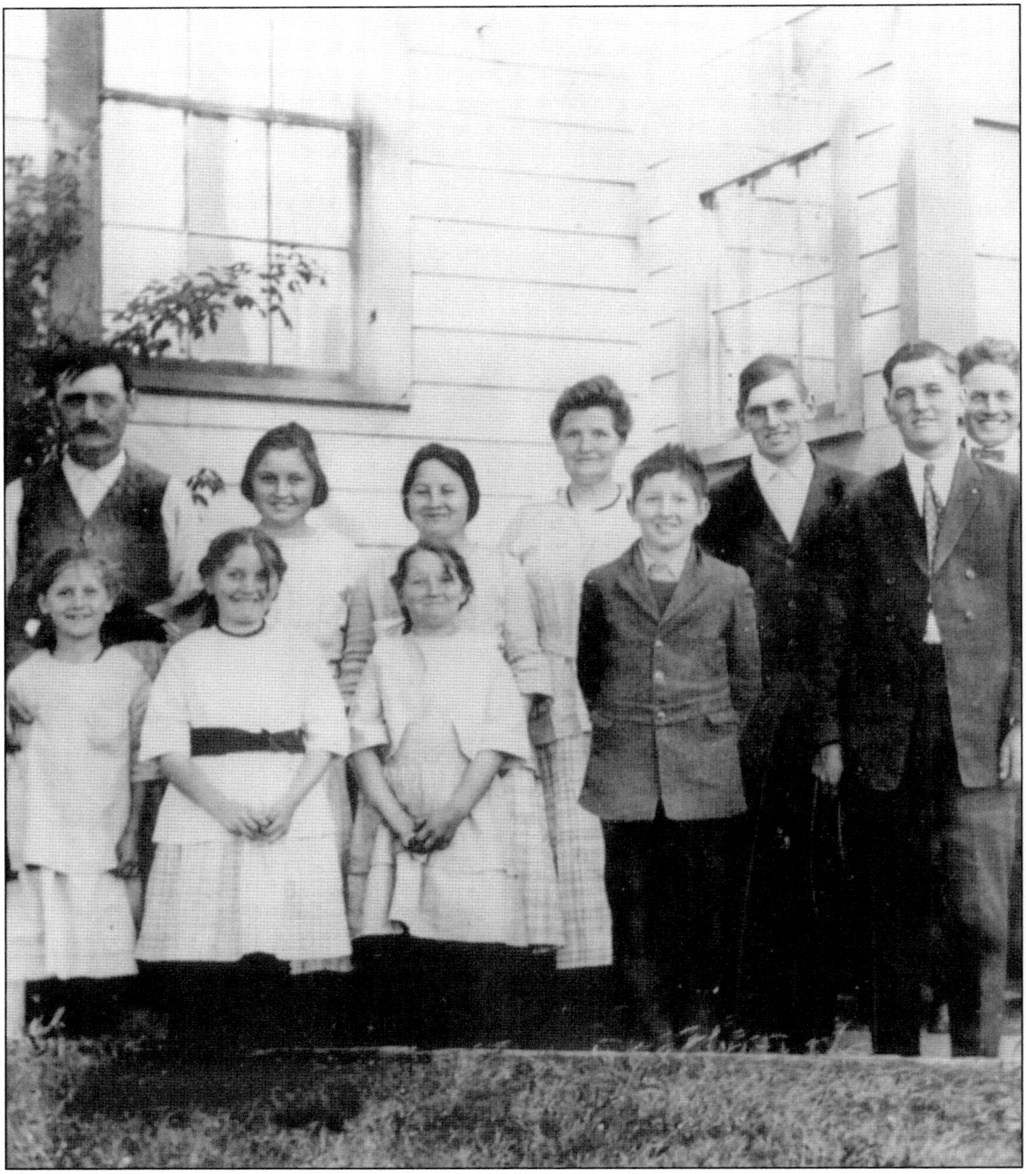

The oldest dairy family still ranching on Point Reyes, the McClures were in the vanguard of a second wave of Irish immigrants to West Marin that began in the 1880s. In 1889, James McClure Sr. (1867–1934) was a carpenter in Enagh, not far from Markethill, Armagh. Most likely sponsored by his uncle David McClure, he immigrated to America, working first at a sawmill on Point Reyes and then as a streetcar driver in San Francisco. Being fired from this job, he returned to Point Reyes and operated dairies for the next decade. His wife, Margaret (1872–1961), gave birth to "Jim" McClure Jr. (1902–1993). After the Radio Corporation of America (RCA) purchased the Marconi Receiving Station in 1920, it took possession through condemnation of the 1,472-acre James McClure Ranch (G Ranch) in 1929 to develop a new receiving station to replace the Marshall Station.

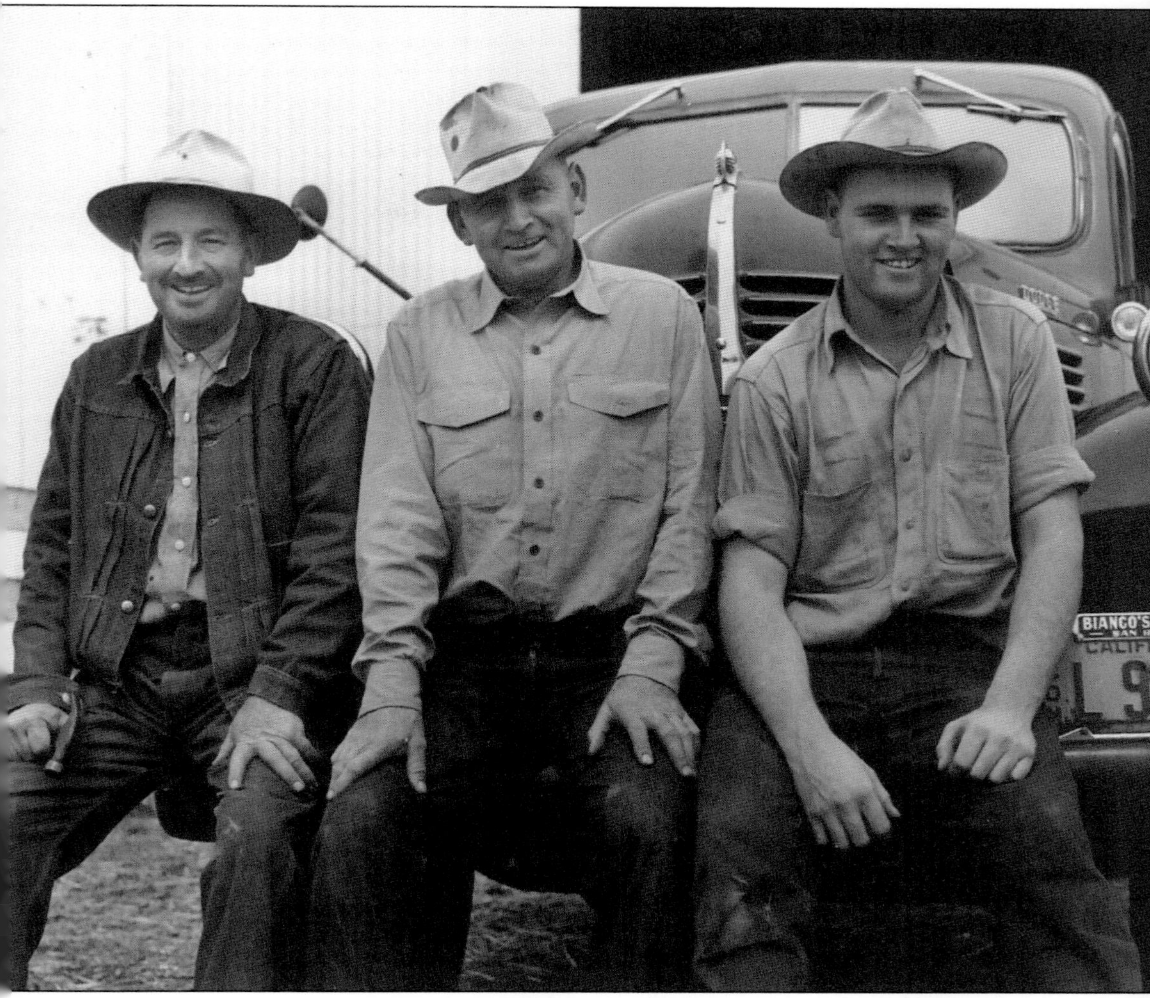

From left to right are Dave McClure (1901–1960), brother Jim McClure Jr. (1902–1993), and Jim's son Ron McClure; Jim Jr. and his wife, the former Helen Gallagher (died in 1967), had Ron in 1930. Woody Williams took this photograph in 1950.

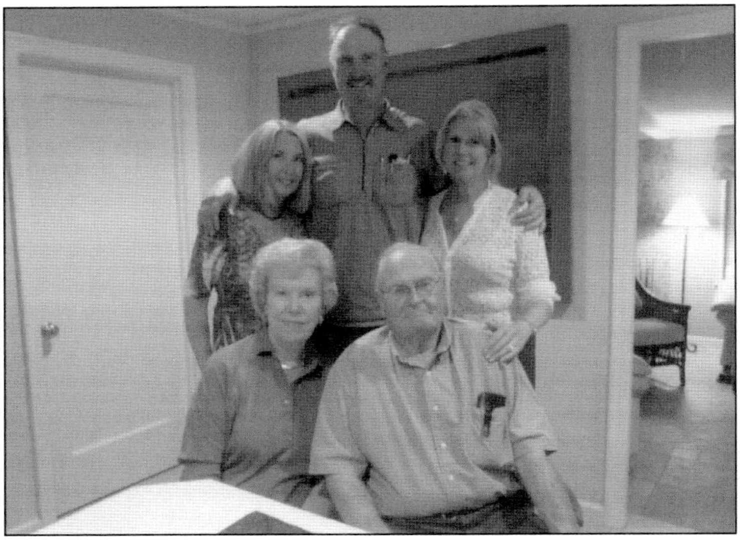

Celebrating their 60th wedding anniversary are Arlene and Ron McClure. Standing proudly behind them are their three children, from left to right, Joan, Bob, and Gayle McClure Crayne. With husband Jim, Gayle McClure Crayne owns Armagh Vineyards, named as a tribute to their ancestral home in Ireland. The McClures are now five generations strong in Tomales Bay.

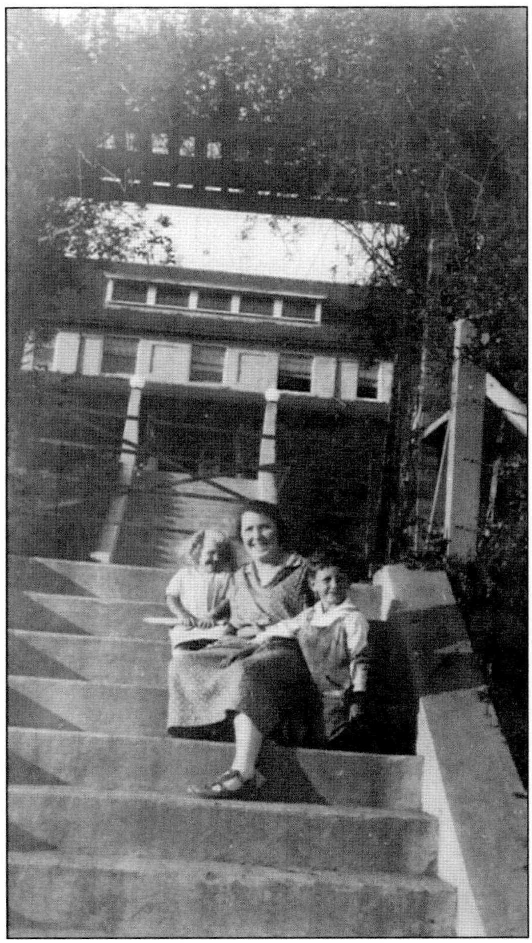

At the steps of the Marconi Station in 1926 are Gelinda Giachini Mazzei (1899–1979) and her two children, Walter and Isabelle. She was born in Colle di Buggiano, in the province of Pistoia, just beyond Italy's most famous spa, Montecatini Terme. Buggiano is 62.5 miles southeast of Marconi's birthplace in Bologna. She married Gualtiero from the same village, and they came to North Beach, San Francisco, on June 22, 1920, where she worked as a seamstress and a factory worker. She taught her grandson Robert how to sew both by hand and by machine. She was also a "kitchen magician," taking the most meager food scraps and transforming them into a meal fit for a king. Taking up squirrel hunting in his teens, Robert would bring the squirrels to Gelinda, who prepared a five-course meal topped off with squirrel meat over polenta.

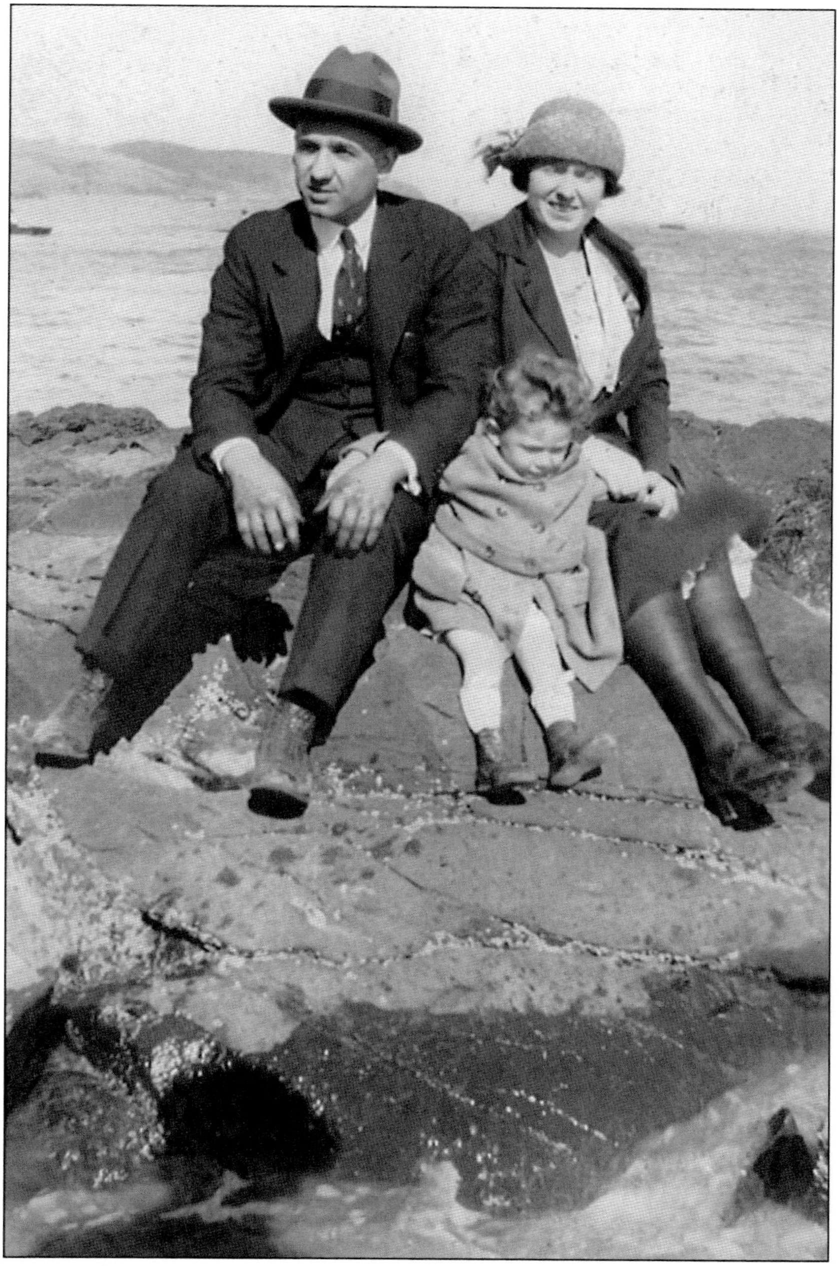

Sitting on a Sunday in Marconi Cove with his wife and son, Gualtiero Mazzei (1894–1977) recalled the poverty of his youth in Buggiano when squirrels, rats, road kill, and baby birds all went into the polenta pot. Marconi became his new destination for bird and mushroom recreational hunting on weekends. He had served in the Italian Army in World War I but was never proud of it. His honorable discharge certificate, dated April 10, 1929, made its way to San Francisco with the stamped signature of Benito Mussolini. In San Francisco, he worked as a handyman in a stockyard. One day, he fell off a scaffolding and broke his back. Unable to do physical work, and with Gelinda's coaxing, he learned a new trade, watch repair. He set up a small business, expanded it into a hardware store, and eventually bought the building. To this day, G. Mazzei and Sons Hardware is still in business at 5166 Third Street, San Francisco.

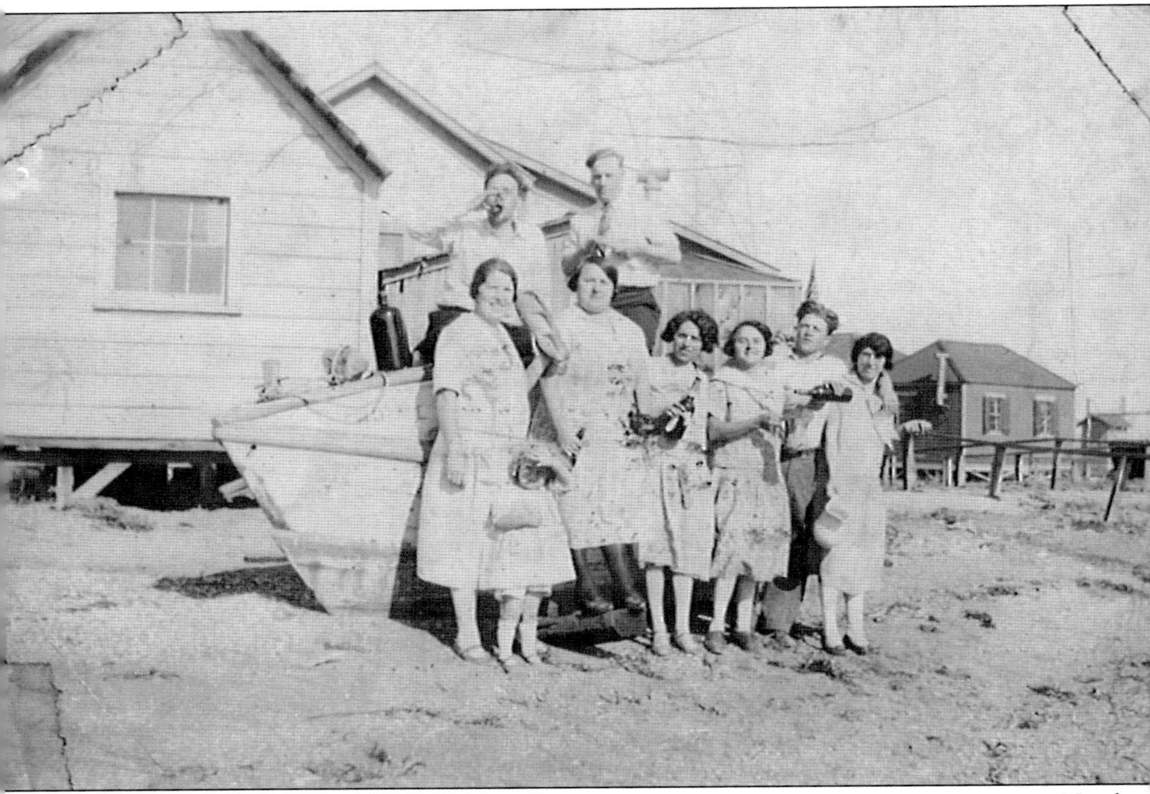

Also from Buggiano, this married couple, it is rumored, won their Marconi cottage in a North Beach poker game. Mario (with a tie) is standing on his boat while Rosie is just below him alongside Gelinda Mazzei. The Checchis had no children, so to keep the cottage "in the family," good friend Walter Mazzei bought it a few years before Mario's death.

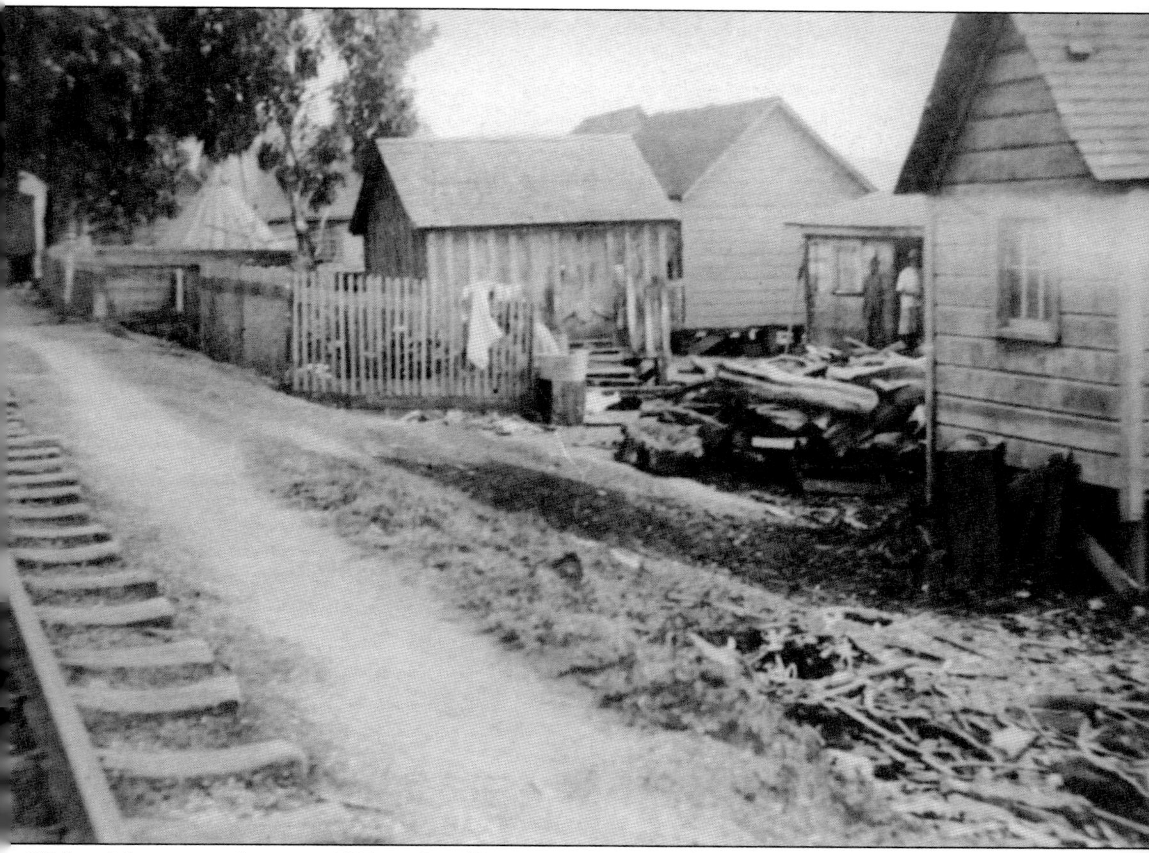

Walter Mazzei was born in 1921 in San Francisco. He attended Mission High School, served as a machinist in World War II, and worked most of his life in his father's hardware store. The "Buggiano cottage" was a regular weekend destination for the Checchis and the Mazzeis. The narrow-gauge railroad served to bring the Marconi catch of herring and turbot back to San Francisco restaurants.

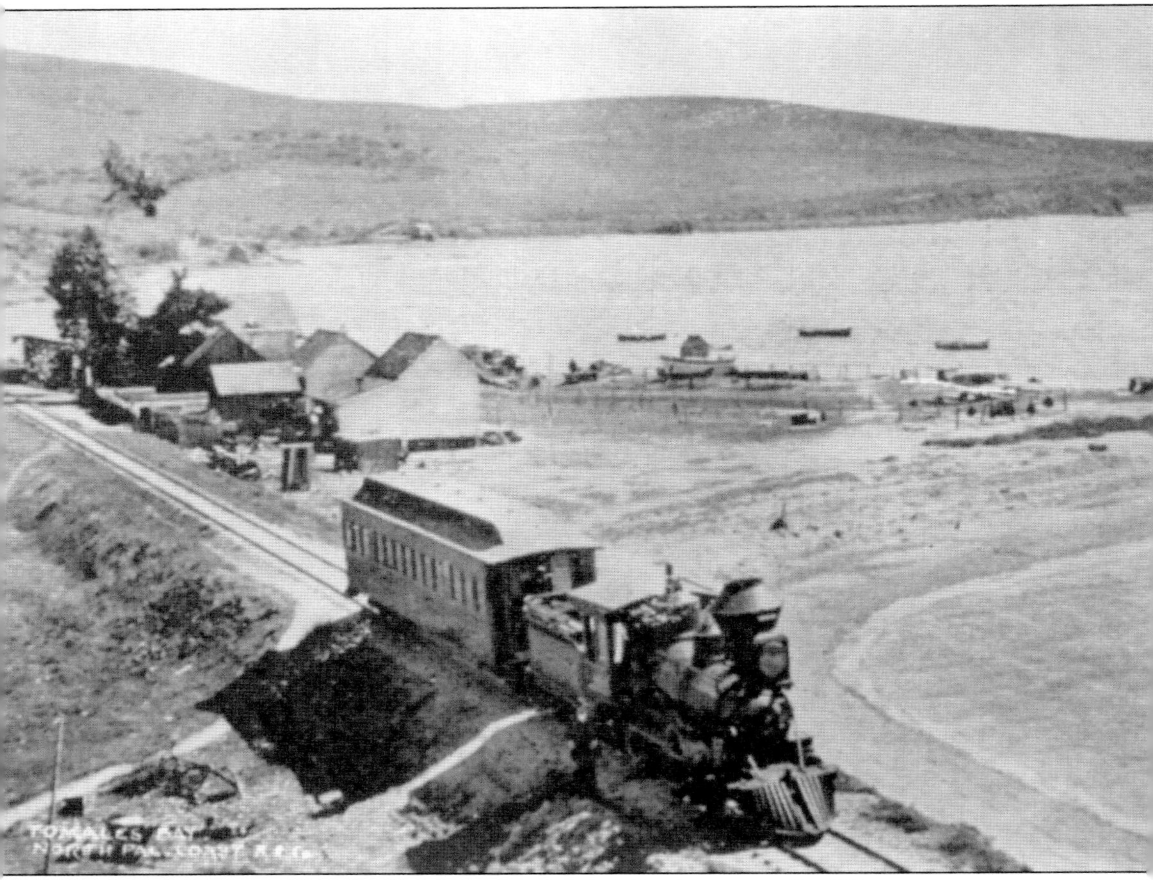

Robert Mazzei, son of Walter and grandson of Gualtiero, recalls, "There were many wooden racks which resembled track hurdles in the open area south of the cottages. These were used by the fishermen to dry and repair their nets. Below, engine No. 7 is just north of the 'Buggiano Cottage.'" It became the "party engine" after No. 9 was wrecked at Austin Creek.

Three

MARSHALL

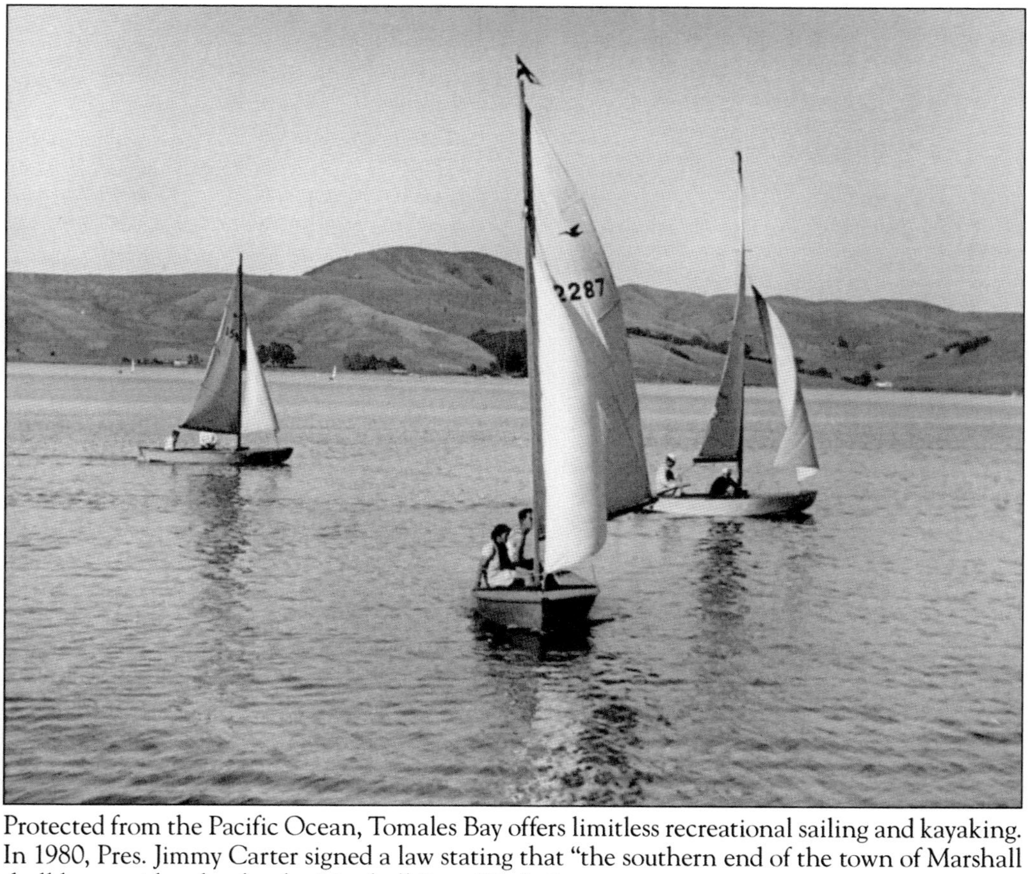

Protected from the Pacific Ocean, Tomales Bay offers limitless recreational sailing and kayaking. In 1980, Pres. Jimmy Carter signed a law stating that "the southern end of the town of Marshall shall be considered to be the Marshall Boat Works."

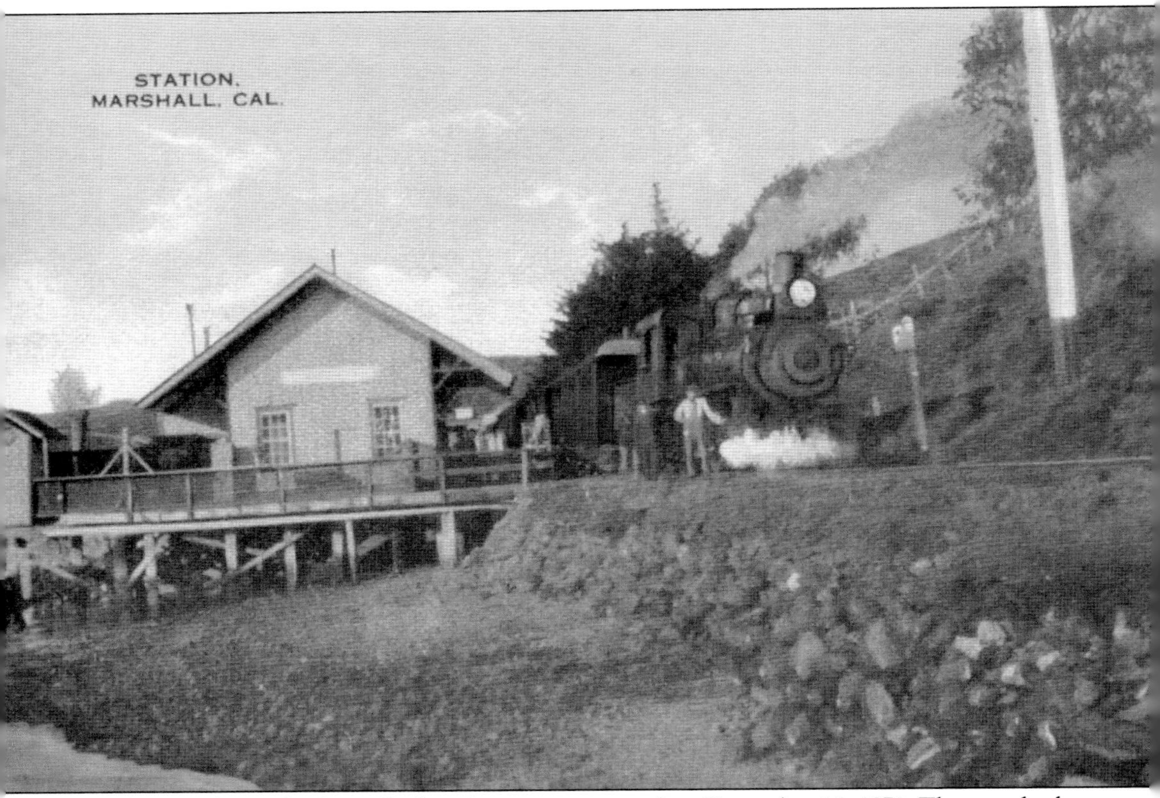

The North Pacific Coast Railroad was incorporated on December 16, 1871. The standard gauge of 4 feet, 8.5 inches, is derived from the original specifications for a Roman war chariot, which was constructed just wide enough to accommodate the rear ends of two warhorses. This standard permitted the interchanging of rolling stock across most of the United States. A three-foot gauge was selected for the North Pacific Coast Railroad based on the successful example of the Denver & Rio Grande Railroad through the Rocky Mountains. A 10-foot rail bed was cheaper than a standard 15-foot one. Narrow gauge meant lighter rails and coaches while still permitting the hauling of timber from West Marin to "Saucelito," present-day Sausalito. Wealthy West Marin businessmen foresaw the advantages of a rail line along Tomales Bay and put up enough money to guarantee it. James Miller and the Marshall brothers offered $10,000 themselves if the project were to pass through Millerton and Marshall. The first consignor of goods was James Fallon, whose 300 sacks of potatoes were destined for San Francisco.

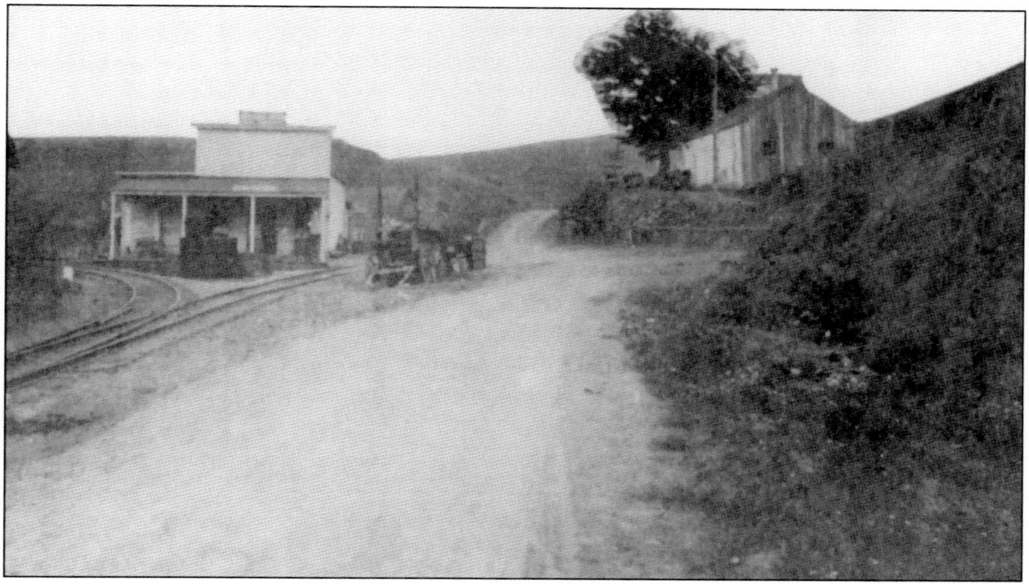

Marshall's first post office was established on February 6, 1872, with Eugene L. White as its first postmaster. Alexander Stitt Marshall was appointed road overseer for the new Tomales District on August 8, 1868. Within one November week in 1869, he bought 369 acres in Tomales from Thomas Carruthers and 750 acres in Tomales from Charles Roberts. With his brothers, he built the Bay View Hotel (Marshall Hotel) in Marshall as a retreat and resting place for fishermen, hunters, and sportsmen alike. In 1873, a store was built next to the Bay View Hotel. It is possible that the post office operated from the Bay View Hotel in 1872 and either the hotel or the Marshall Store from 1873 to 1877. Since the first wall phone in Marshall would not be put in until 1910, the post office was a vital link to the rest of California and the world.

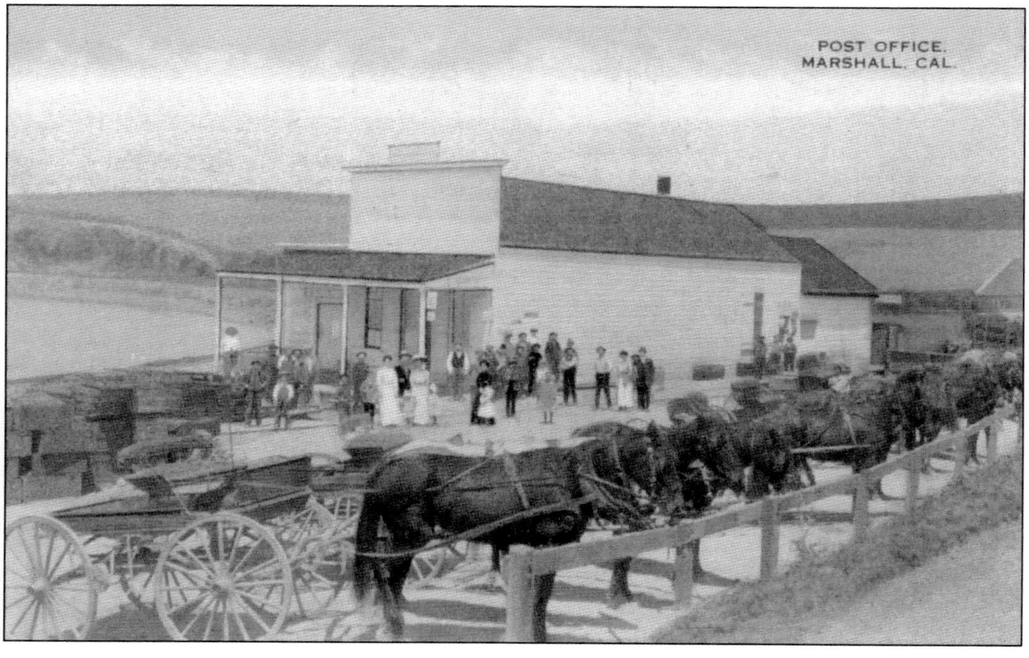

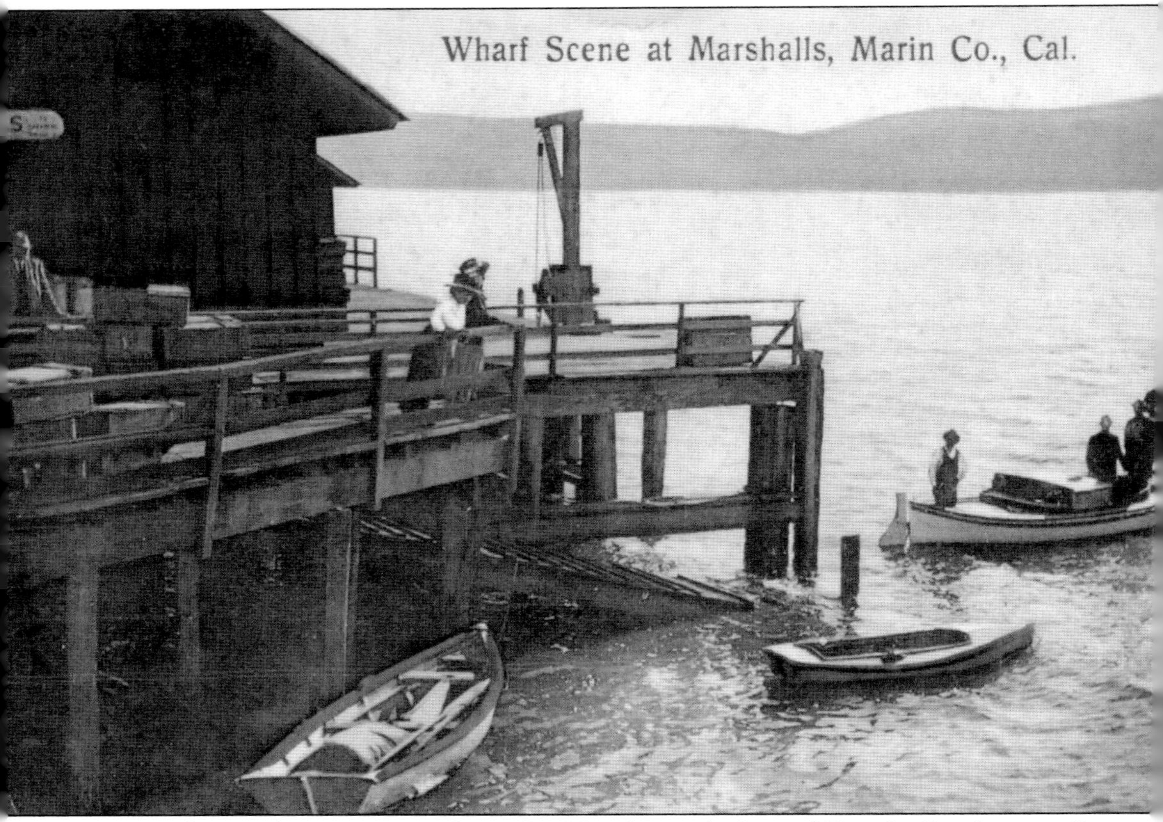

According to the *Marin Journal* in 1888, "On the north shore of Tomales Bay, between Point Reyes Station and Tomales is Marshalls, well known as the point of shipment for the celebrated little clam that is so popular in the San Francisco markets. Near the station as one gets off the train is a gilded sign bearing the name of Howard and Co. This is where a few years ago Charley Howard held forth, doing a prosperous business and controlling the clam trade on Tomales Bay, but his domestic relations are said not to have gone right, and like many others adversity struck him and he departed for other climes." According to Florence Donnelly in 1968, "Men and women of the small colony of Indians turned over the big rocks along the shore to dig up the small clams, which were the great delicacy of the area. The clams were then sold by the diggers for 50¢ to $1 a gunny-sack full. Fish and game laws that outlawed the taking of the clams for commercial purposes left the hapless Indians without any means of support." (Courtesy of Dan Brown.)

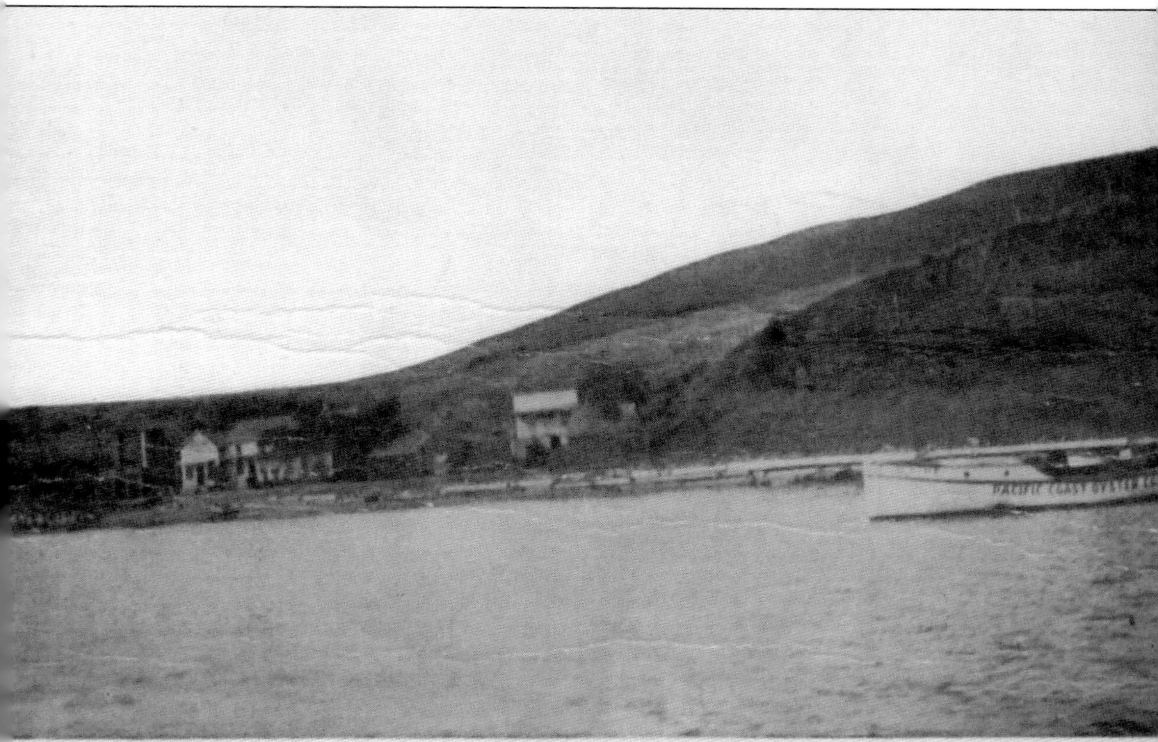

CIFIC COAST OYSTER CO., MARSHALL, CAL.

Oysters and Tomales Bay have been synonymous since 1874–1875, contemporaneous with the North Pacific Railroad Company, which would take them to San Francisco restaurants. Native oysters were sold on a small scale but with limited success. With the completion of the transcontinental railroad in 1869, live eastern oysters and seed oysters made their way to San Francisco Bay, which soon became polluted. Tomales Bay, however, was pristine. Christy Avery writes, "In 1907, Eli Gordon's Pacific Coast Oyster Company planted 450 acres of oysters at Bivalve, a railroad stop opened exclusively for the company on the bay's southeastern shore. The company angered local fishermen when it fenced much of the bay near its beds, and county officials forced the company to remove the impediments. Once the oysters grew to marketable size, the company began daily shipments to San Francisco. The company grew oysters at the beds at Bivalve until the 1930s or 1940s."

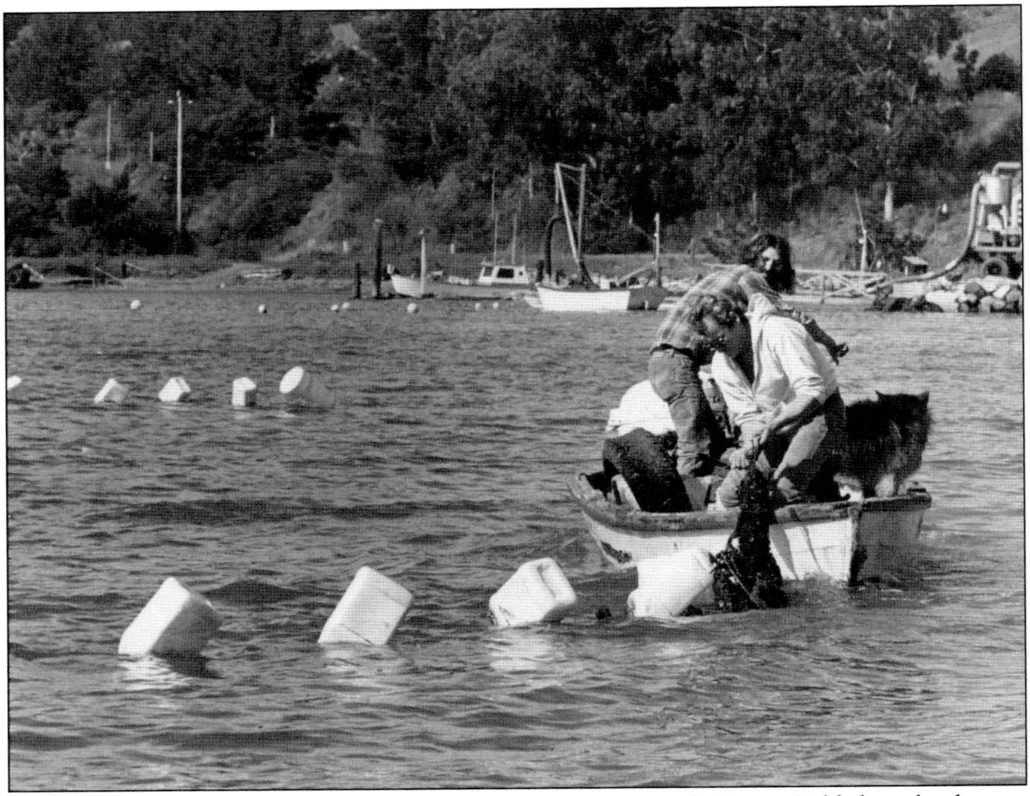

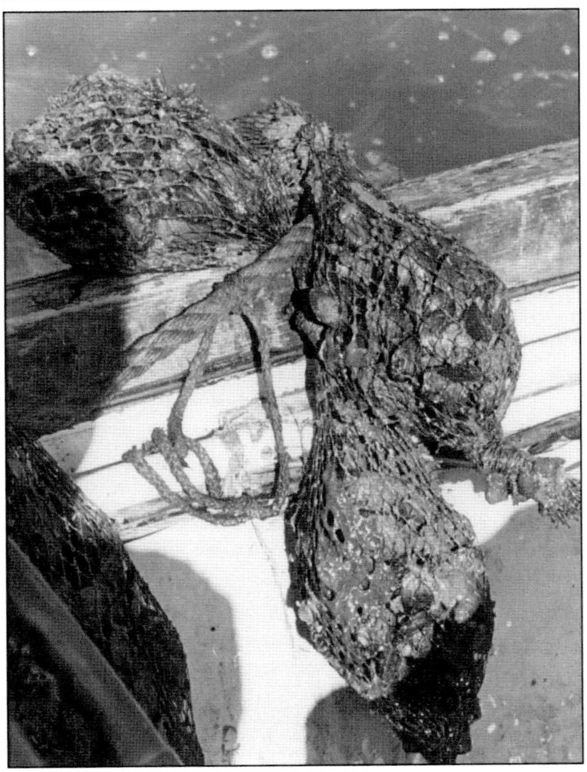

An early Sunset Publishing book celebrated Tomales Bay for its "Cockles Kingdom." While oysters are predominant today, other shellfish have had their day. The Indians at Fishermen's lived by fishing and selling clams to train passengers. In both of these pictures, taken February 25, 1986, Scott Zahl and Michael Matassarin are checking the size of harvested mussels. In *The Wilder Shore* (1984), author David Rains Wallace recollects: "The first place I stayed in California was a little house built on pilings on the east shore of Tomales Bay across from Point Reyes. . . . I had not known a place could be so full of wild animals. Every morning a line of low-flying cormorants seemed to stretch from one end of the bay to the other. The water under the house was alive with long-legged red crabs and orange-fleshed mussels the size of saucers."

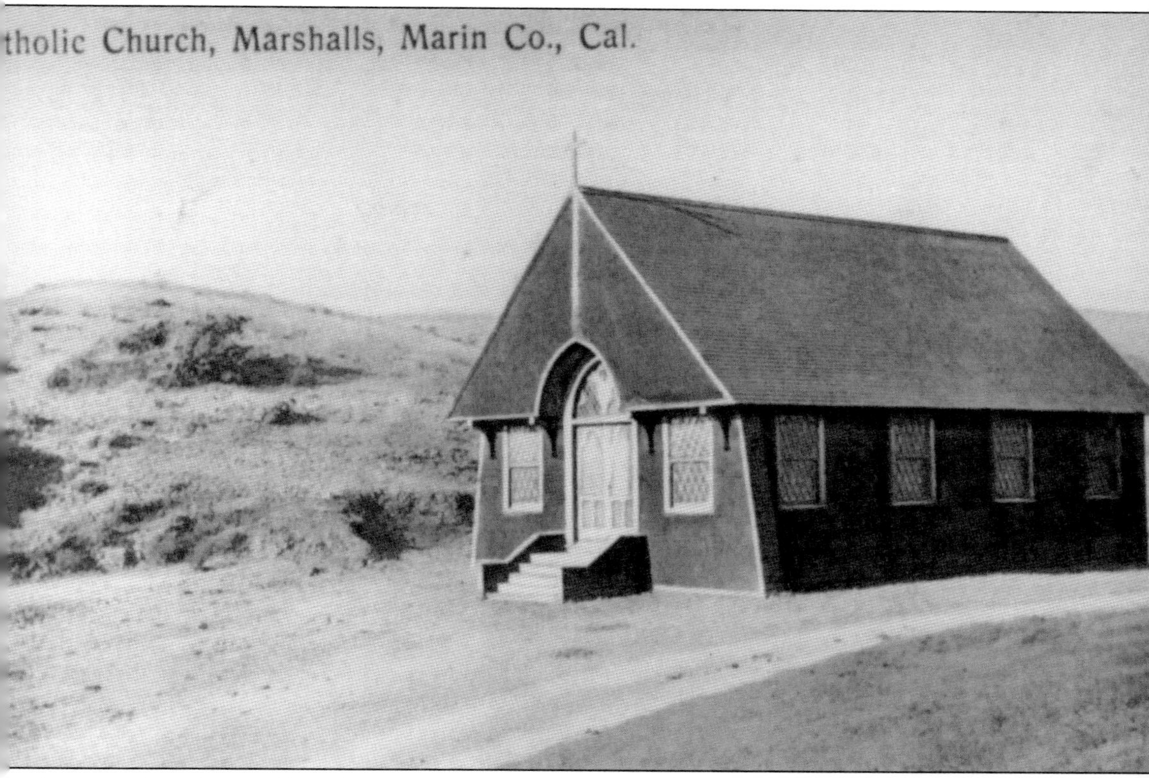

Mrs. James Marshall and Fannie Armstrong, granddaughter of Emma Jane Marshall, the first white child born in Tomales Township, donated the hill site on a bluff north of Marshall overlooking Tomales Bay to the Catholic diocese for $75. The frame church, St. Helen's, was designed by Frank Shea. Cavanaugh Bros. of Petaluma was the contractor, and the final cost in 1900–1902 was $2,000. Archbishop Patrick Riordan dedicated and blessed the church before 1,000 constituents. Jack Mason wrote: "The opening was delayed until the factory-made windows could be shipped by Wells Fargo to the well-known carpenter P. Calegaris. . . . Most of the faithful were down from Cazadero and waypoints on the train. John Keys's daughter Minnie directed Maggie and Cecilia Clark, Valerie and Irene Dado, Maggie Curry and Lizzy Swarts in the choral mass, after which everyone repaired to the sandwich tent in Mrs. Rasmussen's garden."

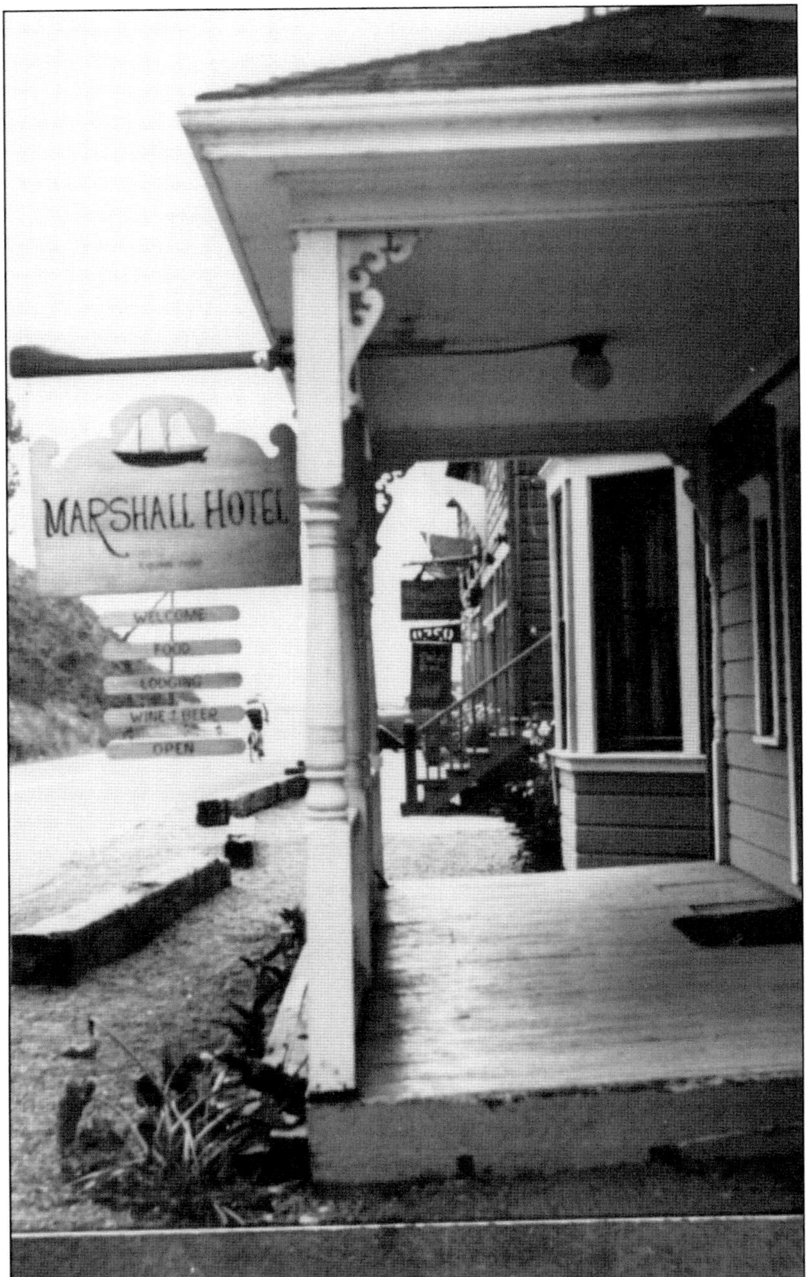

From the *Marin Journal* of October 26, 1899, comes the following excerpt: "A new large and roomy hotel has just been completed at Marshalls. The building is an excellent piece of architectural work and commands a grand sight of Tomales Bay. It was constructed for the Marshall Bros. and compendiously speaking its cost was $3,000. Two years ago, the Bay View Hotel was burned and since then the town has been without any accommodations for the many hunters and fishermen who frequently visit here for the fine hunting and fishing this place affords. Salmon Creek is one of the finest streams in the county for fresh water fishing, being a short distance from here. There is no doubt that with proper management it will become a favorite summer resort because in the hottest days in summer this place is cool and refreshing."

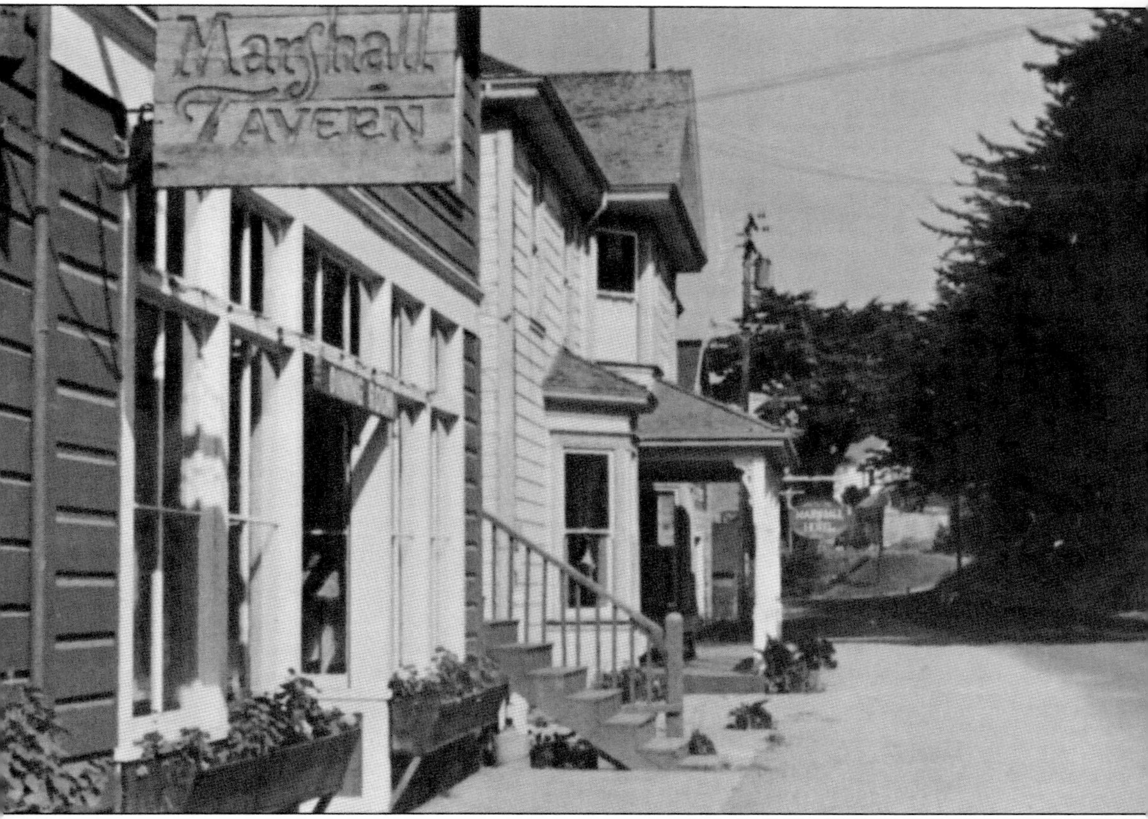

The *Marin Journal* article of October 26, 1899, continues: "Mrs. John Shields, an enterprising woman of this vicinity, has secured a lease and expects to have the building furnished and ready for opening by the first of November." The Shields general merchandise store at Marshall was a favorite gathering place for ranchers and sportsmen alike. John Shields also owned a large dairy ranch here, and it was no surprise when he bought the hotel in 1900 along with the adjoining saloon and livery stable. John Wightman had founded the first store in Marshall in 1867. It was reported to have been located up the wagon road to Petaluma. In 1860, the "Marshalls-to-Petaluma Road" was laid out and served as one of the county's first major roadways. Known often as Marshall's Warehouse Road, it linked Marshall to the inner valley.

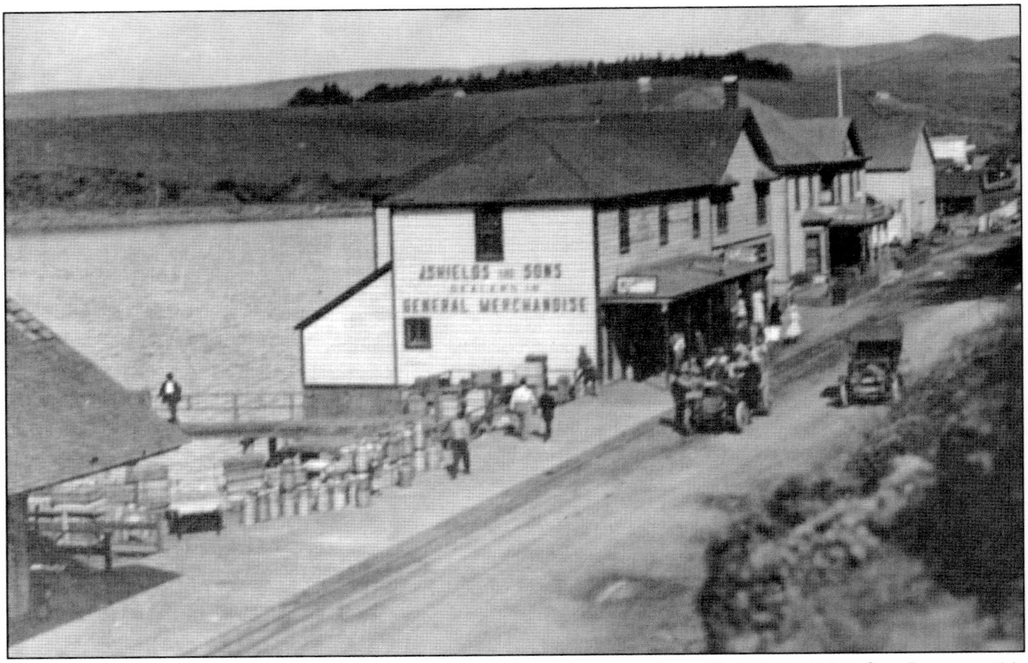

Regular service commenced on the North Pacific narrow-gauge railroad on Monday, January 11, 1875. San Francisco connected with Sausalito through a passenger ferry and also a freight train with an attached passenger car every Tuesday, Thursday, and Saturday at 6:30 a.m. The 47.5-mile trip to Marshall took approximately three hours. The train returned from Marshall to San Francisco between 1:30 and 2:00 p.m. Charles Howard established a mercantile firm in Marshall on May 17, 1877. According to the *Marin Journal*, "A good and commodious depot building was erected by the North Pacific Coast Railroad Company in 1876. The first ticket agent was A.B. Robbins who was succeeded in 1876 by A.W. Dutton." The Marshalls had built the schooner wharf. John Shields and Sons Store, Dealers in Dry Goods and General Merchandise, advertised drugs, boots, shoes, lumber, feed, paints, boat supplies, groceries, hardware and American ladies shoes. The Shields Hotel allowed visitors overnight accommodations to lengthen their stay in Marshall.

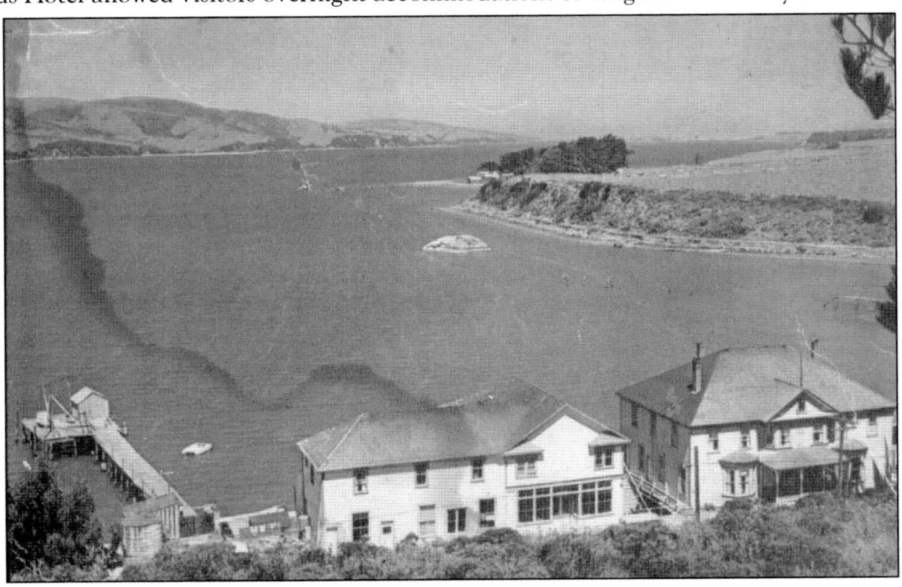

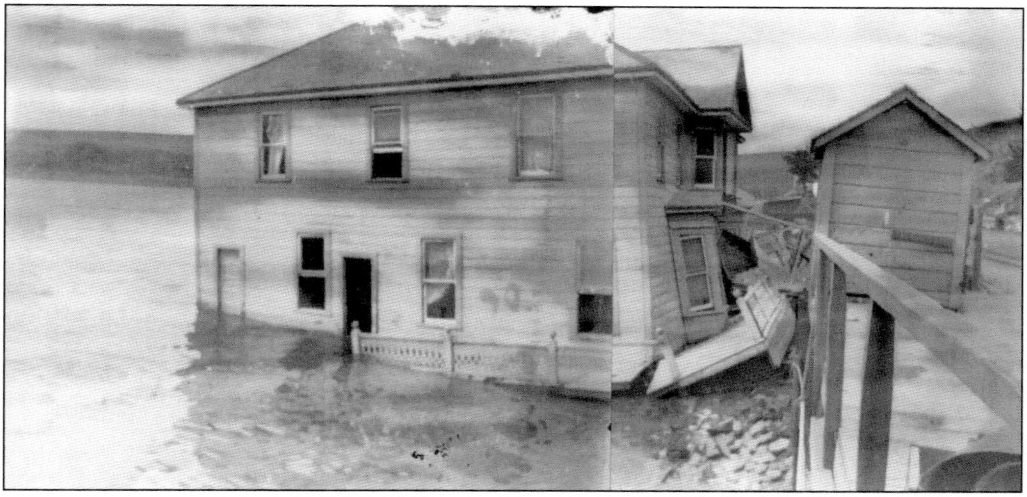

"Tomales Bay is one of California's rewards for putting up with the San Andreas Fault's occasional binges of earthquake destruction," stated *Sunset* magazine. The North Shore Hotel slid into the Bay April 18, 1906, but was retrieved by John Shields. Jack Mason's *Earthquake Bay: A History of Tomales Bay* (1976) is unequaled for its factual documentation. Damage to the railroad was severe, he writes, as it "had just laid 30,000 new ties north of Millerton, and replaced fills, trestles and bridges dating back to the earliest days of the North Pacific Coast," just a quarter of a century earlier. Built on fill along the bay, the railroad tracks shifted, levees broke, and trestles fell. A 1908 study of the earthquake reached the conclusion that: "The earthquake only temporarily modified the bay's landscape . . . Favorite clamming spots were buried in silt. Locals observed that stream channels shifted and springs dried up or increased in flow. Nonetheless, geologists concluded that the earthquake did not cause any major changes to the bay itself."

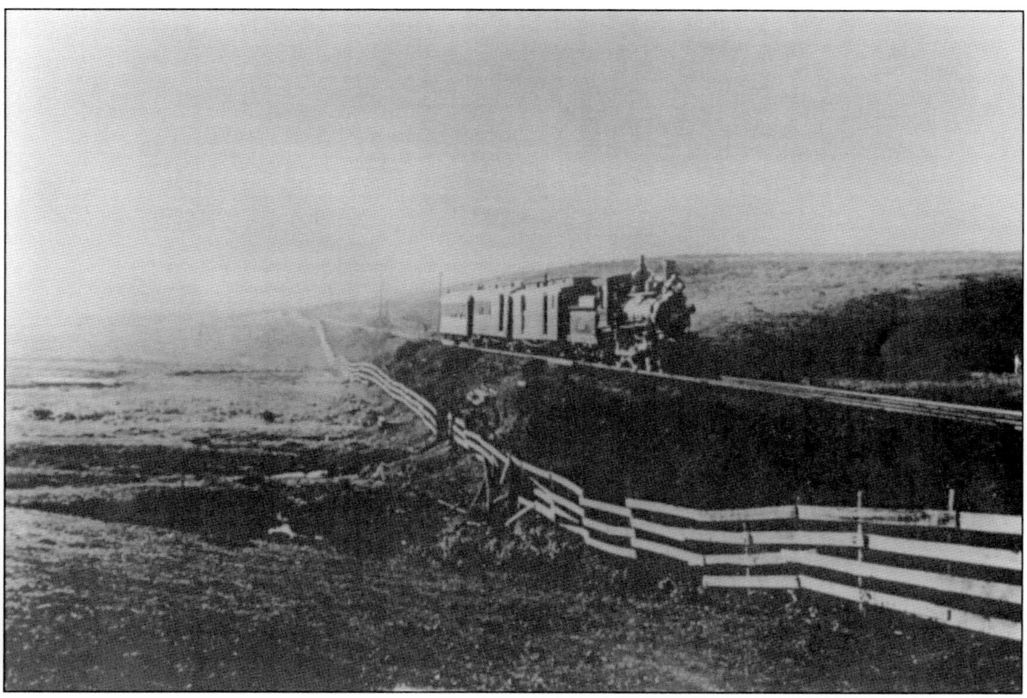

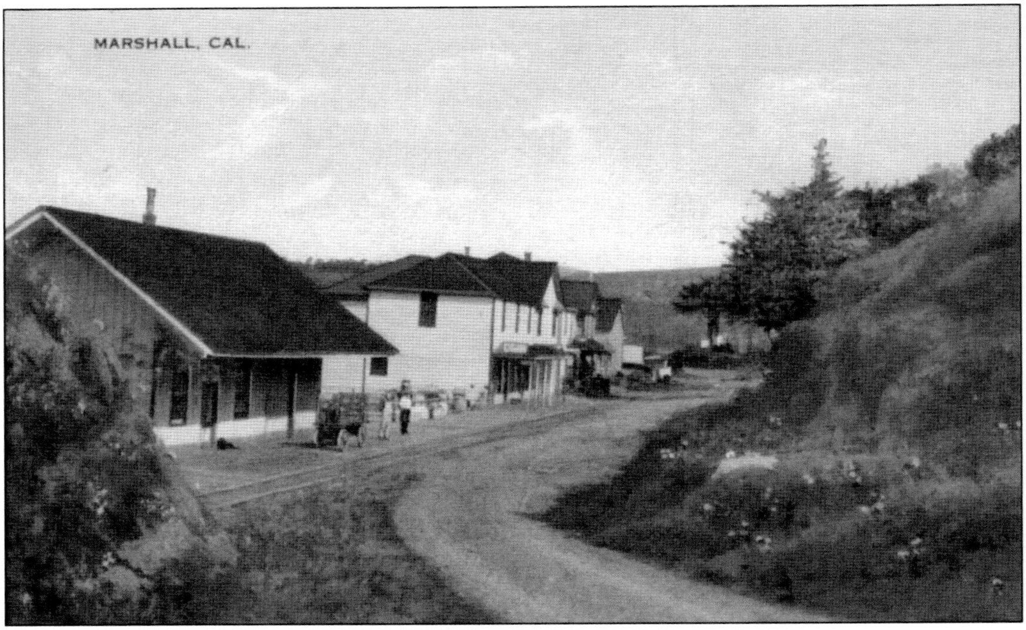

This postcard with a 1¢ stamp was postmarked in the afternoon of December 4, 1910, and reads: "Well I was surprized to get a card from you remember the watermelon? Is your mother with you yet? I suppose Ida is a big girl now, isn't she. This is a picture of our Marshalls Town. Will close with best regards to you and Joe. I remain yours, Willie Bell." Richard Behrendt of San Francisco published this postcard, printed in Germany, for J. Shields & Sons, General Merchandise, in Marshalls. (Courtesy of Dan Brown.)

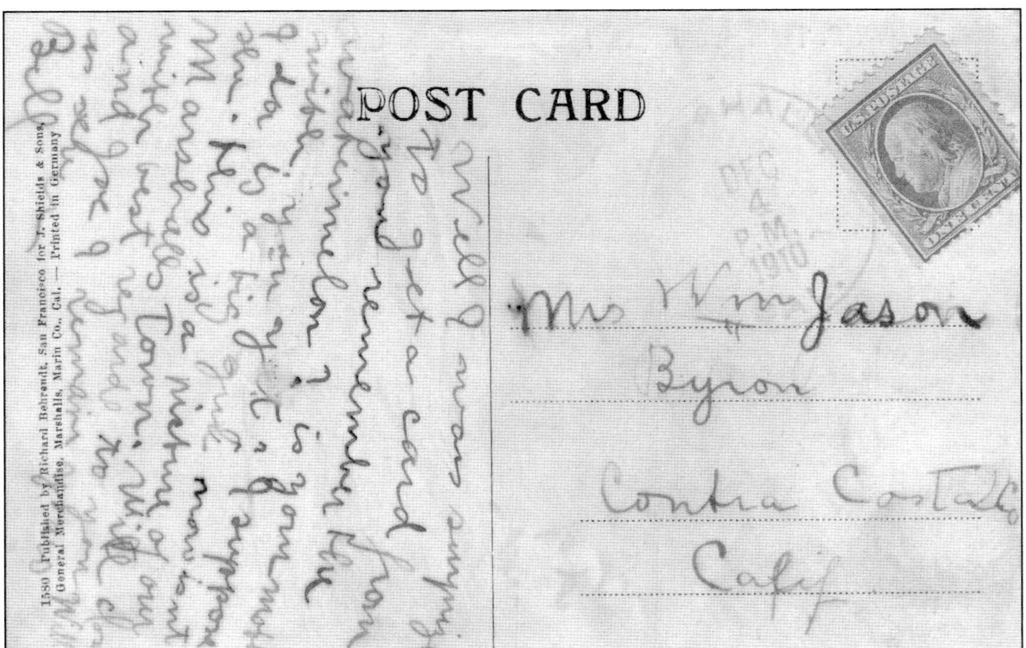

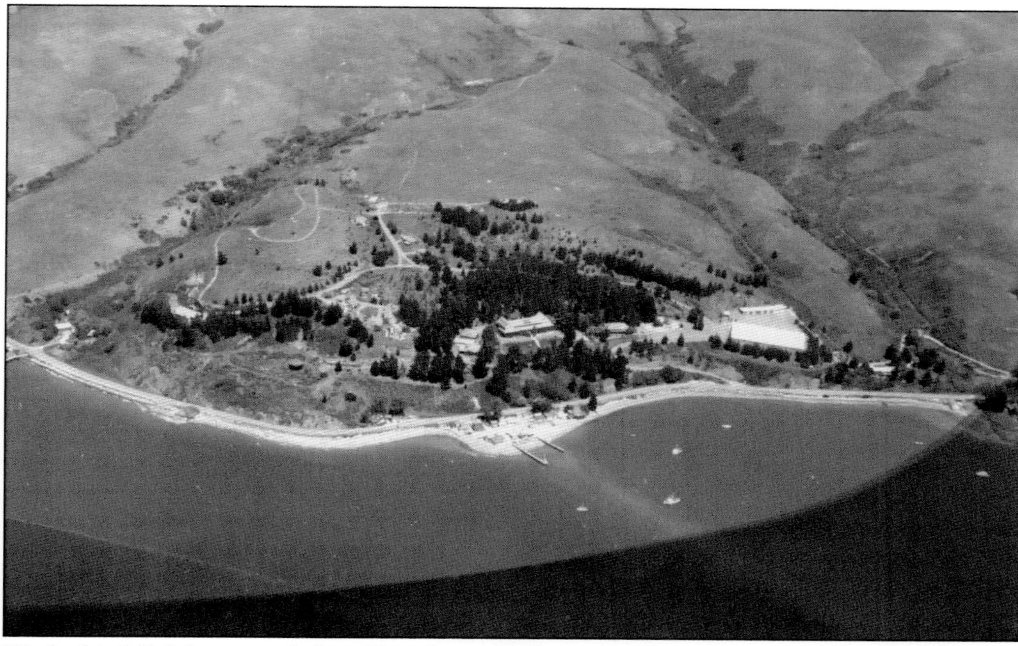

"Early this fall, I drove south from Tomales on Highway 1. Swinging into the broad curve toward Marshall, I should have been transfixed by the appearance of Tomales Bay and, before it Point Reyes. Instead, my car entered a stand of eucalyptus and I was transfixed—by the leathery trunks along the road, the silvery-gray branches and leaves above. . . ." reported John King in the *San Francisco Chronicle*, November 30, 2011. If King had continued his drive and traveled back exactly a century, he would have been able to stop at Charlie Salmina's grocery store in Marshall five minutes later for a Coca-Cola and a gasoline refill costing him 15¢ a gallon, plus 4¢ tax. A phone call from the store to San Francisco would cost another 25¢. Bachelor brothers Charlie and Felix Salmina had a well provisioned mahogany bar that ran half the length of the store. Charlie died in 1947 and Felix in 1968.

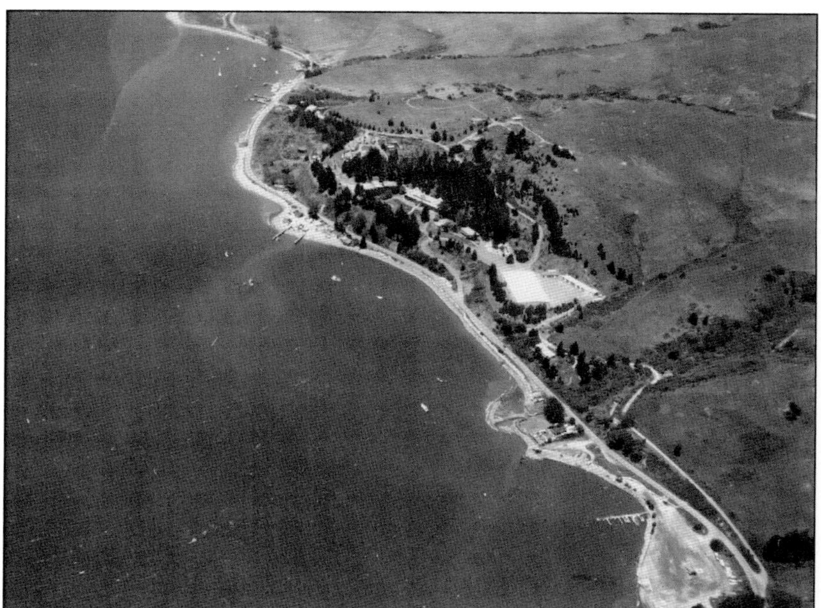

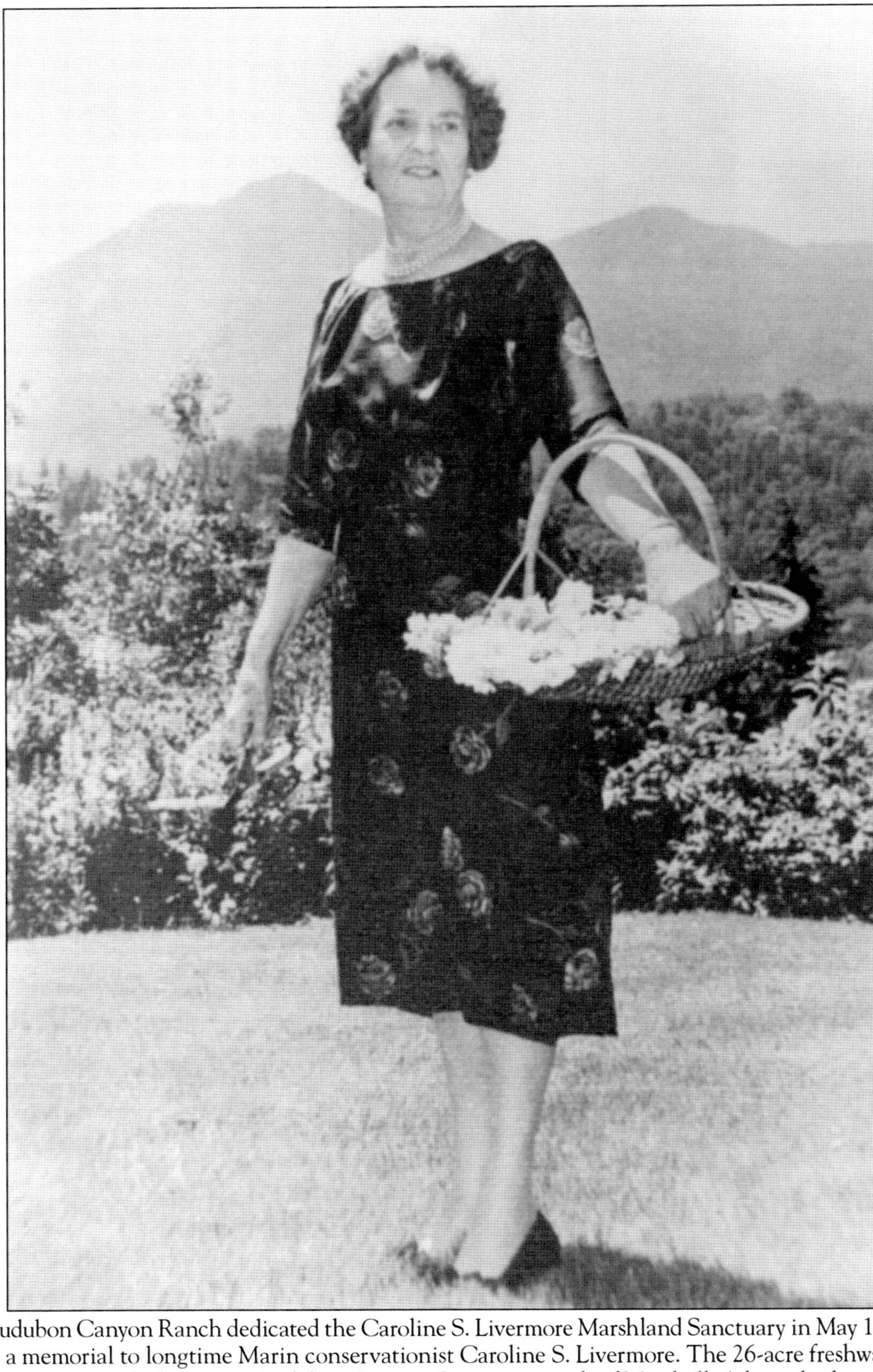

Audubon Canyon Ranch dedicated the Caroline S. Livermore Marshland Sanctuary in May 1983 as a memorial to longtime Marin conservationist Caroline S. Livermore. The 26-acre freshwater marsh is located adjacent to Audubon Cypress Grove just north of Marshall. A berm built in the mid-1870s for the tracks of the North Pacific Coast Railroad keeps out water from the bay.

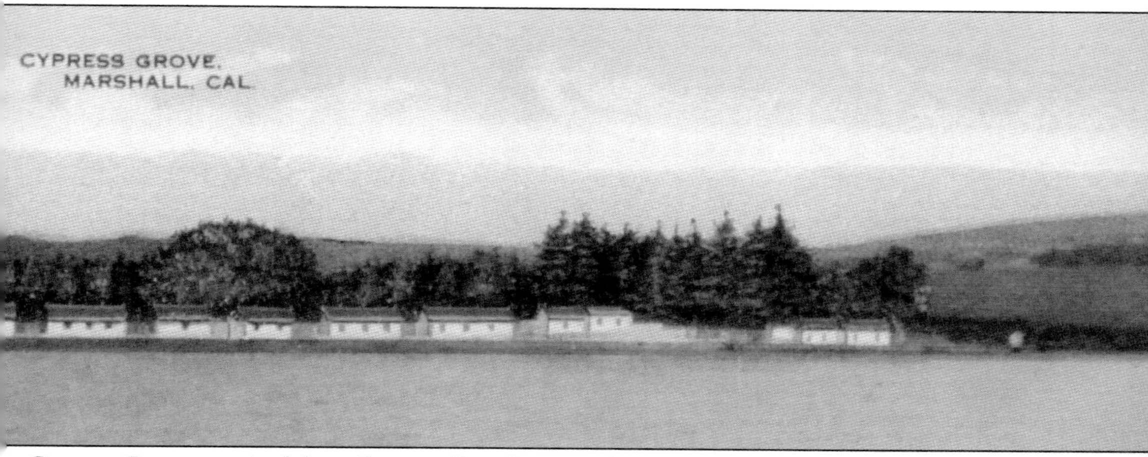

Cypress Grove, an Audubon Canyon Ranch research center, operates as a 139-acre wildlife sanctuary. Developers planned a 1,800 home subdivision on the 1,000 acres surrounding the site in the 1960s, but activists defeated the plan while working to preserve the Tomales Bay shore. (Courtesy of Dan Brown.)

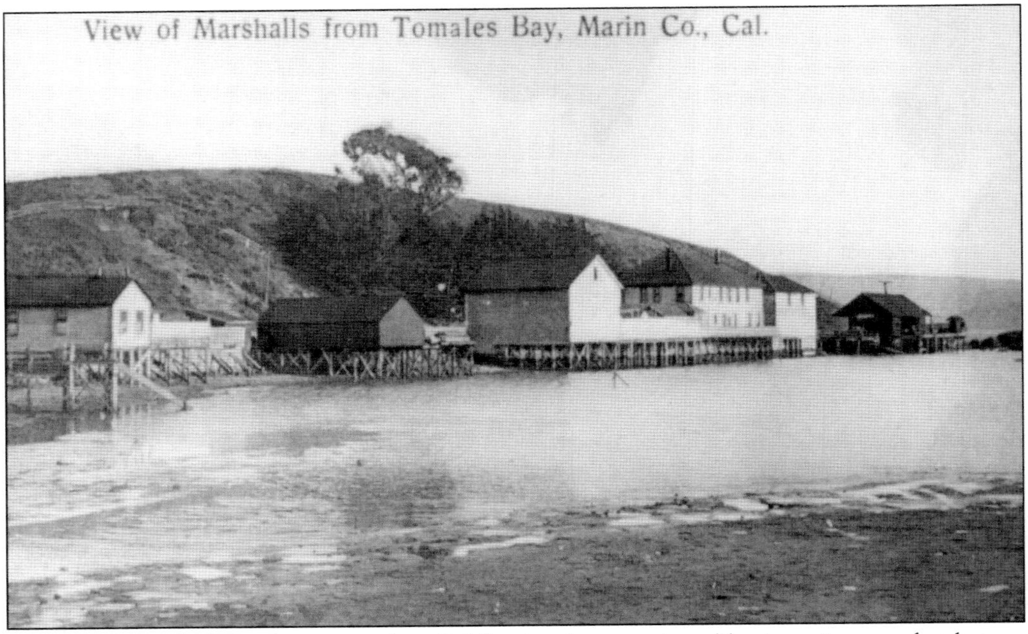

When the Marshall brothers moved to California, they continued business in a market but on a much grander scale. They drove 60 head of pureblood Durham cattle across the plains from Kentucky to Marshall in 1853, and then after a profitable sale, Samuel returned to Kentucky to repeat the procedure in 1854 with $3,000 in gold tucked in his belt. Today, Marshall consists of about 35 homes, some of which are second homes, alternating with a few businesses such as the Marshall Boat Works. The highway population number of 50 is an inside joke, representing the 35-mile-per-hour speed limit plus 15-foot elevation above sea level. Pat Simmons Kilgallin is pictured here with her three children, from left to right, Marsha Haydel, Janet Short, and Greg McKeegan. She is Alexander Marshall's great-granddaughter by way of her grandmother Florence Marshall Gregory and her father, Marshall Romeyn Gregory.

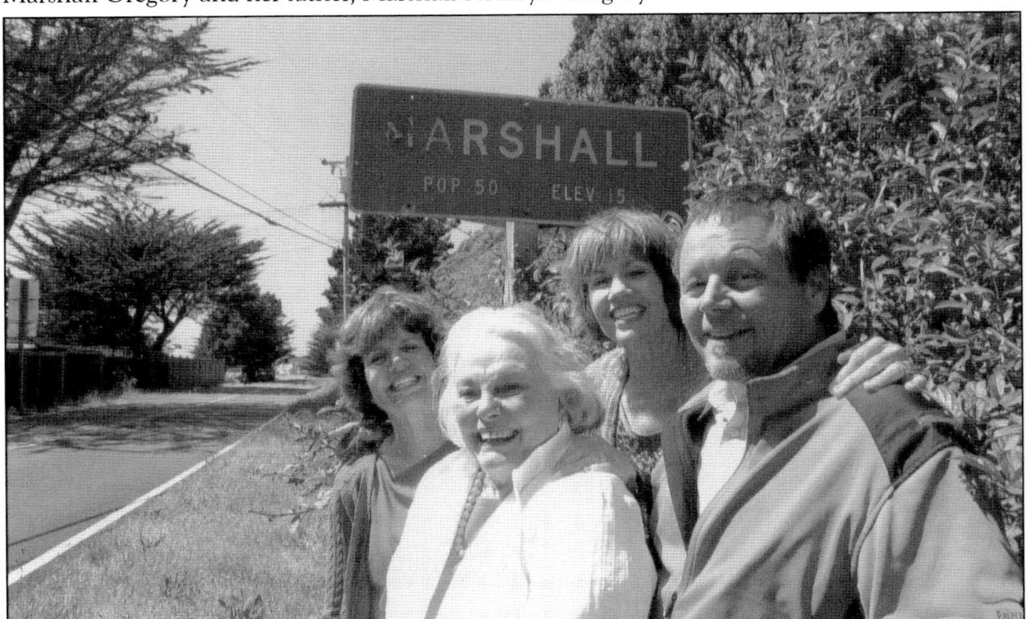

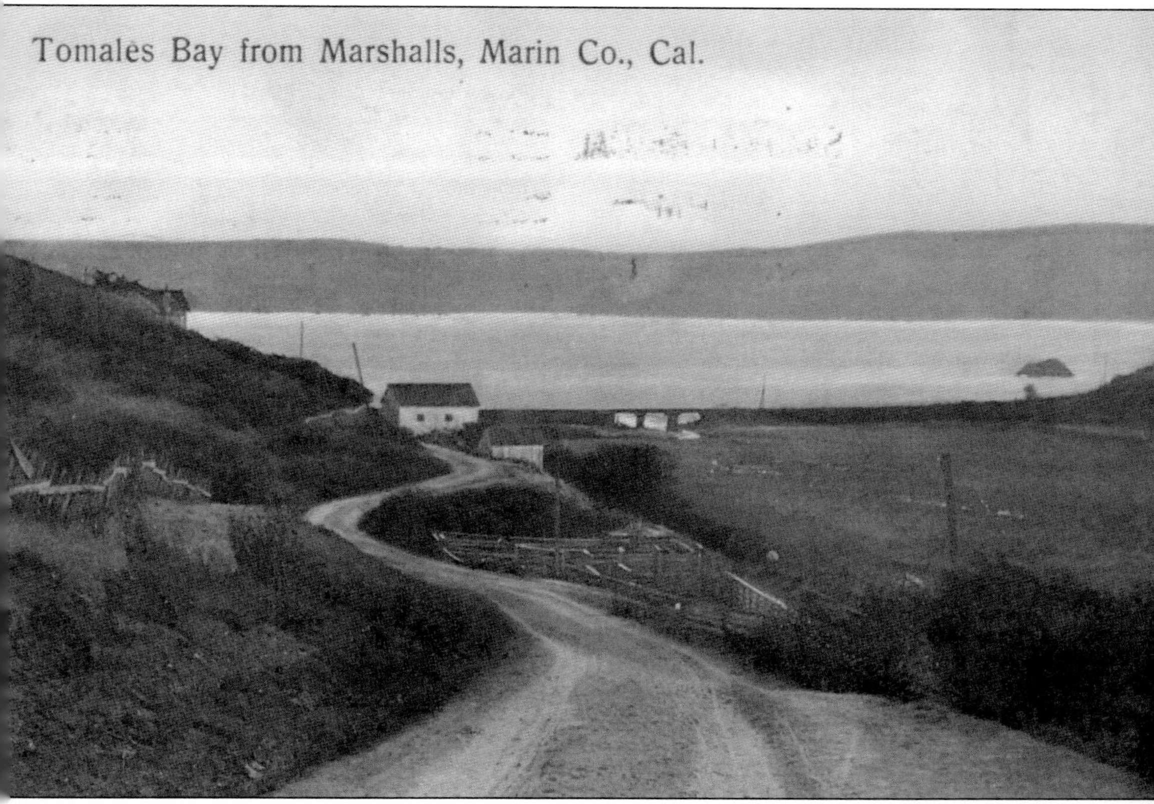

According to Pat Simmons Kilgallin: "One of the favorite legends in our family was the love story of my great-grandfather Alexander Stitt Marshall. His family had a large ranch in Markethill, County Armagh, Ireland, and raised cattle and horses. The word Marshall can be traced to two ancient words 'marhaz' or 'horse' and 'skalkaz' or 'servant.' Thus Marshall means horse servant or groom. In 1853, in Kentucky, Alexander fell in love with Fannie Brown, met with her parents, and asked for her hand in marriage. They declined, saying she was too young. I can only guess that she was 15 or 16 and Alexander 23. With great sadness Alexander left with brother Samuel and their wagon train. Fannie, however, was not going to give up quietly. She immediately went on a hunger strike and after a week or so her frantic parents sent a rider out to find Alexander and bring him back. They married March 4, 1854. Their first child, Emma Jane, was the first white child born in Tomales Township." (Courtesy of Dan Brown.)

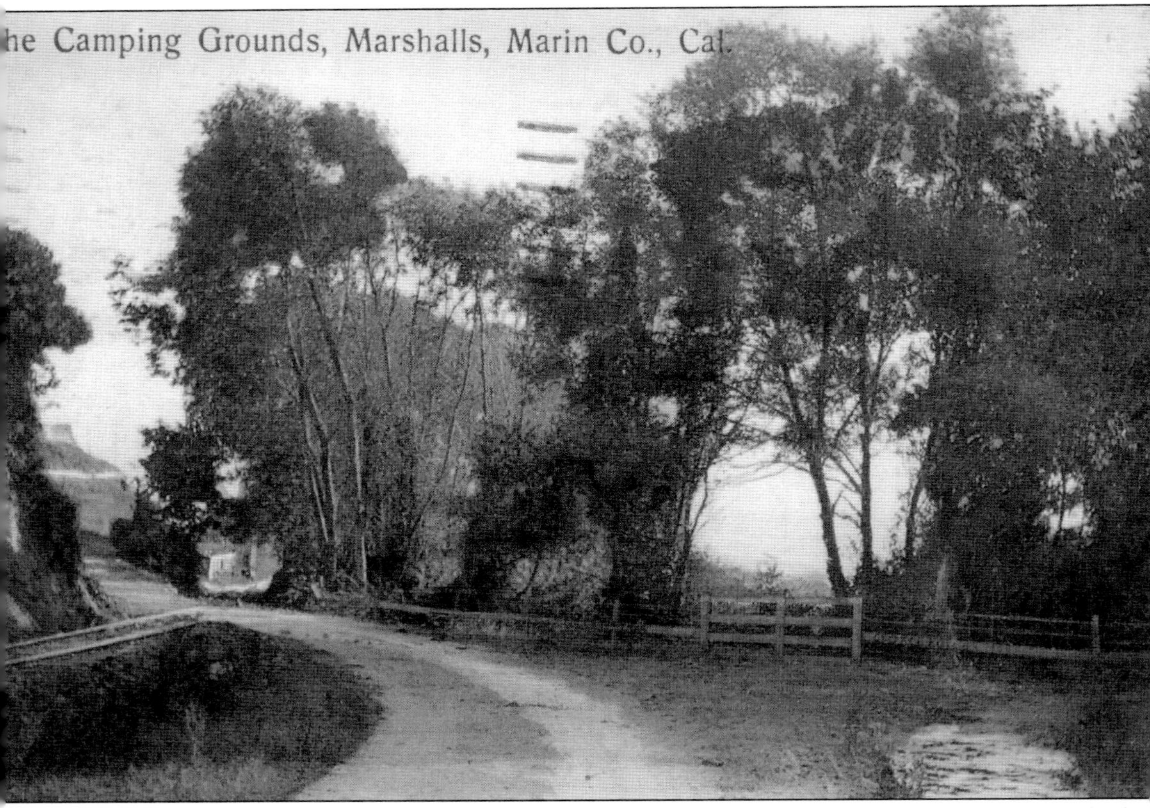

This child, Emma Jane Marshall, would marry the Irish-born W. Armstrong in 1875. They had two children, Fannie and James Joseph Marshal Armstrong. Emma had two sisters, Fannie and Lizzie. A year after Emma's birth, in the District Court of the 7th Judicial District, Marin County, on May 10, 1856, John Keys and Jeremiah Blake testified for the plaintiff, Alexander Marshall, in a suit against his brothers Hugh and Samuel Marshall. The suit involved rightful ownership of the 119 head of American Cattle, one saddle, 18 dry cows, steers and heifers worth $40 a head, 26 milk cows at $65 a head, two ploughs, one barrow, and two stoves (one being new with a crack and the other secondhand), worth $30 together. Alexander contended that Fannie was owed part of the above for services rendered crossing the prairies in 1854. The judge agreed. On April 14, 1857, Alexander charged Hugh with fraud larceny. Fannie died November 30, 1861, and was buried in the Tomales Cemetery. (Courtesy of Dan Brown.)

Four

Nick's Cove

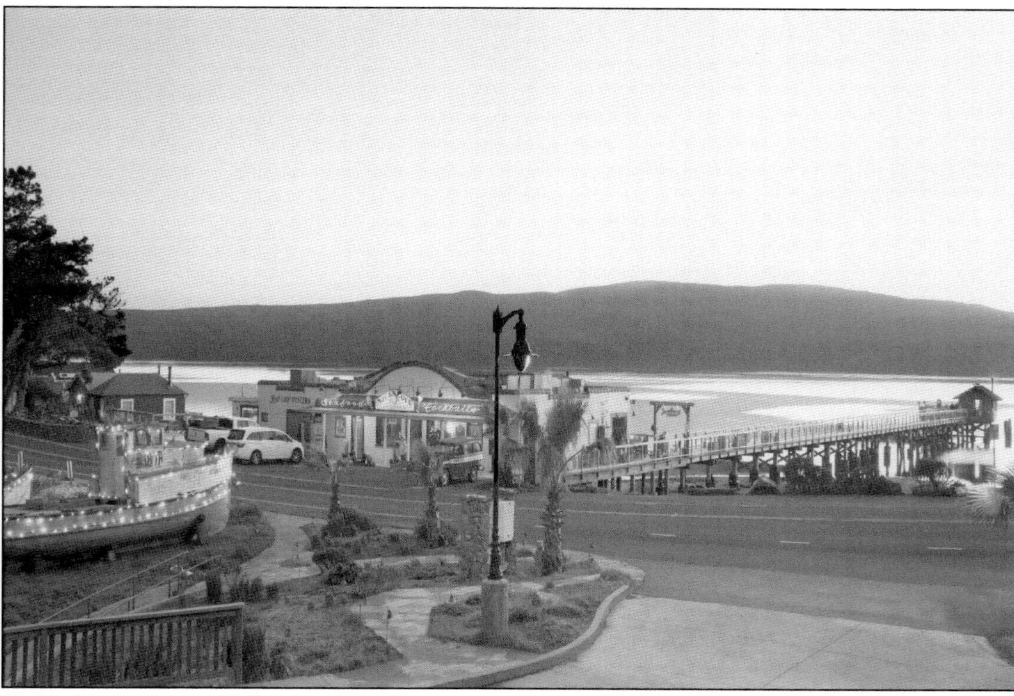

Nick's Cove, also spelled Nicks Cove, is an unincorporated community 3.25 miles south-southwest of Tomales at an elevation of seven feet. The name honors Nick Kojich, who, in 1931, opened a seafood restaurant here. As a combined hotel and restaurant, Nick's Cove has become a landmark destination for visitors and locals. It was featured in the 2001 film *Bandits*. (Courtesy of Frankie Frankeney.)

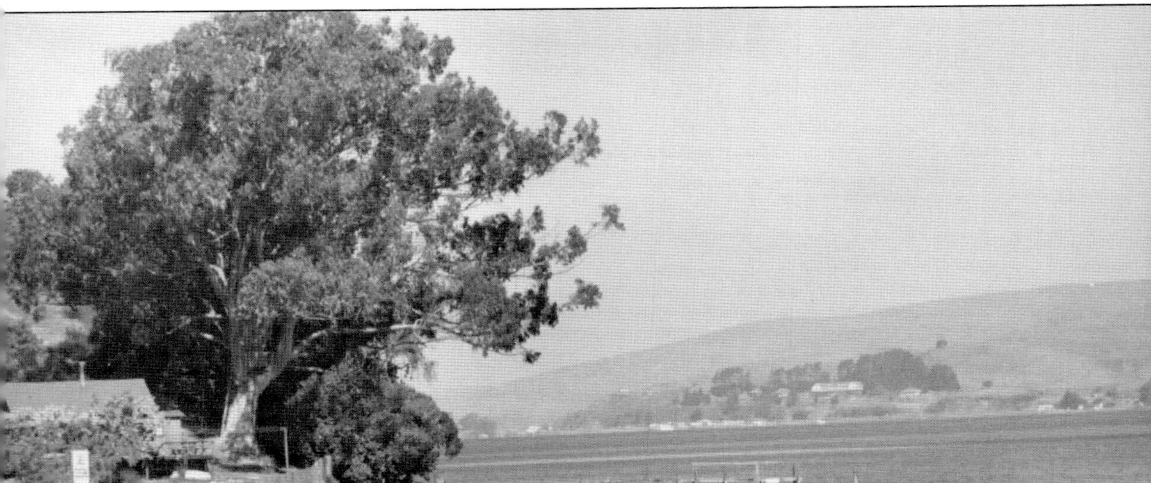

No history of Nick's Cove and Marshall would be complete without the following names and the years they came to Tomales Bay: Nicola Vilicich (1900), Anton Smilcich (1908), Nick Kojich (1920), and Tony Konatich (1931). Nicola and Anton emigrated from Croatia in an era when it was controlled by Austria. The Balkan Wars of 1913 led to the assassination of Austria's Archduke Ferdinand at Sarajevo and the commencement of World War I. In this same period, Turkey controlled Serbia. Following the defeat of Austria and Turkey by 1918, Croatia and Serbia struggled with unification problems until the umbrella of Yugoslavia covered them both by 1929. Croatian immigrants looking for gold headed to Amador County, California, in the 1850s. Later, they fished the Pacific coast from Alaska to Mexico. Few Croatian women immigrated to the United States during these early years, and so many men married Irish or other Catholic women. Marcus Tanner noted, "Ireland and the former Yugoslavia are separated by more than geographical distance but their histories have certain common elements."

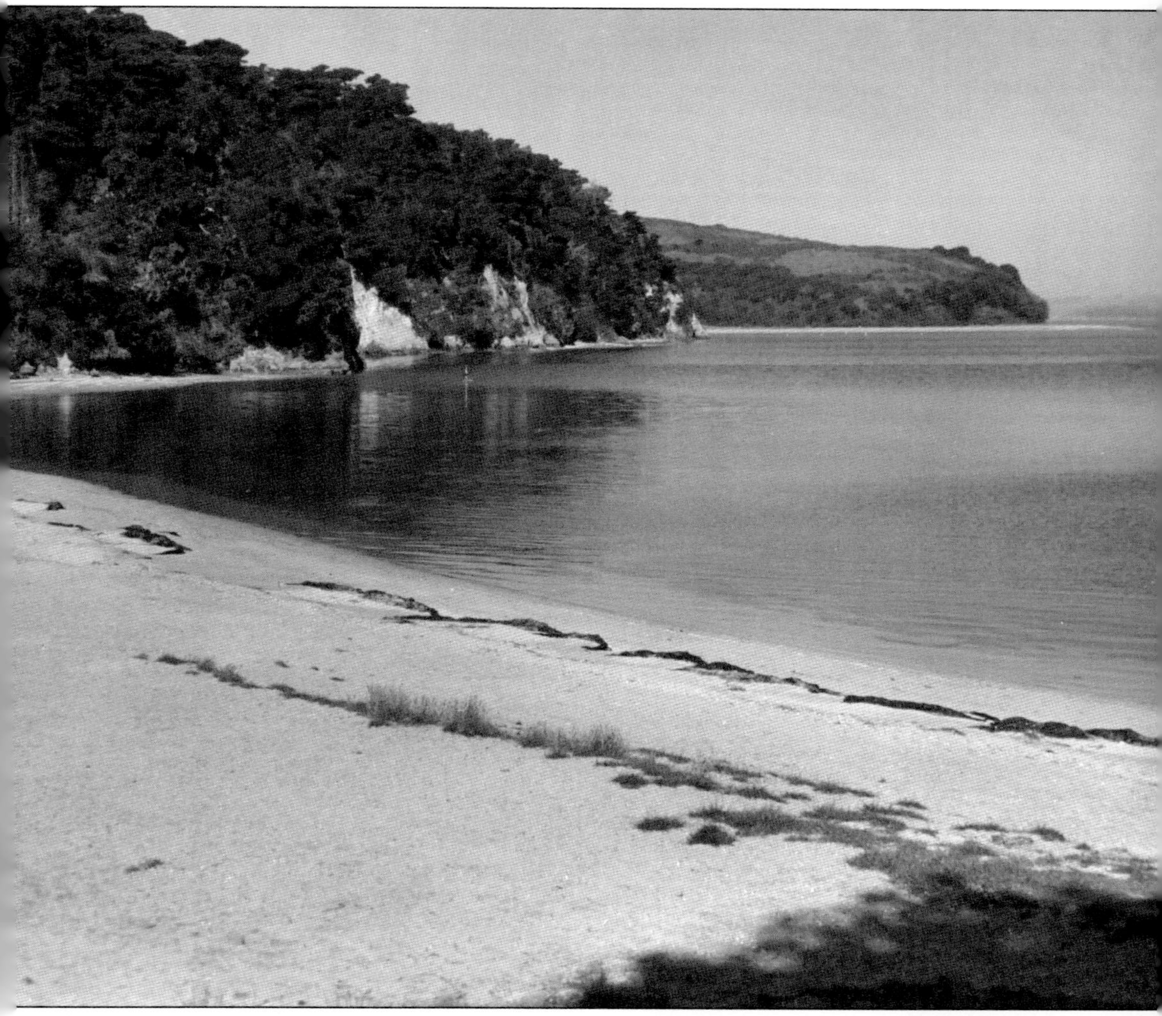

Serbian immigrants came mostly from the coastal areas of Dalmatia as early as the Gold Rush. They also worked as fishermen, oystermen, and shop and saloon keepers. By 1860, the Serbian Orthodox Church in America was founded in San Francisco. From the tiny Croatian island of Iz in the Zadar Archipelago off the Dalmatian coast, and the island of Hvar, farther south in the Adriatic, came the fishing families of Vilicich, Smilcich, Kojich, and Konatich. John Vilicich remembers his father explaining that he emigrated from his country to avoid military service. He loved fishing and did not want to waste 10 years in the Army when he could be doing something he loved. He sent for his fiancée two years after arriving, and John was born in 1919 on Tomales Bay's west shore. In 1927, Nick Vilicich bought property at Rancheria Point, just above Reynolds, and built the largest boatworks on the bay. John has operated the boatyard since 1946, the same year he retired from the Navy.

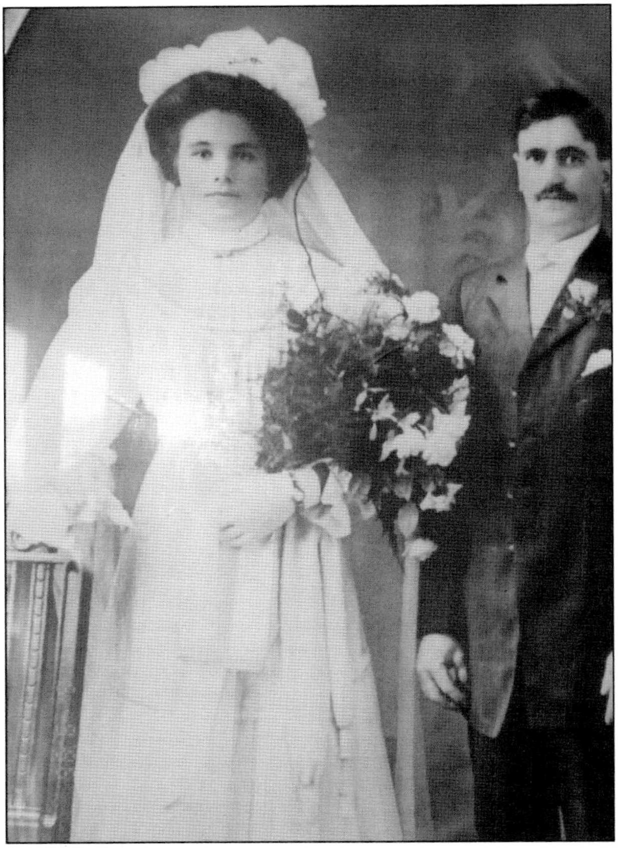

Gregory Matkovich came to the United States early in the 20th century, working first in coal mines near Chicago in order to finance the immigration of six brothers and sisters. Around 1906, the family moved to Oakland. Hearing of the thriving settlements in Tomales Bay and frustrated with work in Oakland, the Matkovich brothers moved there in 1911. That same year, Gregory married Nicolina Krstnich, with whom he had three children, Elizabeth, Andrew, and Leona.

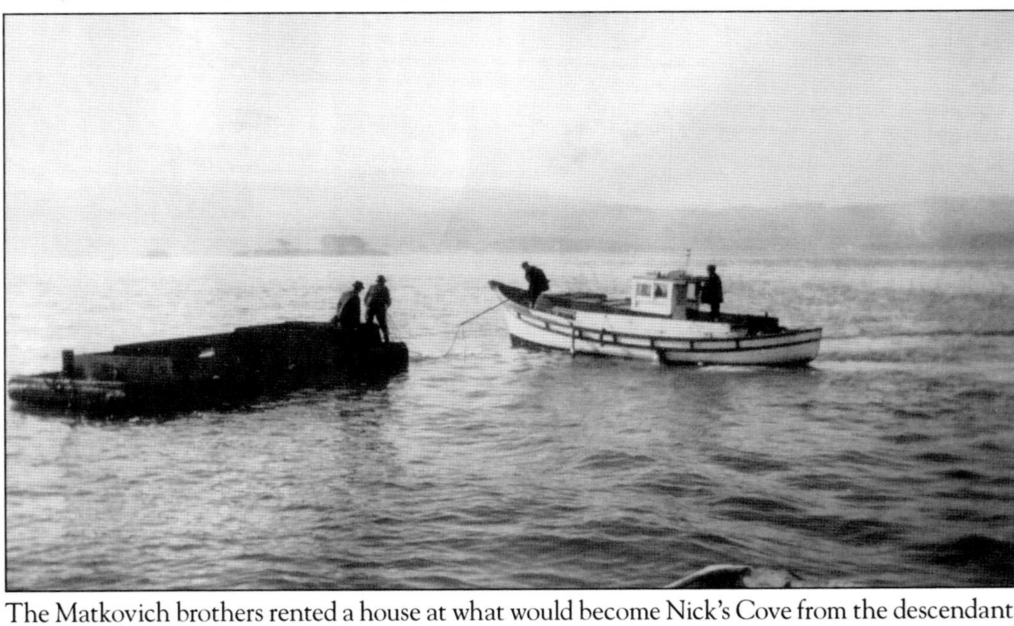

The Matkovich brothers rented a house at what would become Nick's Cove from the descendants of Jeremiah Blake, who had bought it in 1862 from Abraham Lincoln's chief of staff, Henry Halleck. The brothers' fishing fleet consisted of several boats, including a scow. The men tended nets of Italian hemp, which they made themselves.

The Matkovich brothers were not the only ones fishing Tomales Bay. Twenty fishermen and six fishing boats were already based in Marshall with another 12 fishermen and six boats based at Inverness. Following the examples of Nickola Vilicich and Nickola Cosmi, who had leased land at White Gulch from the Pierce family, the brothers moved from the east side of the bay to the west around 1917–1918.

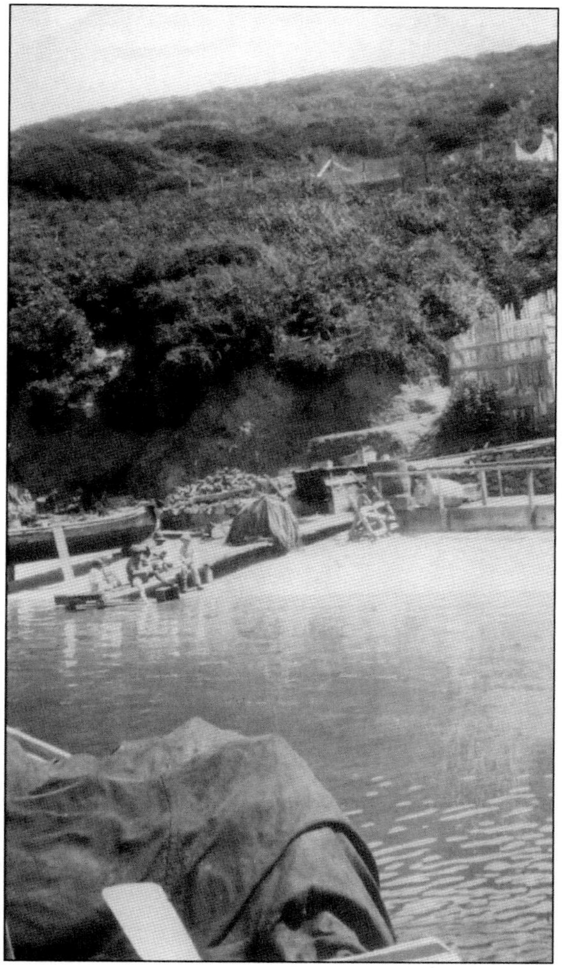

Nickola Vilicich and Nickola Cosmi built a four-bedroom home here as headquarters for their fishing business. In 1909, Cosmi had married and moved to the cove north of White Gulch while Vilicich stayed in the home to raise chickens and turkeys. In 1927, this home burned down, and Vilicich moved to Marshall, where the boatworks company was established. Cosmi's home had burned down in 1921. (Courtesy of Patricia Clark.)

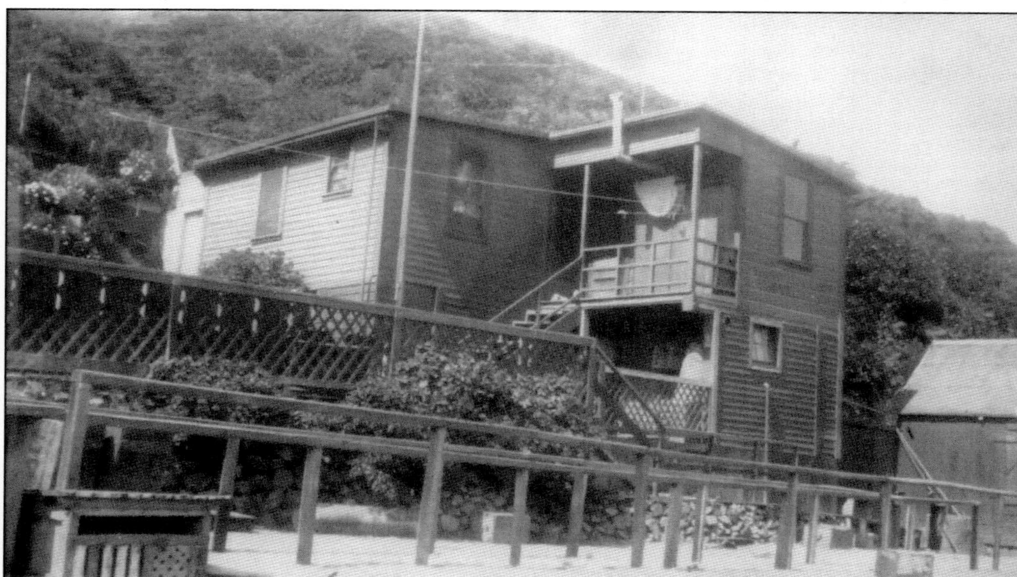

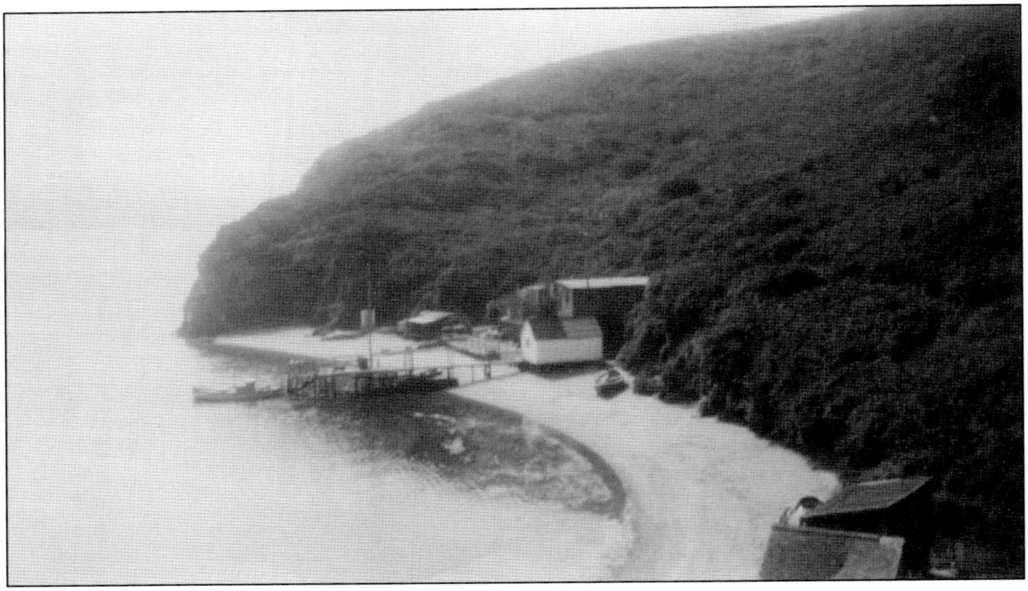

New immigrants improvised with their homes as with their fishing business. They were their own architects, as their ancestors had been on the island of Otok Hvar, Vrboska, Dalmatia, thousands of miles away in the very Old World. The architecture was simple and rural in a coastal vernacular style. Adaptation was necessary, such as the use of a classic Monterey double-ender boat such as is used at Fisherman's Wharf in San Francisco. Herring was a basic catch in the Adriatic and was equally available in Tomales Bay. Old-timers recalled when it sold for 50¢ a sack and when, in one period of two months, eight to nine tons were loaded onto the Marshall trains for hungry European immigrants in San Francisco as well as markets in Asia and even Europe. (Courtesy of Patricia Clark.)

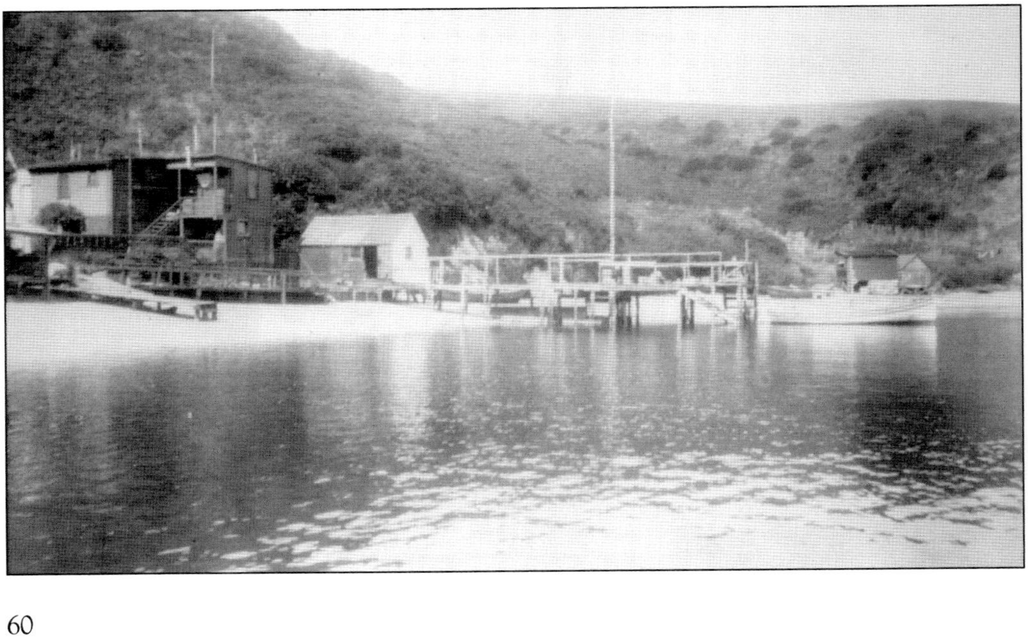

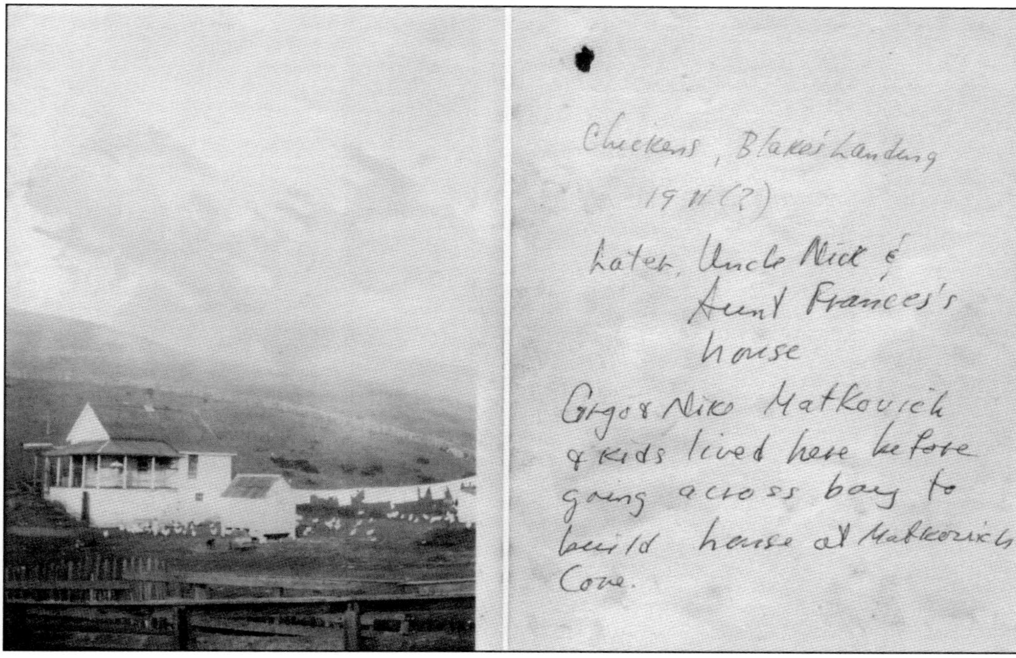

Gregory and Nikolina Matkovich and their children lived here with an army of chickens before going across the bay to build their house at Matkovich Cove. Later, it became the home of Nicola "Nick" Kojich and Frances Matkovich, who moved from Oakland, where he reportedly operated a public house. (Courtesy of Patricia Clark.)

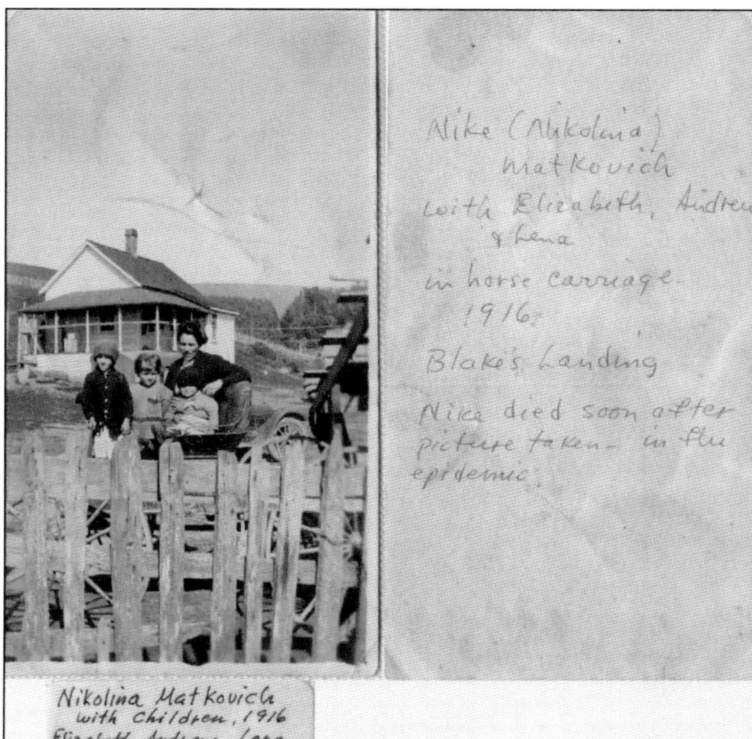

Nikolina Matkovich is in a horse carriage at Blake's Landing in 1916 with her children, Elizabeth, Andrew, and Lena. She died only seven years after her marriage in the devastating flu epidemic of 1918.

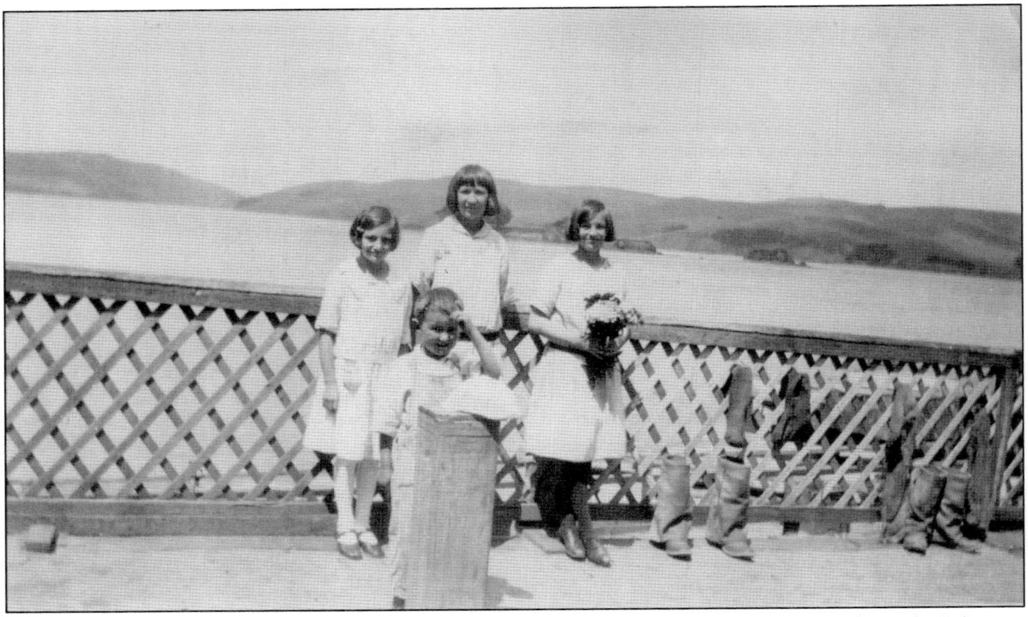

These four new Americans of Croatian ancestry are, from left to right: Lena Matkovich, Johnnie Vilicich (in front), Mary Vilicich, and Elizabeth Matkovich (with flowers). Today, Johnnie (born in 1919) is the owner of the Marshall Boatworks. It is worth noting that large fishermen's boots are drying to the right of the four children.

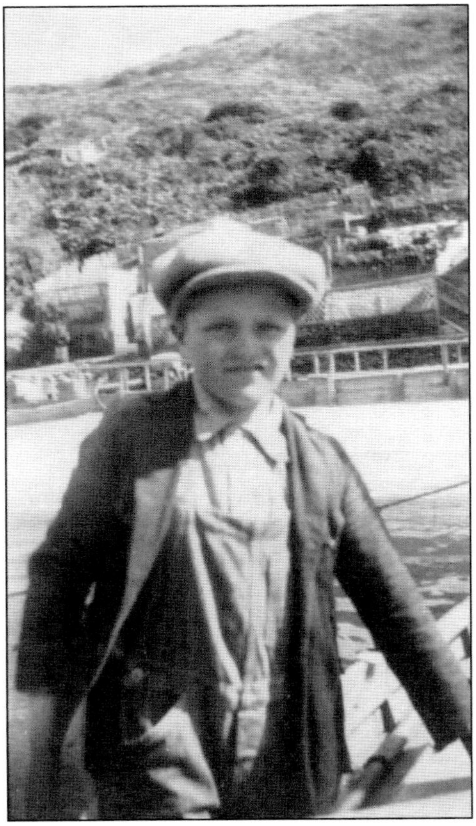

Andrew Matkovich, named after his uncle, was the son of Nikolina and Gregory. As a young boy, he worked alongside his uncles and father in their fishing business. He was born in one of the cabins now used as a rental cottage at Nick's Cove Restaurant and Cottages. He later married Dorothy, and they became partners with Nick and Frances Kojich at Nick's Cove Restaurant. Andrew and Dorothy remained owners after the Kojichs died. Andrew died in 1969.

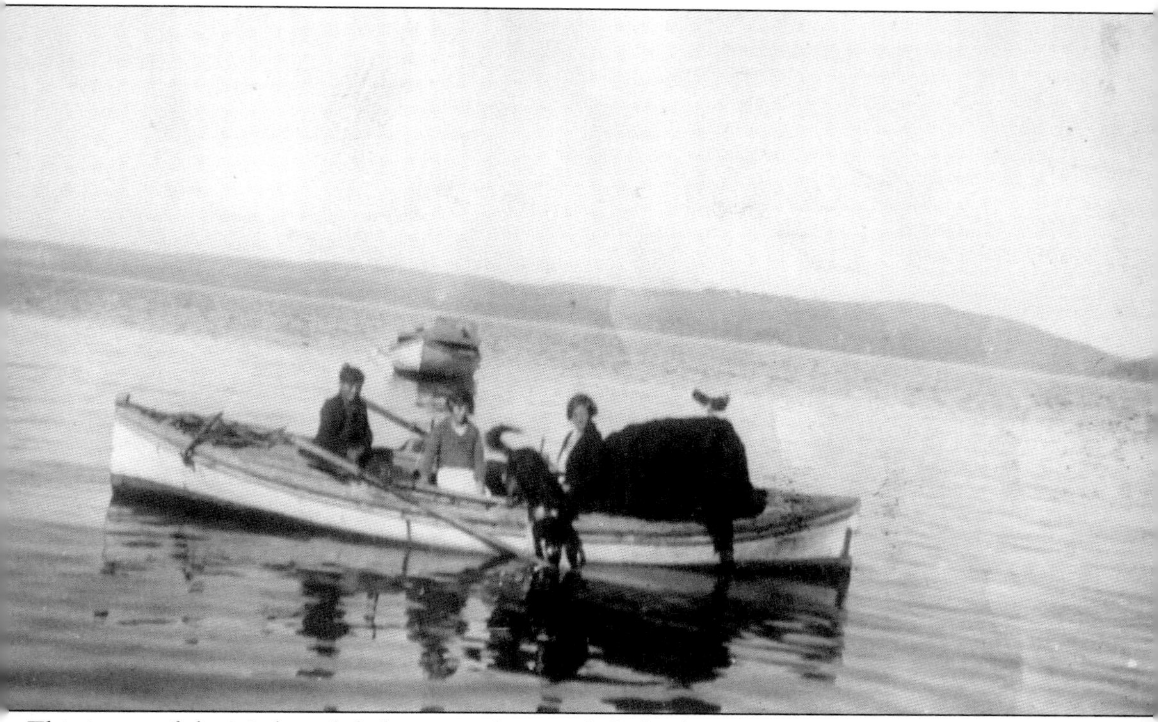

This image of the Matkovich kids in a rowboat with Duke diving into the water and a Banty hen sitting on top of the fishing nets epitomizes a continuity of hunting activity on the bay going back to the Miwoks. This Bantam chicken, meaning small in size, could be a mud hen or duck, which Miwok men would shoot with bow and arrow from the shores of the bay. Brown pelicans and great blue herons were also captured for food, feathers, and ceremonial artifacts. Loons and cormorants, scaup, and scoter feast on herring spawn. In winter, flocks of Brant geese with white markings and neck rings occupy the surface of the bay from the Miller Park boat ramp to Hog Island and beyond. Hunting season is open at Tom's Point, just two miles to the north, but these geese are smart enough to stay in the protected zone of Nick's Cove.

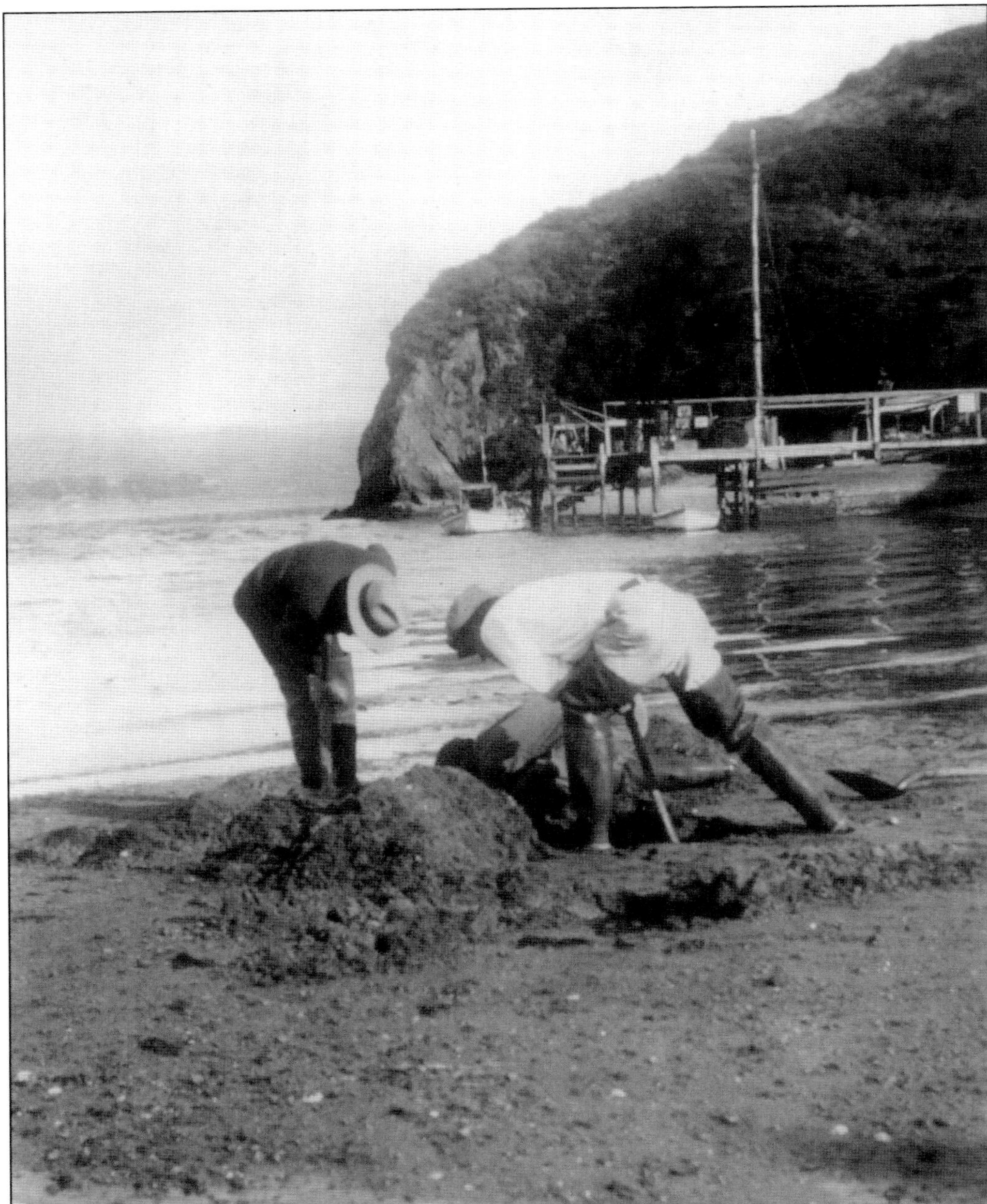

White Gulch residents Nickola Vilicich and Nickola Cosmi gathered clams and oysters to sell when the weather was too rough to fish. The habitats of the more common clams are distributed based on the nature of the substrate. The Washington or butter clam occurs in coarse sand or coarse mud. The white sand clam occurs in medium to fine-grained sand or sandy mud. The gaper or horseneck clam occurs in finer mud. Because Tomales Bay is an estuary, each of these clams is omnipresent, but abundance varies depending on the availability of suitable habitats. Almost $3 million worth of oysters, mussels, and clams was produced in Tomales Bay in 2004. The Chinese were significant abalone farmers in the 19th century, inventing a hook to pry the snail from a rock. Cleaned, dried, and salted, abalone was merchandised to Chinese communities far and wide in the western United States.

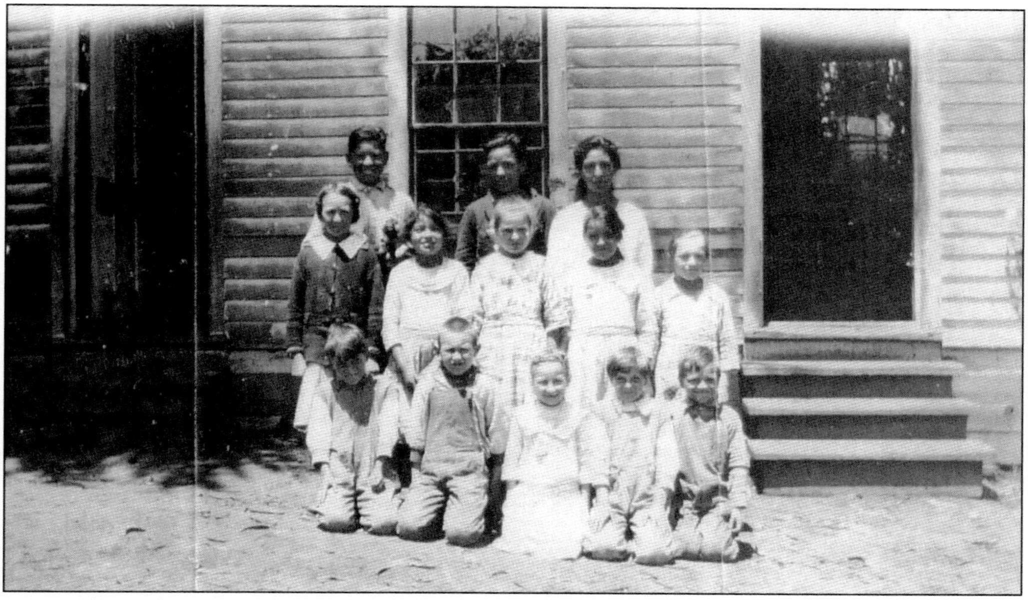

Pictured are, from left to right, (first row) Reno Cosmi, Frank Vilicich, Katherine Vilicich, Vincent Cosmi, and Andrew Matkovich; (second row) Mary Vilicich, Edna Pensotti, Leona Cosmi, Rose Pensotti, and Elizabeth Matkovich; (third row) Clarence Pensotti, Tony Pensotti, and Frances Pensotti.

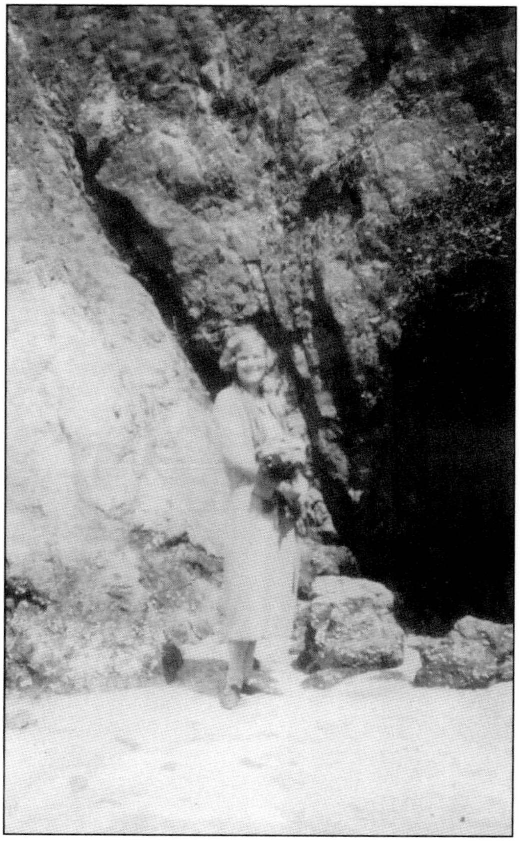

In 1859, Solomon and Sarah C. Jewell Pierce purchased a tract of 2,000 acres on Tomales Point and immediately moved their family here. Abram Jewell Pierce, the eldest son, was 18. His parents built a home on the north shore of White Gulch, developed a most successful dairy, and built a school. Kay Vilicich (Wing) wrote that the Indians who went to school with her here in 1920 were 100-percent Miwok.

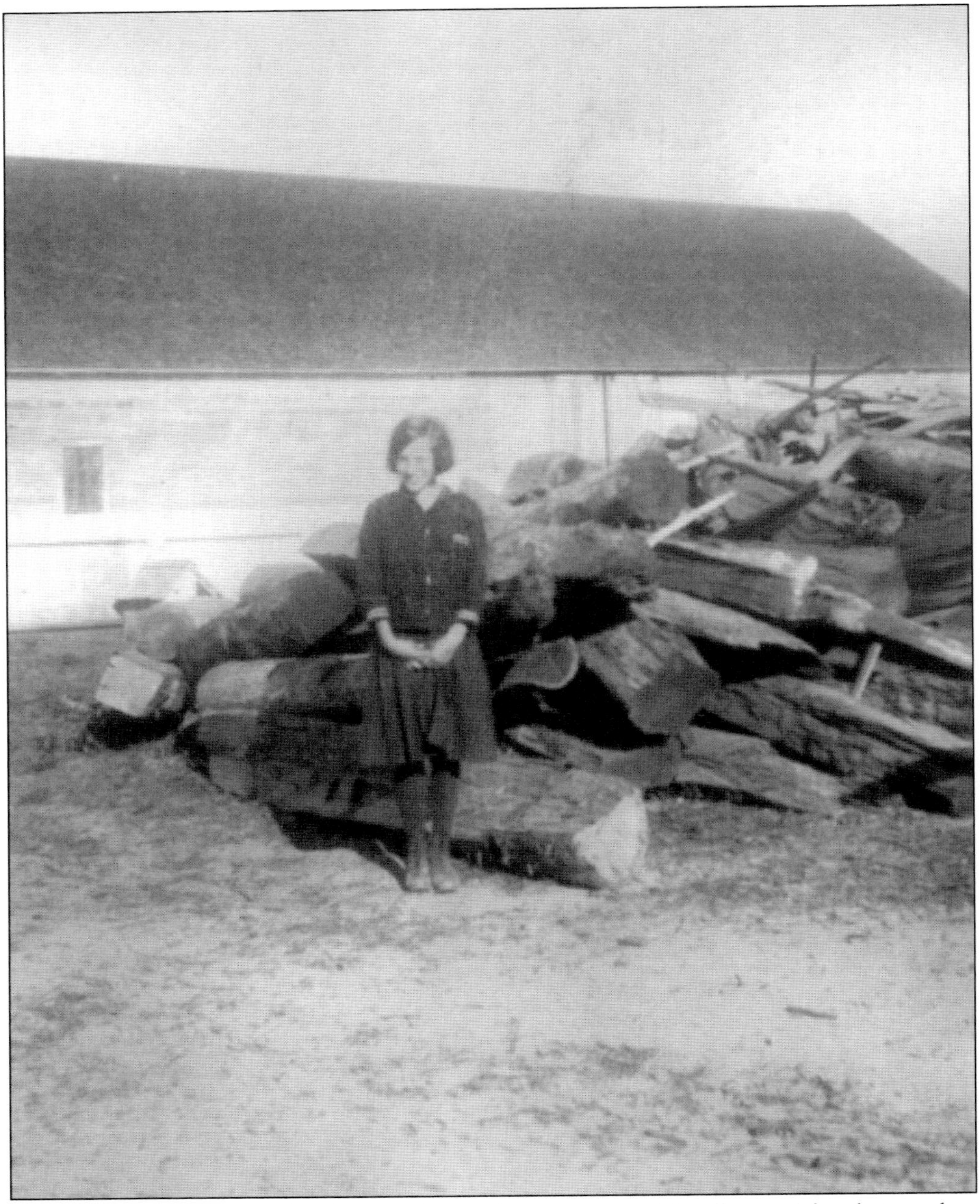

Elizabeth Matkovich stands beside a woodpile at the Pierce Point Schoolhouse. After their mother, Nikolina, died in the 1918 flu epidemic, their father, Gregory, raised Elizabeth, Leona, and Andrew "Andy." While the men were busy fishing on the bay, Elizabeth worked hard maintaining their home and cooking. Her daughter Patricia Nikolina Clark has captured Elizabeth's childhood in the rugged yet idyllic coves of Tomales Bay in an evocative and reminiscent work of fiction. *Fisherman's Daughter* (2012) is published by Bridgeline Books. Dewey Livingston, Marin County historian and curator of the Jack Mason Museum in Inverness, writes, "The small cove in *Fisherman's Daughter*, now preserved within Point Reyes National Seashore, is a lovely place, peaceful but empty. Written with loving care, Clark's dramatic tale of a young girl's life here brings the spirit of this isolated beach to life." (Courtesy of Patricia Clark.)

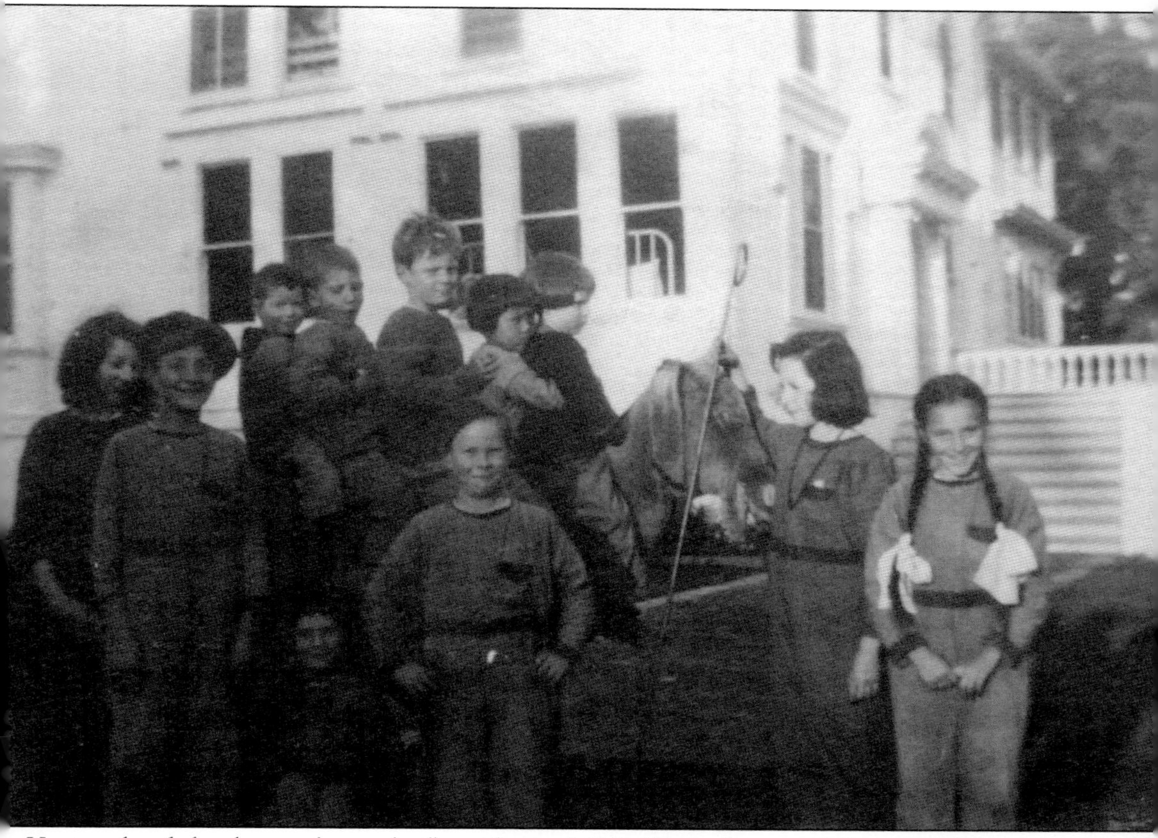

Having already lost her mother to the flu epidemic of 1918, Elizabeth successfully survived pleurisy and pneumonia at the Stanford Convalescent House in the 1920s. The remoteness of West Marin and limited access to doctors and hospitals was a precarious situation for children and adults alike. In the author's note to her novel, Patricia Nikolina Clark writes, "When this story takes place, the automobile had recently been invented and the telephone was still a novelty. Life was slower then, simpler, and full of promise for these immigrants, who nevertheless faced great challenges in adapting to their new country. But they brought with them their religious beliefs, determination and skills that helped them survive and raise their families along the shorelines of Tomales Bay, in a string of sandy coves once known as Little Yugoslavia." Clark has been writing for children for more than 20 years with *Goodbye, Goose* and *In the Shadow of the Mammoth*, which preceded *Fisherman's Daughter*. (Courtesy of Patricia Clark.)

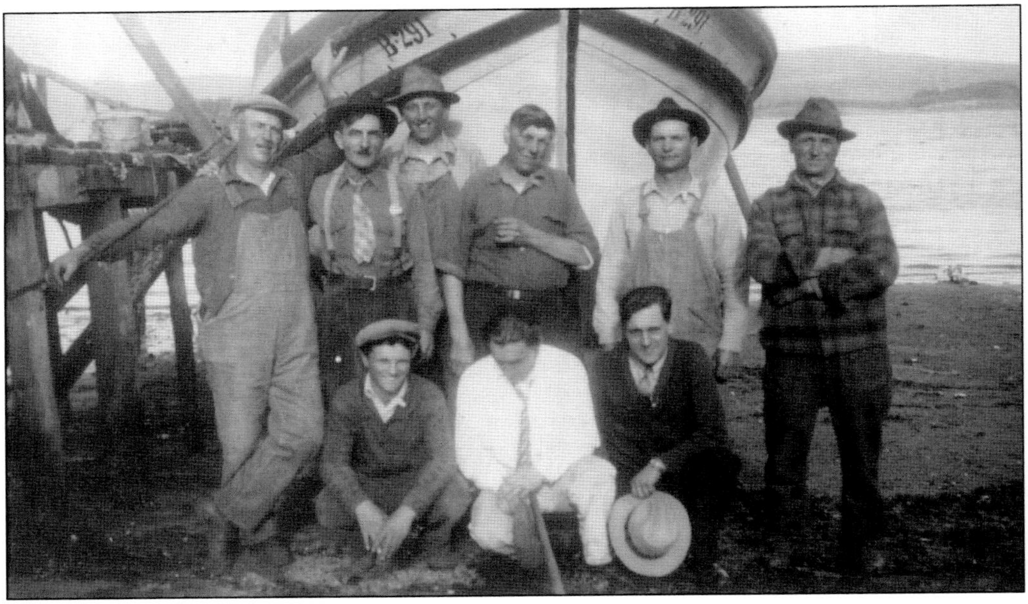

Presumably, Elizabeth Matkovich took this candid photograph in the late 1920s with her annotations on the back: "Resting in the back row in front of Nick Kojich's boat are Uncle Nick, Mo Pusich, Uncle Andrew, Uncle Mike, Uncle Steve and Papa. In the front row are Andy, her brother, and the Pusich boys." Nick had fished previously out of Monterey in the open Pacific. Tomales Bay was not as violent, though occasional squalls could be deadly. Through the years, the winter herring run has been the leading species of the Tomales Bay fishery, but other species landed include salmon, crab, sole, shark, and lingcod, with lesser numbers of surfperch and smelt. Jack Mason wrote that "a minimum of 1,600 tons of herring enter Tomales Bay each year to spawn, and lay at least 163 tons of eggs, primarily upon eel grass, which comprises 75 percent of the vegetation of the bay." (Courtesy of Patricia Clark.)

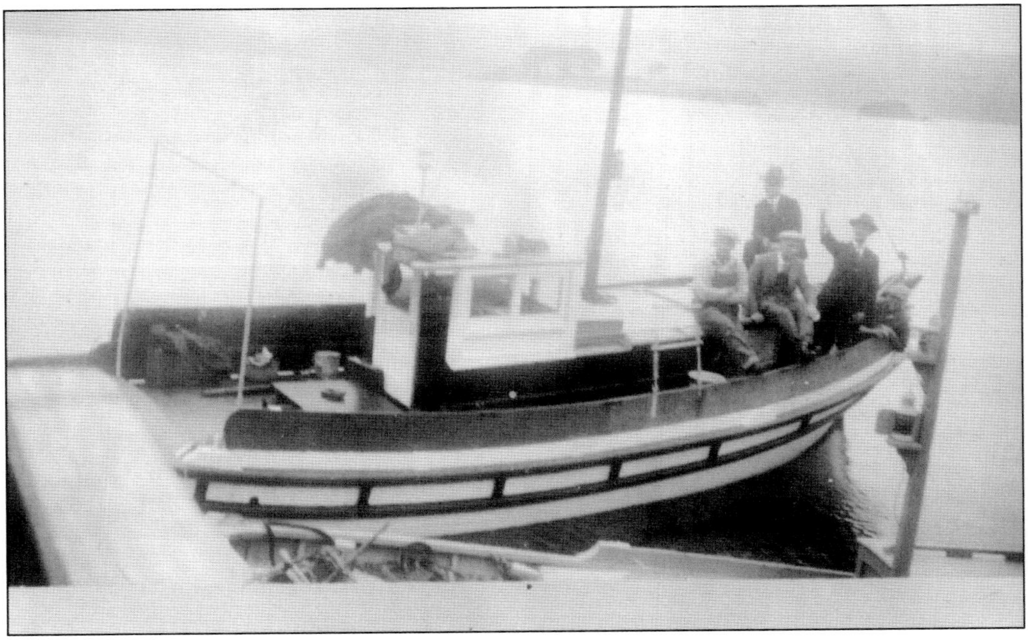

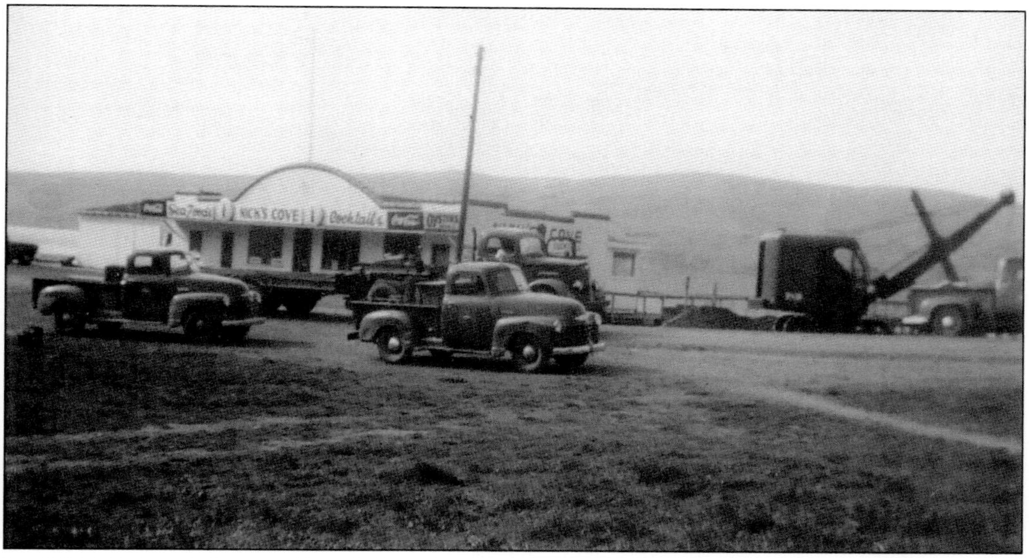

In 1931, Nick and Frances Kojich bought a parcel of the old Jeremiah Blake Ranch complete with an old herring smokehouse from Blake's heirs. According to Jack Mason, the terms were simple—"$1,000 down, $50 a month." Kojich moved his building, including the house and "joker shed" from the Pierce Ranch cove to his new property using a barge. He built a pier with a dock house from materials salvaged from the old pier across the bay. Three other cabins were built or moved to the site. Utilizing the old herring plant, the Kojichs decided to open a small seafood restaurant on their property.

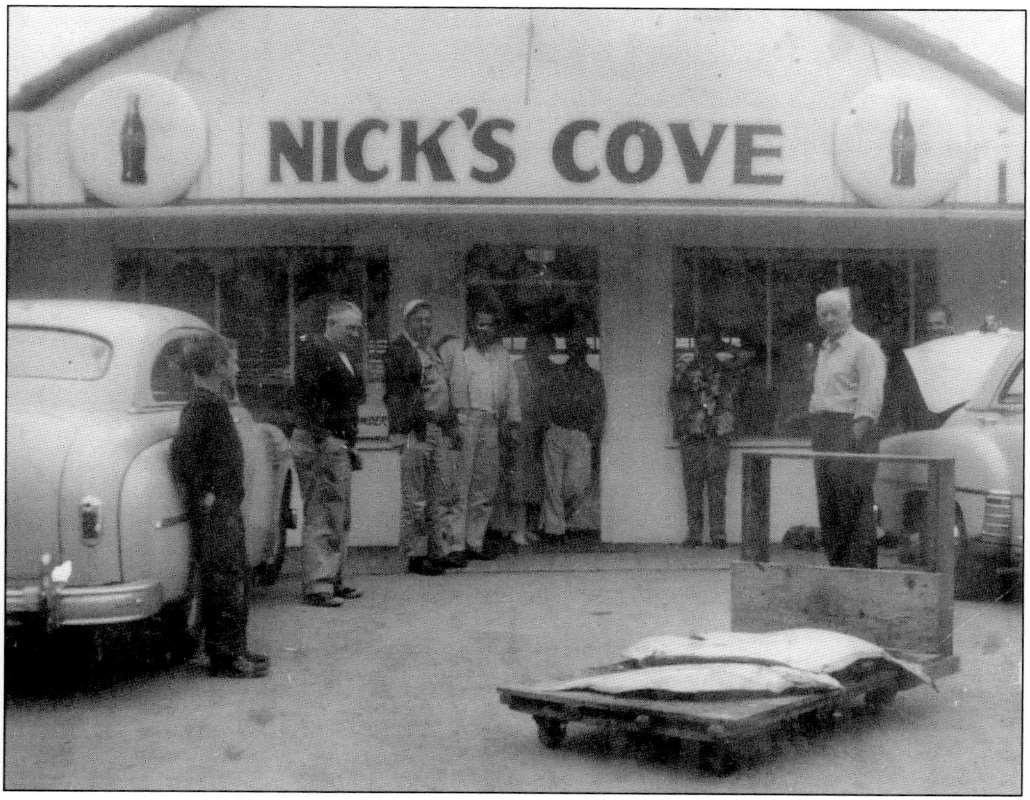

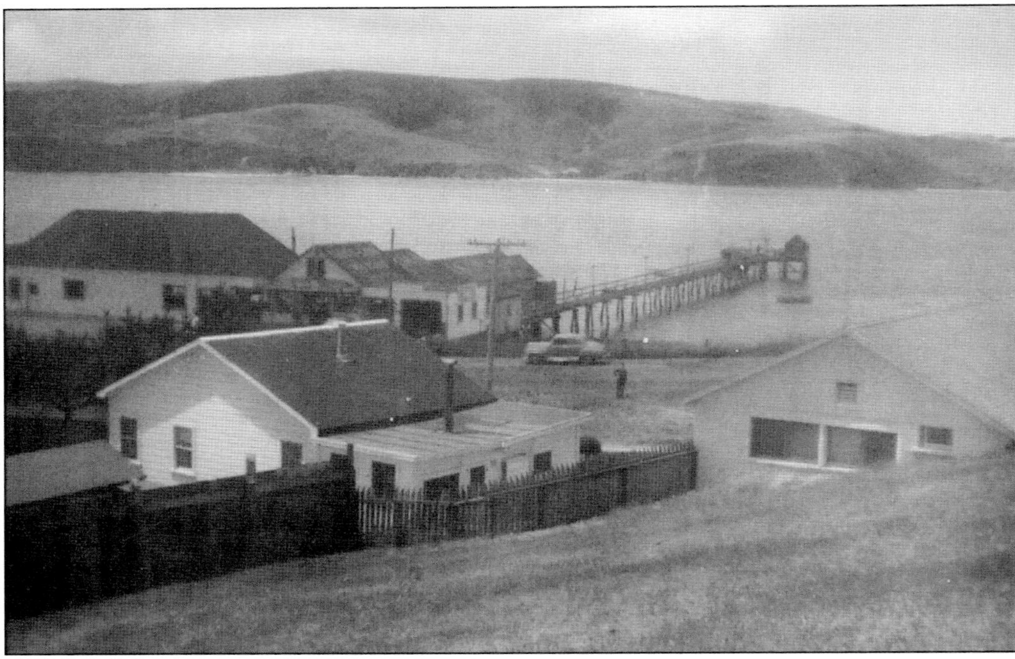

Herring from Tomales Bay made a particularly good smoked and salted product due to its large size. In the 1930s, smoked herring was produced at both Nick's Cove and at Consolidated Fisheries' Blake's Landing plant. Nick and Frances Kojich's small seafood restaurant was not a full-sized restaurant but sold shrimp and crab cocktails and the like. The bar they built in 1933 burned in 1950 and was replaced with the help of Frances's nephew and business partner Andrew Matkovich, whose widow, Dorothy, sold out in 1973 to the Alfred Gibsons. Highway traffic since the 1930s brought a surge in tourists looking for food, lodging, and adventure. They found all three at Nick's Cove.

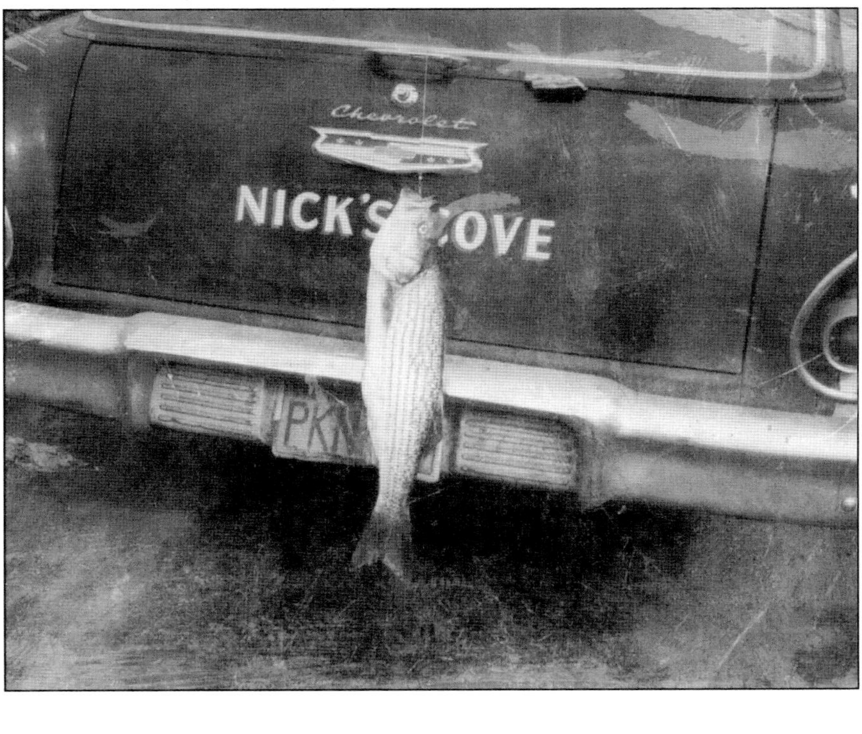

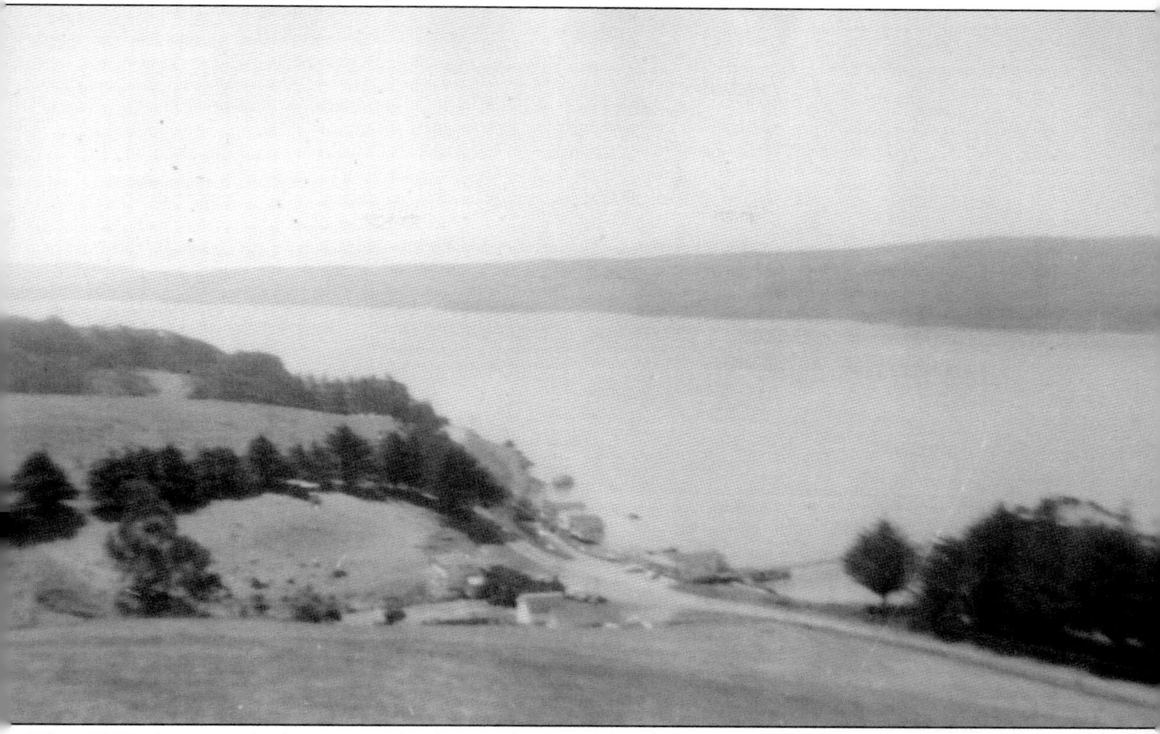

This 1950 photograph shows rental cabins, which used to be on the other side of the bay in the center, including one belonging to Elizabeth Matkovitch. Miller's cabin is in the trees. Today, it is Miller State Park. The highway, now Highway 1, was widened and paved in 1933. Nick's Cove proved especially popular with residents of the Sacramento Valley, where summer heat was always oppressive. For David Rains Wallace, the bay represented semi-controlled adventure: "When I rowed across the bay, herds of sea lions swam alongside and belched their fishy breath at me, and anxious-looking harbor seals seemed to pop up everywhere I looked. . . . Tomales Bay seemed to belong to the seals as much as to the people. I felt I'd ridden a time machine back to the Pleistocene, when the planet was bursting with big wild mammals. The bay and the grassy hills around it seemed charged with a tremendous potential and excitement." (Courtesy of Patricia Clark.)

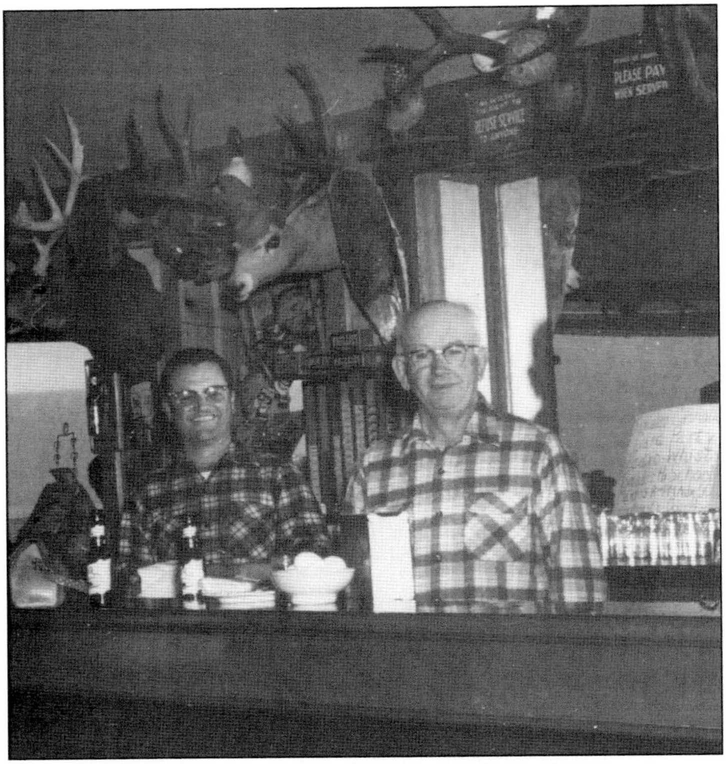

With the end of Prohibition in 1933, the rumors of Nick's bootlegging ceased, and he was able to open a legitimate bar and greatly improve profitability. He and Frances rented the bayfront cabins on a long-term basis, attracting people from San Francisco and Sacramento. One cabin closest to the restaurant was occupied by Frances's bachelor brothers Andy and Mike until 1953. The small cabin was later joined to the adjacent one with a wood frame addition placed between the two in order to provide space for one of the restaurant's cooks who had a large family.

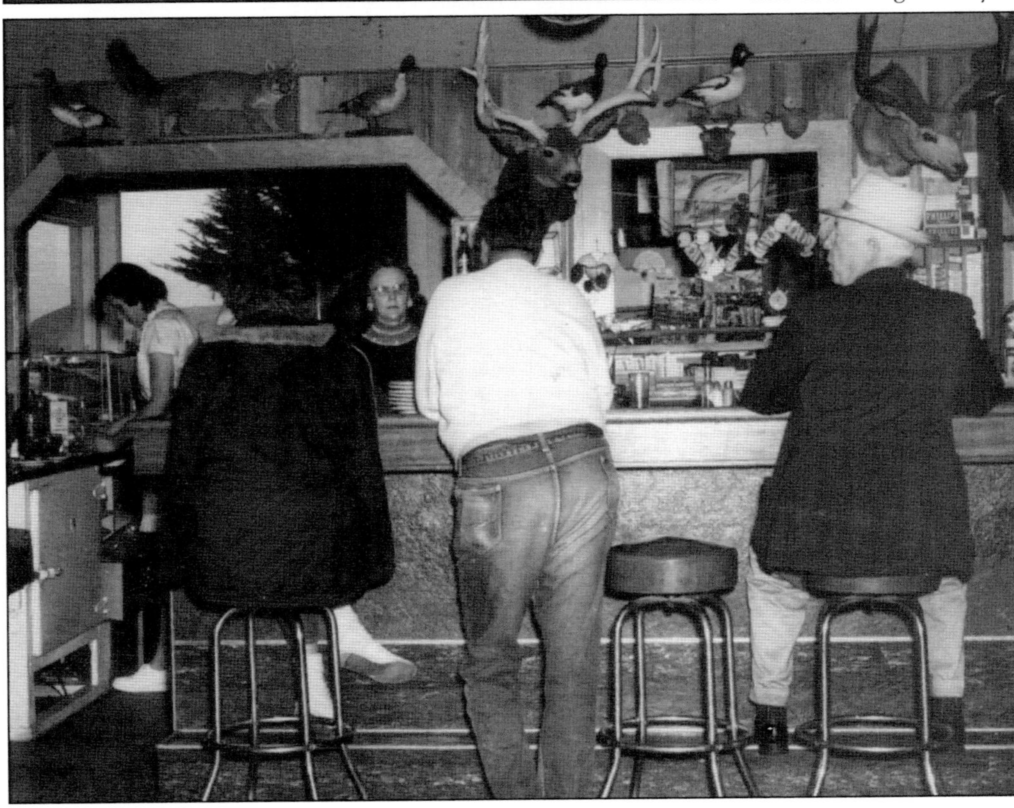

In the 1950s and 1960s, boaters could tie up at the pier for a restaurant visit, and fishermen could sell their catches, which ended up on the menu. The Kojichs also rented out small boats with oars and/or motors. They hosted events and parties such as the annual Stingray Derby and Shark Derby. Sportfishing was so popular in California that, by 1954, the sportfishing catch exceeded that of commercial fishermen. Tomales Bay fishermen caught silver salmon and steelhead in the fall, jacksmelt and surfperch in the winter, halibut in the summer, and flounder and the occasional striped bass all year long. The two derbys were created to eliminate "predators" that took bait and/or catches from fishermen before they could reel them in. According to Christie Avery, "In 1970, 30,000 pounds of shark and stingray (twice the sportcatch of all other species in the bay combined) were caught and turned to fertilizer."

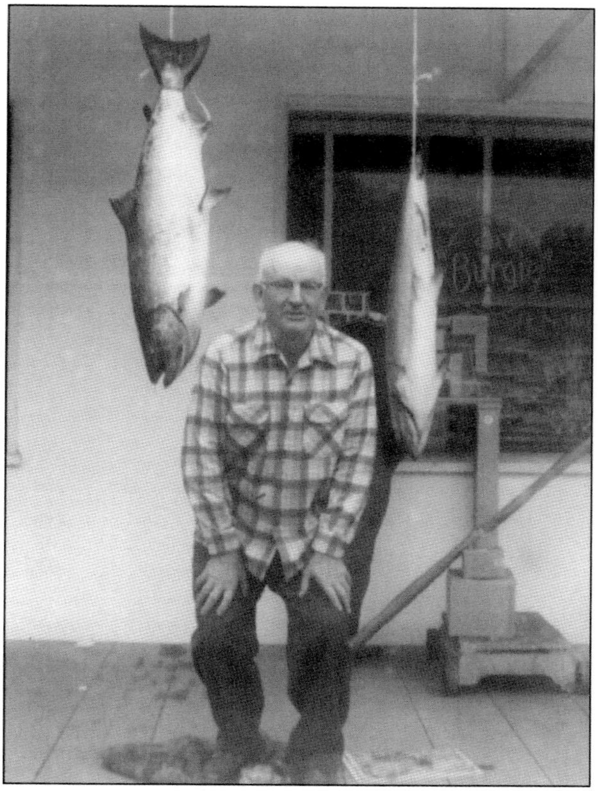

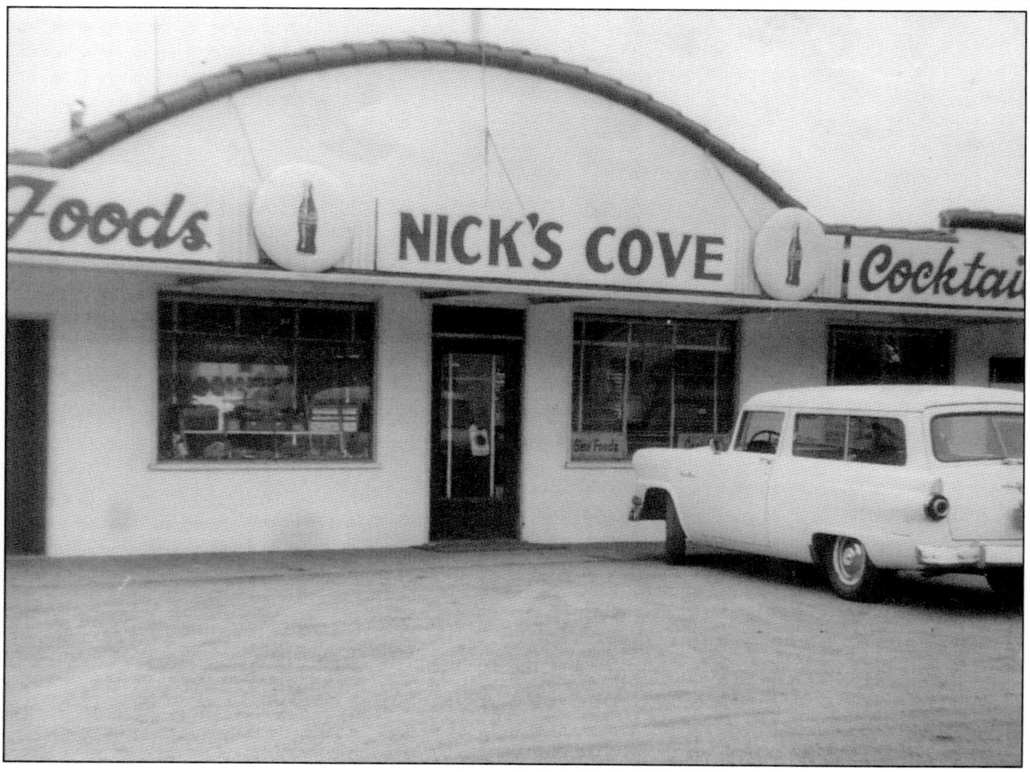

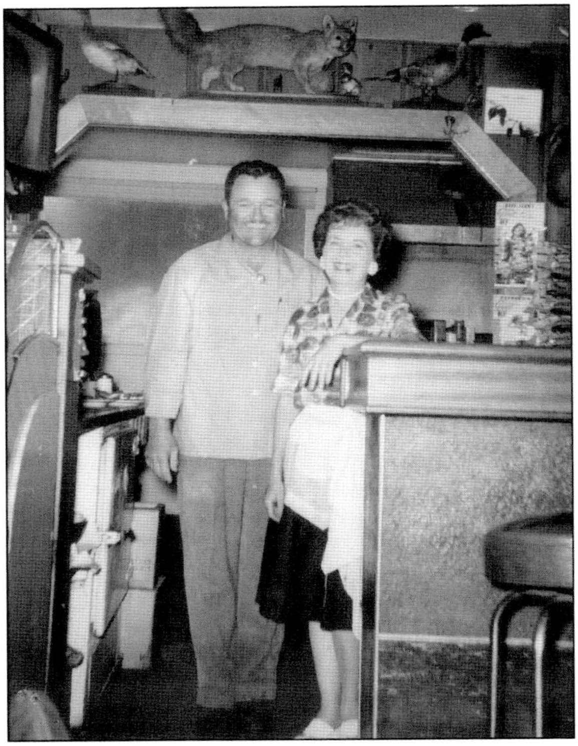

Nick and Frances Kojich remained at Nick's Cove until they died, with Frances predeceasing Nick. With an early eye to keeping the restaurant in the family, they asked Frances's nephew Andrew and his wife, Dorothy, to be business partners. Andrew Matkovich was a son of bay pioneer Gregory Matkovivh and had been born in one of the cabins now used as a rental cottage. They developed a full menu, still specializing in seafood, and as Nick and Frances could now enter retirement peacefully, Andrew and Dorothy (pictured here) took over the business fully and raised a family. In 1973, Dorothy, a widow of four years, sold Nick's Cove to Alfred (pictured at right, below) and Ruth Gibson, ending more than 40 years of family ownership.

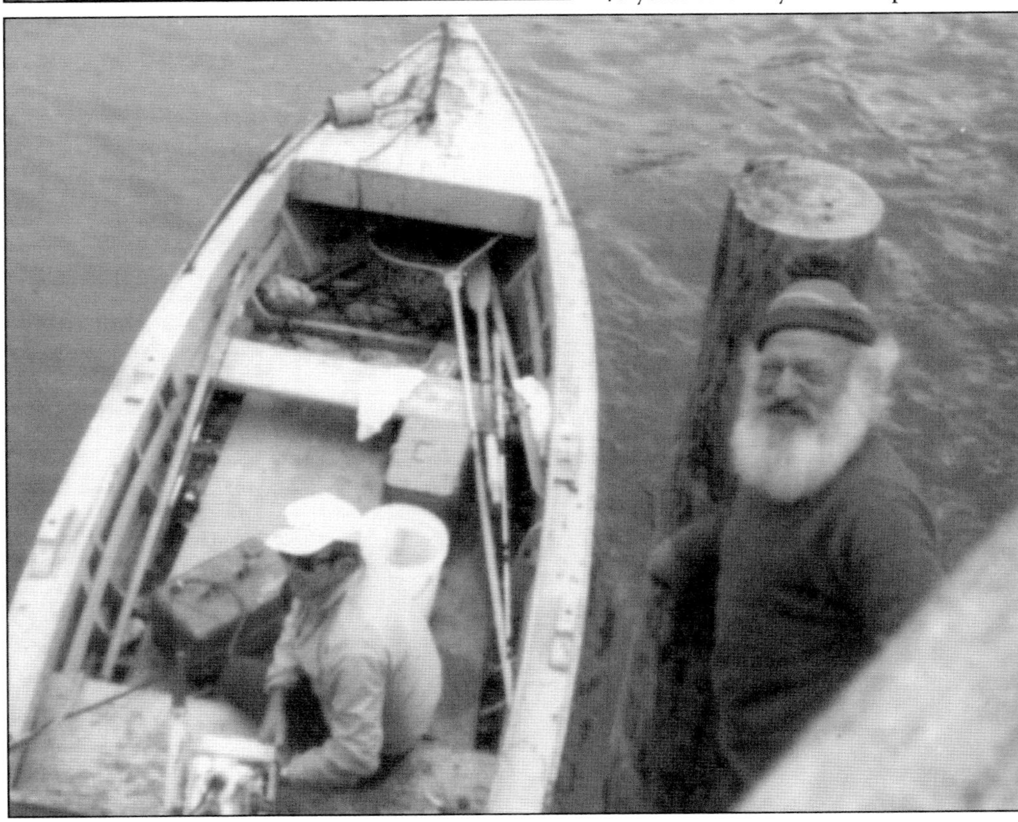

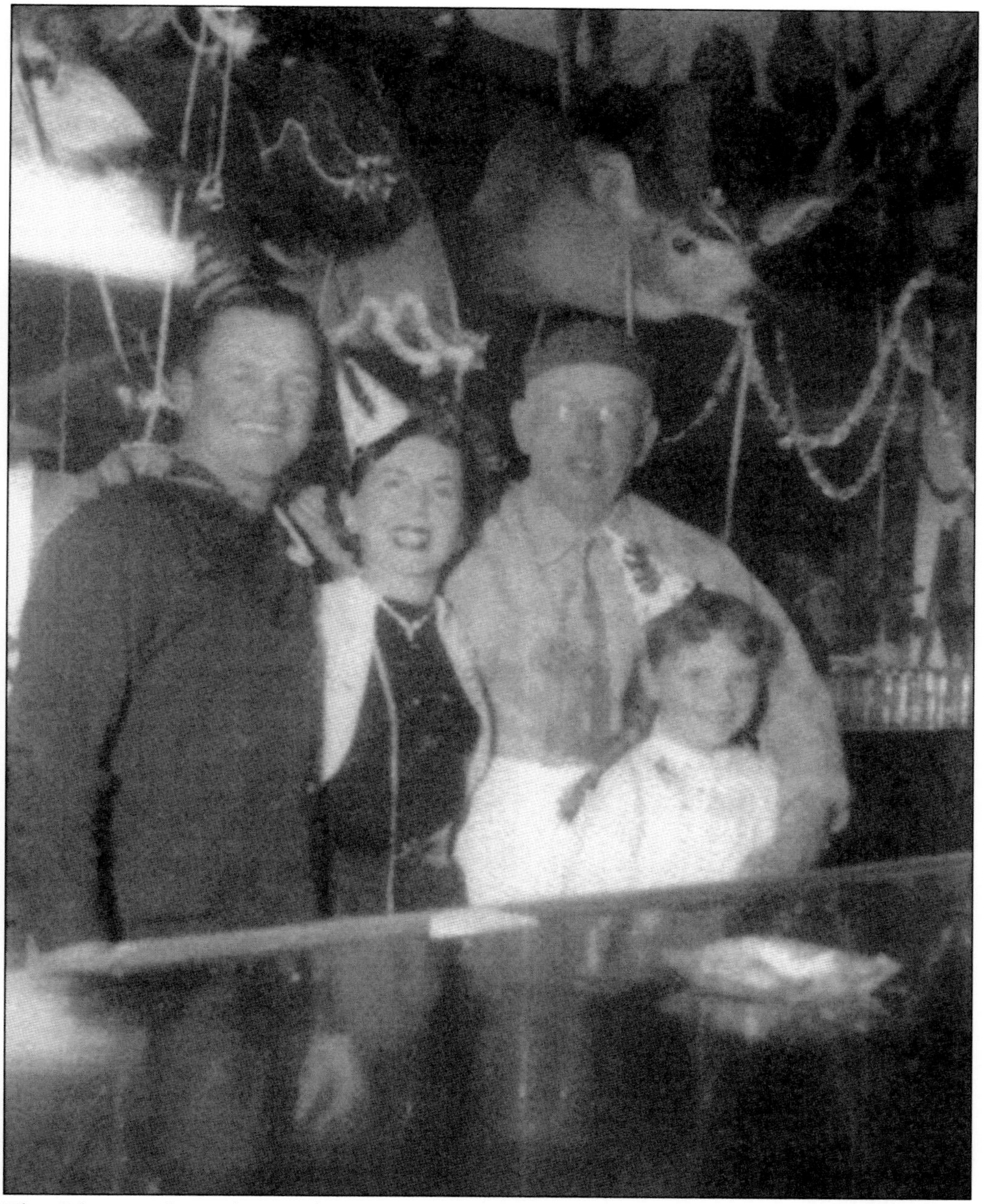

The Gibsons inherited more than a restaurant. In the past 40 years, Nick's Cove had become a home away from home for locals and visitors alike. Christmas cheer, as in this photograph of Andrew, Dorothy, and Nick, continued all year long. Now, the cabins were rented on a weekly, weekend, and nightly basis to hunters, fishermen, nature lovers, and unsuspecting travelers who stumbled upon a restaurant/motel full of character and scenic beauty. Some of the Gibsons' guests included university professors, writers, sportsmen, kayakers, and a private pilot who rented one of the cabins every time he flew into the Bay area. The cabins also accommodated family members at times, for example the Gibsons' daughters who worked in the restaurant, and patrons too drunk to drive home. After Al's death, Ruth Gibson continued to operate the restaurant and rental business although under greater adversity as time passed.

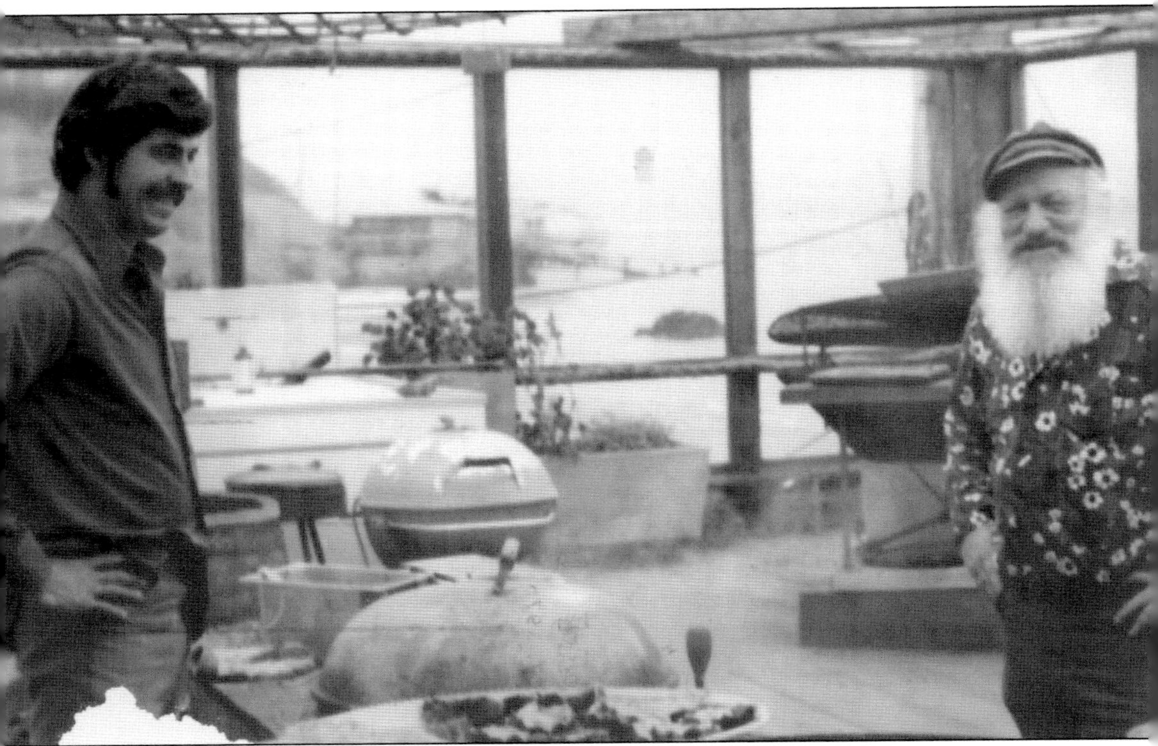

Ruth Gibson encouraged friends and family to stay and help with the business and to keep her company. At one point, fearful of being taken advantage of while living there alone, she slept in a different cabin every night to foil a crime. In the 1990s, the restaurant was open fewer hours until finally closing. Ruth Gibson continued to rent the cottages until a needed septic system proved too costly. She sold the property in 1999 to Pat Kuleto. Pictured above is husband, Al, with Anastacio Gonzalez. In her encyclopedic and definitive book *Oyster Culture* (2011), Gwendolyn Meyer relates that Anastacio "had never seen an oyster large enough to barbecue until he was presented with a sack of them one summer evening in 1972 at the Tomales Bay Sportsmen's Association's Shark and Ray Derby. At the end of the day he and his fellow fishermen were cooking their catches at Nick's Cove, where they convened every evening during the two-day annual event. . . . He concocted a sauce based on one his mother served with barbecued shrimp back in his Mexican hometown of Valle de Guadalupe."

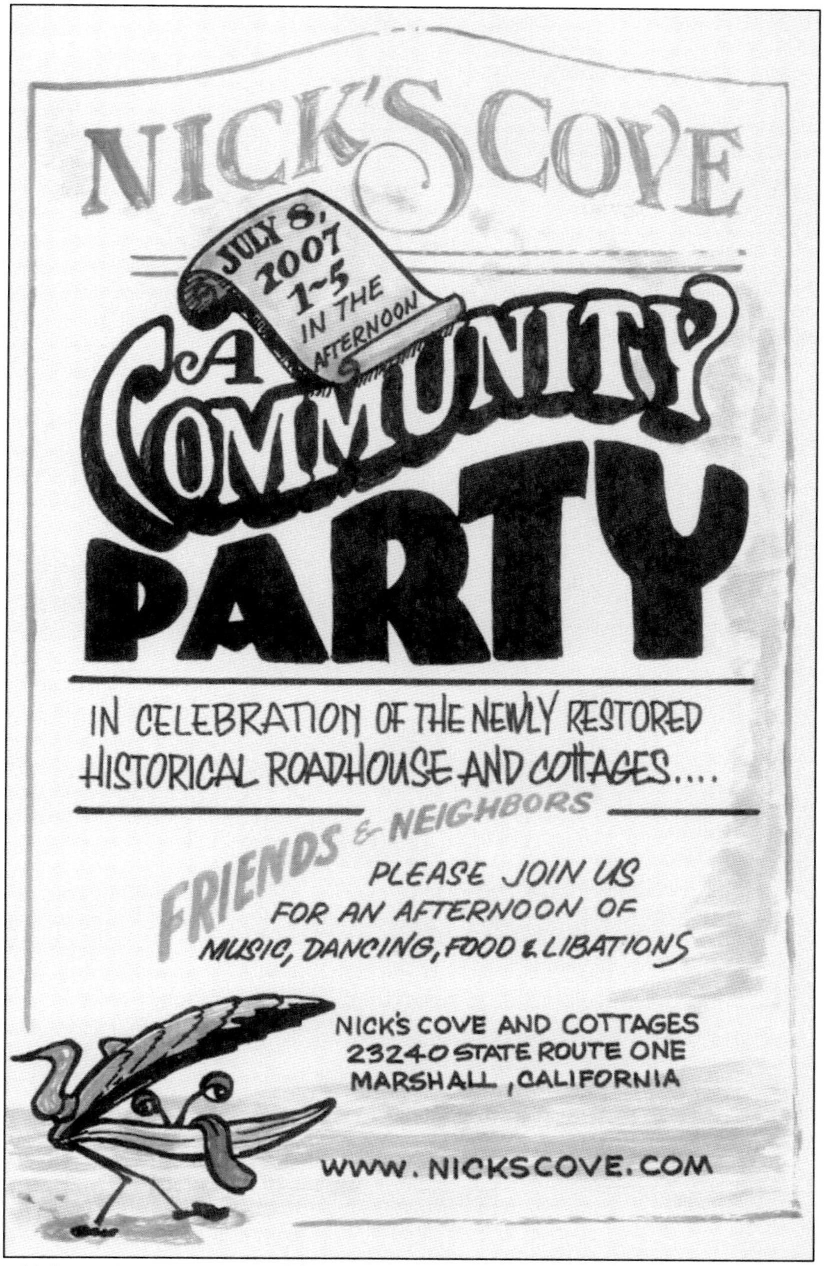

"Because of Mexico's economic problems many immigrants come here (Tomales Bay) hoping to save enough money to return to Mexico and set up a business or buy a ranch. A lot go back, but many Mexicans, like the Portuguese, Irish, Yugoslavs and Italian-Swiss before them, have found themselves growing roots in their new homeland. Their kids are in school. They want to stay. They have to stay," stated Anastacio Gonzalez. When Pat Kuleto purchased Nick's Cove in 1999–2000 from Ruth Gibson, he was continuing the immigrant tradition. Though born in La Crescenta, an unincorporated suburb of Los Angeles, it was only when he visited northern Italy and his family's roots that he knew his destiny. Born in 1945, he is credited with being the first American to bring recognition to restaurant design as a distinct form of interior design. By late 2009, he had designed nearly 400 restaurants.

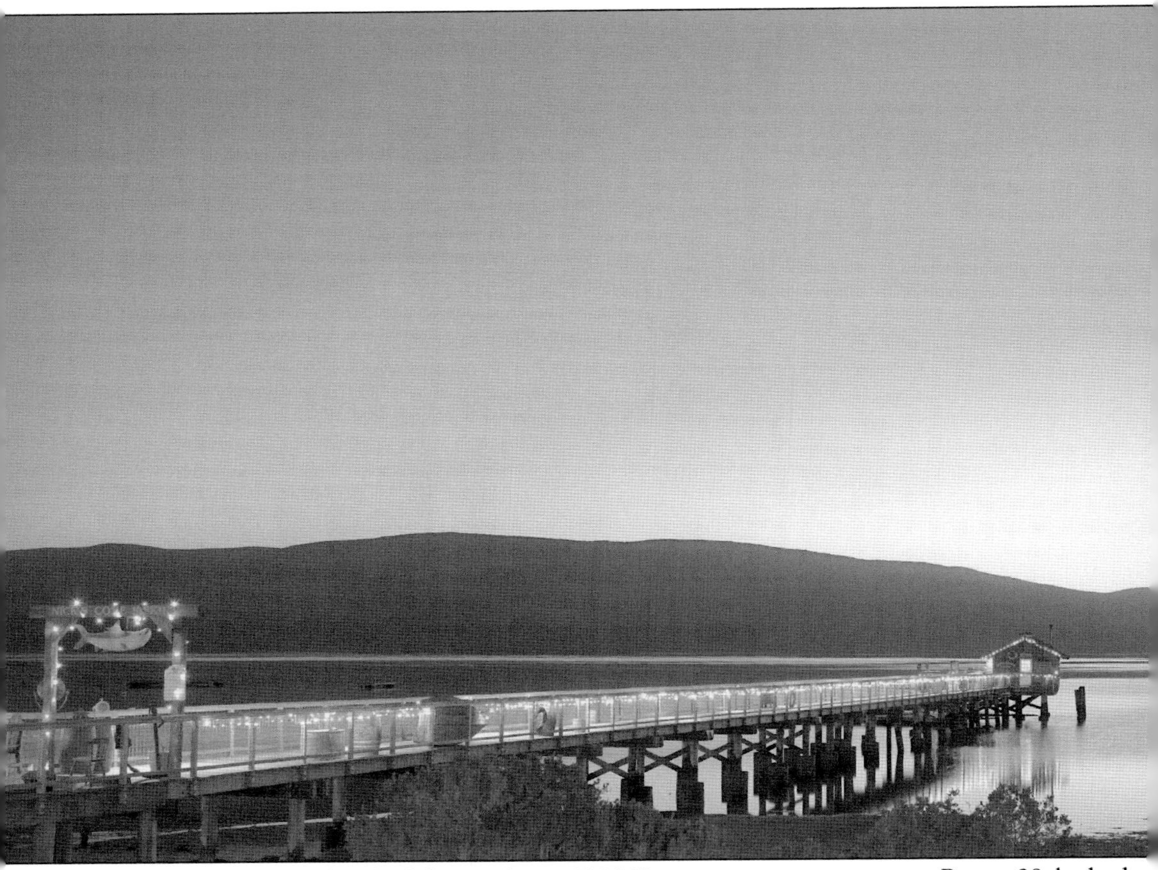

By July 2007, Pat Kuleto had designed over 100 US restaurants coast to coast. By age 28, he had already designed 60 restaurants. Nick's Cove proved to be his most challenging venue to date. He restored the property to a rustic 1930s appearance at a cost of $14 million and then reopened it July 8, 2007, with a community party as an inn of 12 cabins and a 130-seat restaurant. The eight-year project involved environmental litigation since the restaurant's kitchen was above a streambed. The California red-legged frog, an endangered species, was discovered on the property during construction. The restoration of a dilapidated building and reconstruction of this fishing pier proved very costly. Simultaneously building his own winery in Napa during this period allowed him to build a wine list at Nick's Cove, previously inconceivable. Nevertheless, the recession of 2008 and beyond, plus electronic and interminable communication problems, signaled a no-win situation. New owners, a group of silent investors, finally purchased Nick's Cove from Kuleto. They launched a totally different menu, with more small plates and slightly more modern fare. (Courtesy of frankenyimages.com.)

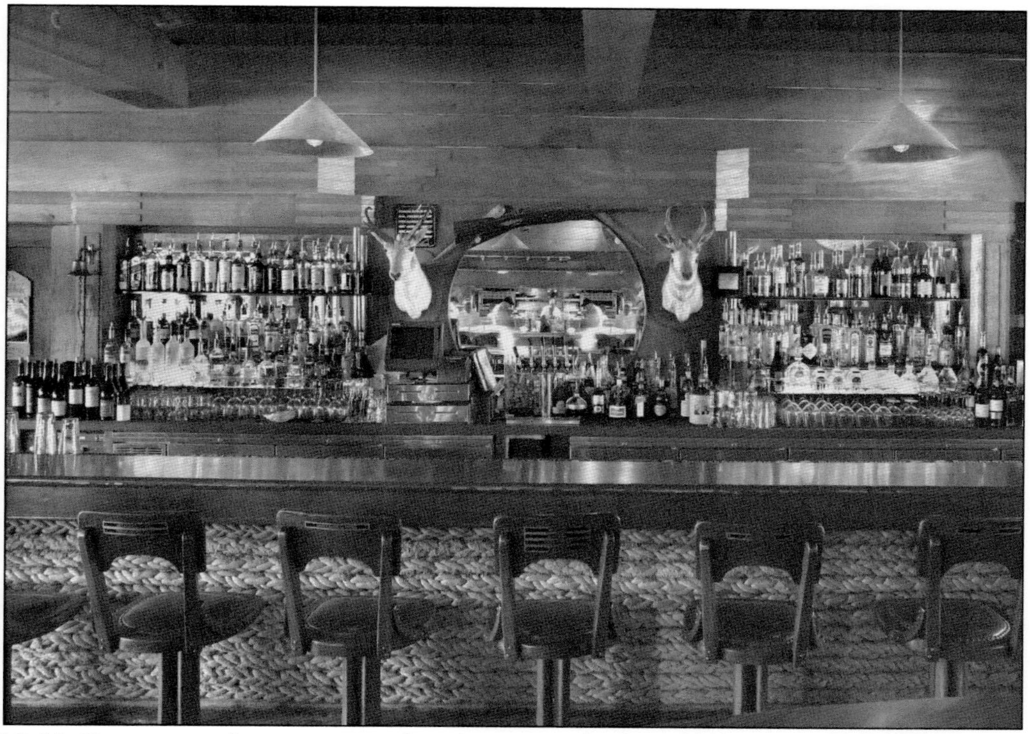

Nick's Cove was unfortunate enough to begin as a food establishment during Prohibition's implementation of the Volstead Act. With the end of Prohibition, beer and hard liquor were the predominant sources of alcohol. When Pat Kuleto opened Nick's Cove, he described the large bar as an "altar that legitimizes the drinking experience" in the same way that an open exhibition kitchen allows diners to watch their food being cooked. The symbiotic relationship of both was exemplified in an appetizer of octopus soaked in sake followed by crabcakes served with sherry aioli. Nick's chocolate martinis would end the dining adventure. Today at Nick's Cove, Dean Castelli extends the cocktail experience with his invention of the Marshall Manhattan. Starting with a dark oatmeal stout, he adds wintery spices of cloves, cinnamon, and allspice to create a syrup that replaces the customary sweet vermouth of a standard Manhattan. Added to one's preferred bourbon, a new classic awaits. (Both courtesy of frankenyimages.com.)

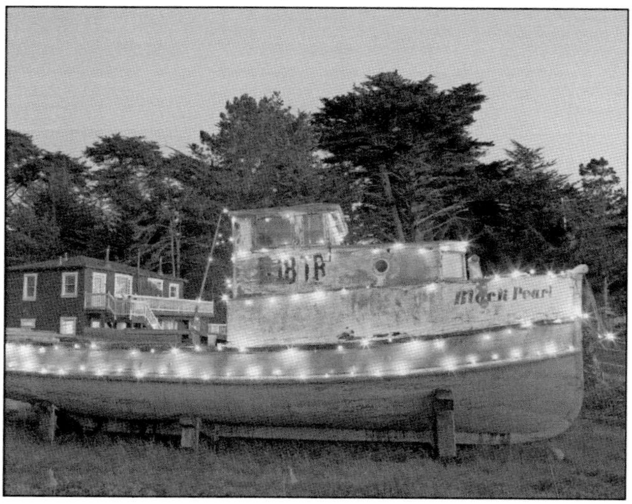

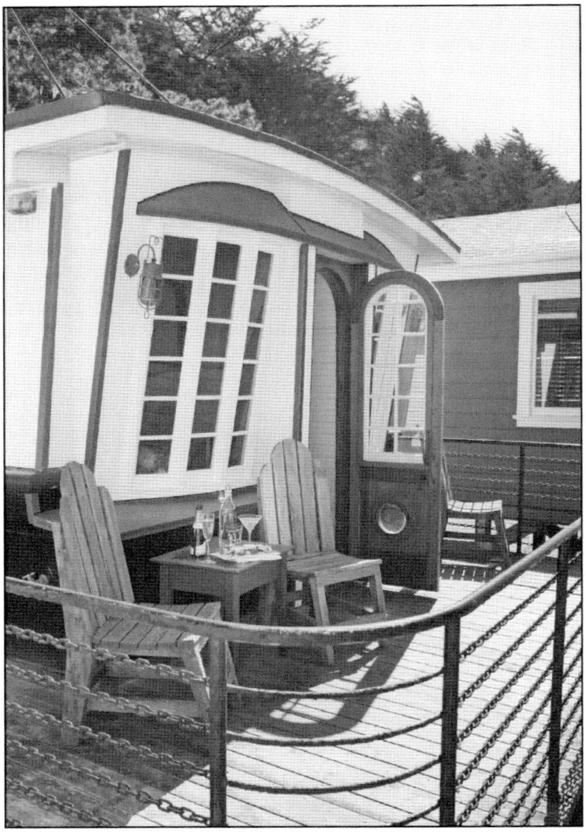

Nick's Cove is over 80 years old but does not show its age in any deleterious way. The similarity of Tomales Bay to the Adriatic Sea, with its mild winters and shallow waters, made the location a prime spot for the large Yugoslavian immigrant community. Not to be overlooked is Tony Konatich, who gave Tony's Seafood restaurant in Marshall its name. Son Felix explained, "Since my father was a seaman, it was easy for him to come. He just got off the boat in America in 1922. Fourteen years later, he could afford to send for me." The current owners of Nick's Cove have taken special care to maintain the integrity of its traditional architecture in recognition of the cottages' historical importance. These cabins reflect the coastal vernacular style common to the community. They have been carefully preserved while simultaneously improving their decor to accommodate luxe-rustic amenities without damaging their historical qualities. (Both courtesy of frankenyimages.com.)

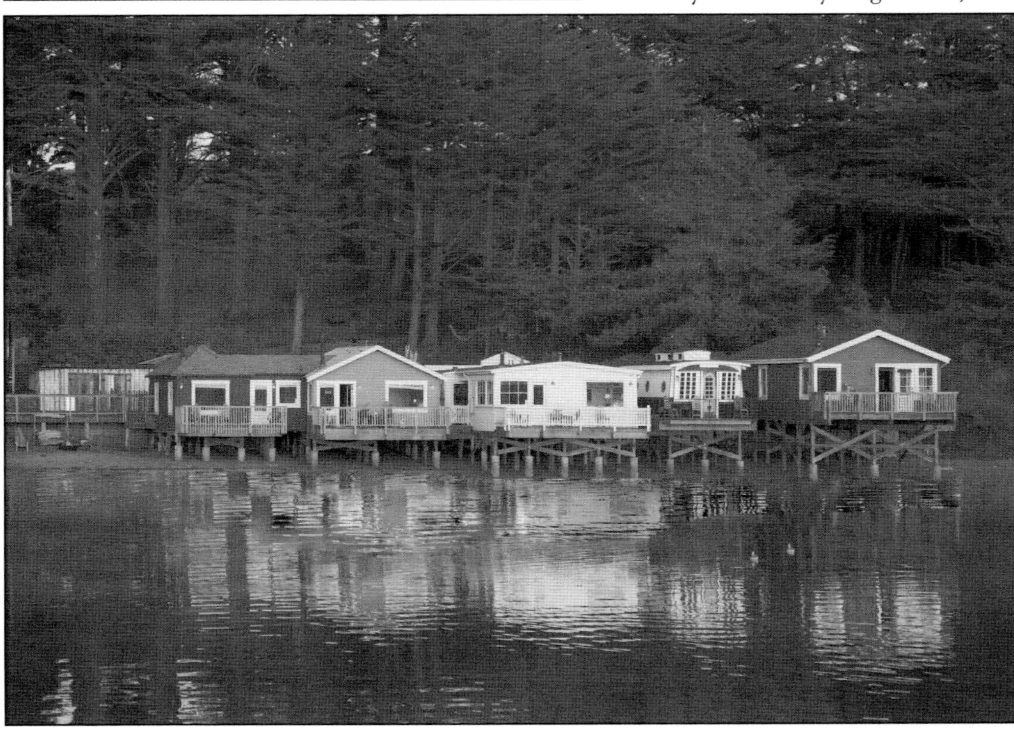

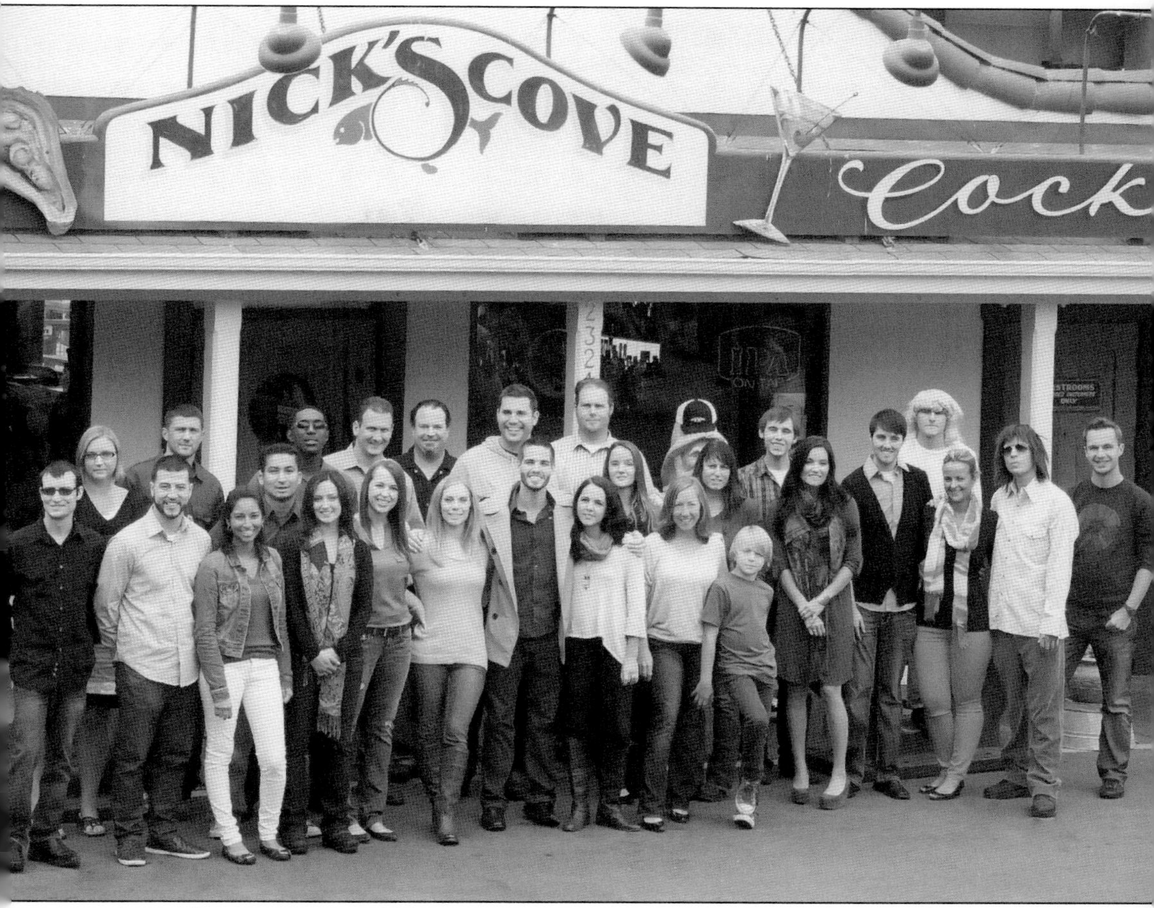

It may take a village to raise a child, but it takes a staff of 27 to run Nick's Cove restaurant, oyster bar, and cottages. Pictured are (first row) server Tavez Emery; runner/bartender Danny Martin; host Aubrey Cutris-Peno; servers Kate Graham, Frankie Carlon, and Rose Partington; bartender Casey Marr; expediter Rachel Tatum; general manager/director of operations Dena Grunt; and next generation staff Bohdan Grunt (son of Dena Grunt); (second row) accounting and human resources coordinator Katrina Garret; server Manuel Orantes; busser Kacey Gusto; private dining manager Kathryn Marando; server Jill Morris; lodging host Trevor Jenkins; lodging supervisor Tanya Markowitch; server/trainer David Jones (in wig); and server Daniel Felski; (third row) maintenance master Jake White; server Faron Bailey; restaurant and lodging manager Dean Castelli; sous chef Robert Holmes; executive chef Austin Perkins; sous chef Kua Speer; busser Tyler Jenkins; and line cook Cameron Jensen (in wig). (Courtesy of Erin Wrightsman.)

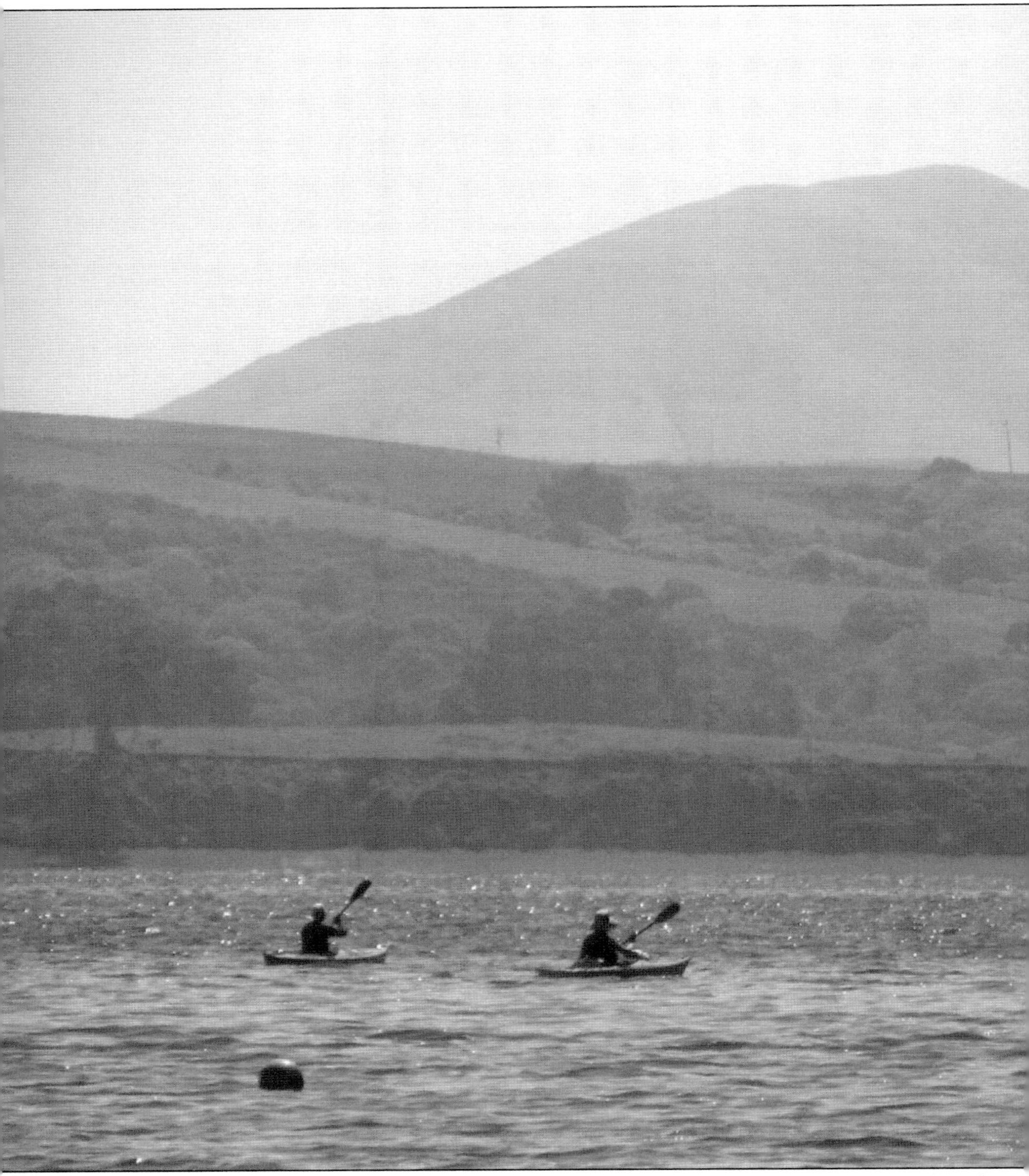

Kayakers enjoy Tomales Bay and views south to Black Mountain, perhaps unaware that they follow in the wake of Coast Miwok. The Coast Miwok considered the stunningly symmetrical peak as special—sacred, even. The bay gets its name from the Tamal-ko (coast people), one of three Miwok tribelets that called this coast their homeland into the 1800s, until various aspects of encroaching civilization doomed them. "Tamales" and "Tomales" are found in various documents of the 1840s, with the latter spelling taking hold by about 1850. The Miwoks made *Sakas*, or tule canoes, out of bundles of sturdy, hollow tule reeds in various lengths from 12 to 16

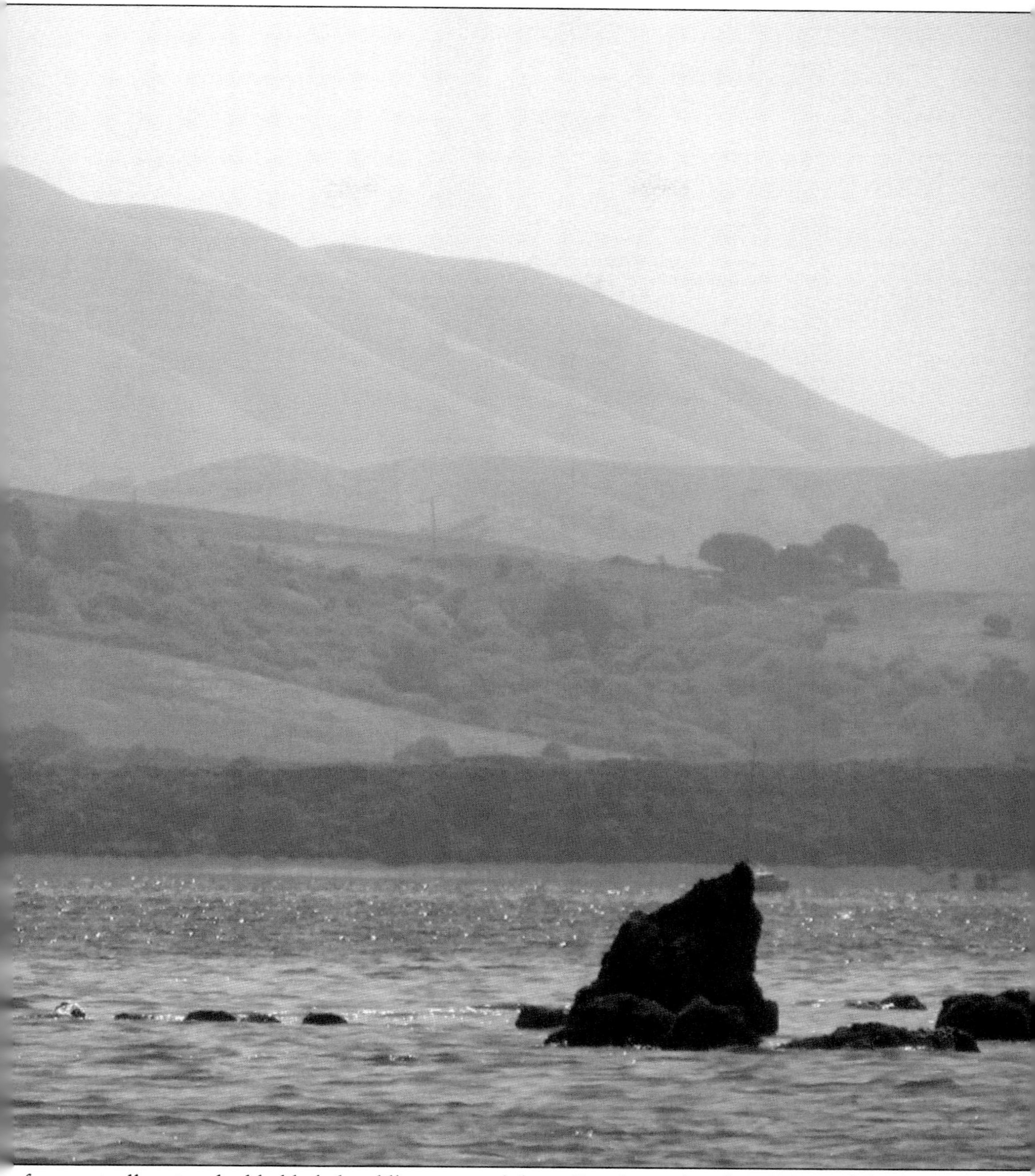

feet, typically using double-bladed paddles to propel them. Fast-forward to the 1980s, and the first kayak company on the bay was named Tamal Saka, an appropriate nod to those who came here first. The advent of the plastic kayak hastened the bay's popularity as a paddling mecca. Also in this period came the Marin Agricultural Land Trust, or MALT, which has protected the area's privately ranched hills from development, including the iconic Black Mountain. (Photograph and caption courtesy of Brett Poirier.)

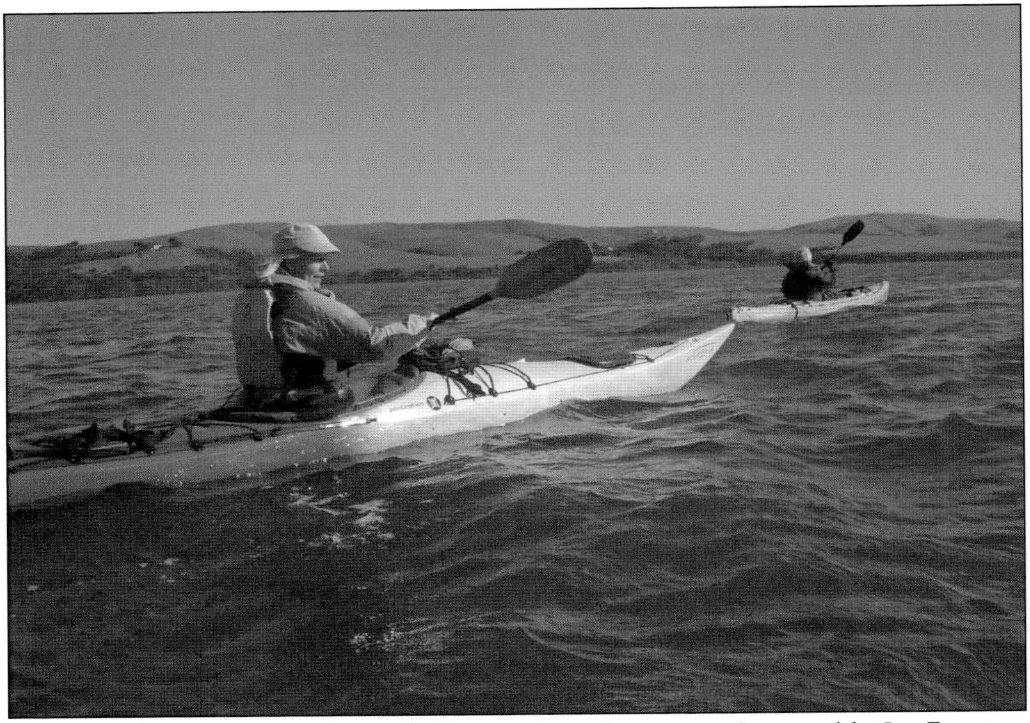

By the late 20th century, Tomales Bay had become better known as a playground for San Francisco Bay area residents than for its natural resources. By 2005, a total of 11 kayaking companies operated on the bay, and paddlers camped by permit, mostly along Marshall and Tomales beaches. Two West Marin–based outfitters, Point Reyes Outdoors and Blue Waters Kayaking, offer guided kayak trips from Miller Park at Nick's Cove. Mostly on weekends, these year-round outings spend several hours on the bay with pass-bys of mid-bay Hog Island and also White Gulch, a treeless crease in Tomales Point that shelters herds of elk. Winter kayakers often see the primal connection between herring runs and bird and seal activity, with the laws of nature played out. Summer and fall evening trips usually are treated to underwater bioluminescence displays. (Photographs and caption courtesy of Brett Poirier.)

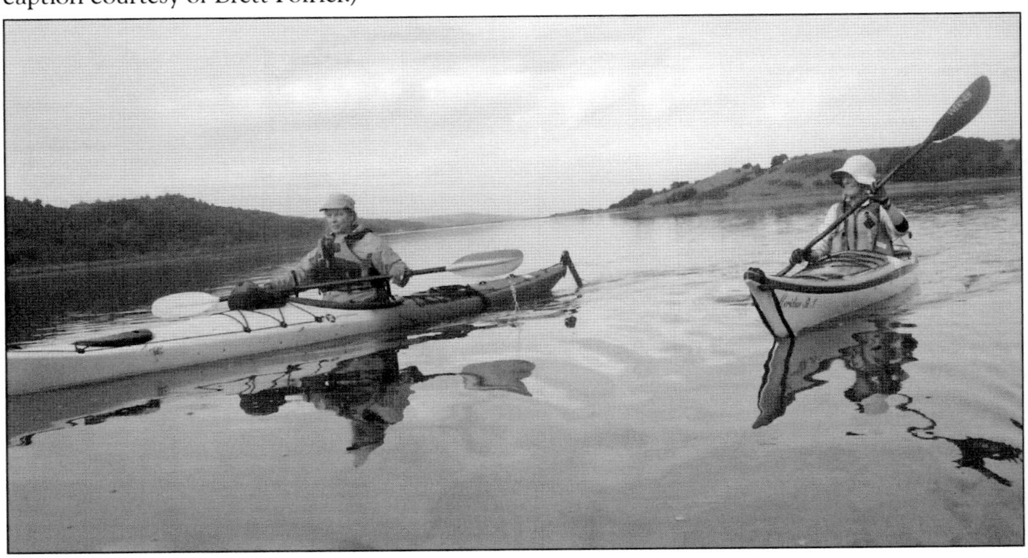

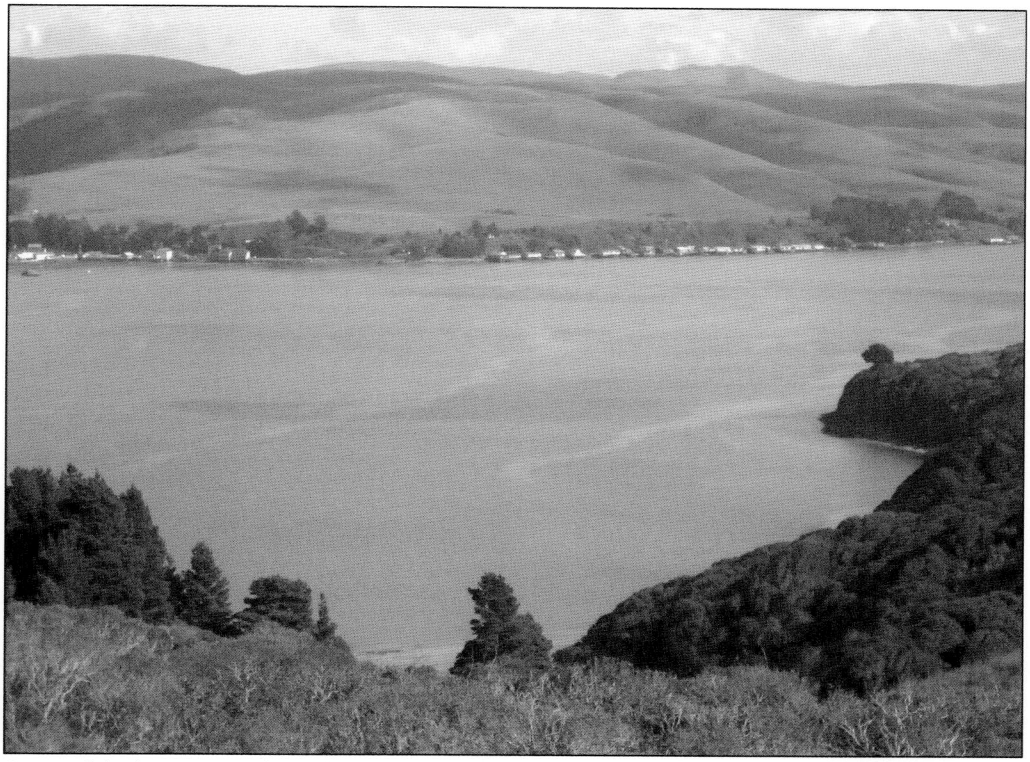

Some of the best views of Marshall and its surroundings are from the parkland heights on the west side of Tomales Bay—and by recreational boaters plying this midway point on the 12-mile-long estuary. Many shoreline buildings are constructed on pilings and even atop remnants of the original railroad grade. The strip of homes visible in both photographs, south of the Marshall Tavern, all went up around 1950. The rolling hills have been ranched since the Mexican land grant era of the 1830s. It is suspected that the Coast Miwok intentionally burned much of the bay's uplands annually to sustain grass communities and prevent brush and woodlands from encroaching. Spanish explorers of the 1700s, hoping to find sources of timber along this coast, viewed the windswept grasslands as useless. (Photographs and caption courtesy of Brett Poirier.)

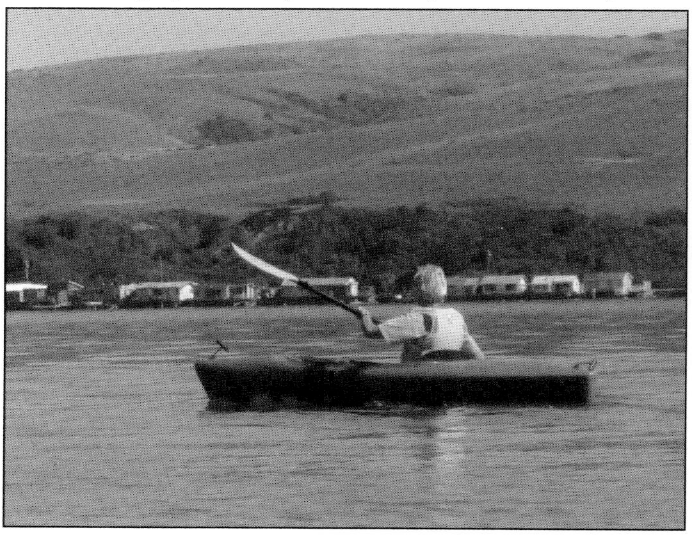

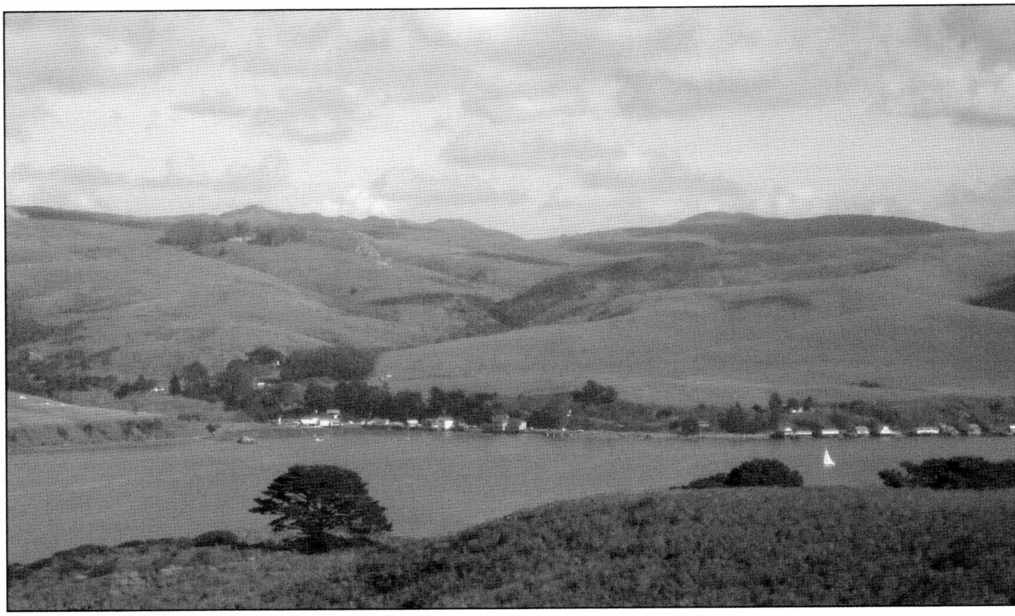

Day hikers on the bay's west-side heights, usually en route to Marshall Beach, enjoy sweeping views of the Marshall shoreline and the ranched hills beyond. The photograph above shows a rare remnant of the old railroad grade at left, just north of Hog Island Oyster Company, sheltered in its tiny cove. Most shoreline stretches of the grade have eroded into the bay or been covered by buildings and the construction of Highway 1. The 1875 railroad, which seeded so many little towns along its way north from Sausalito, found Marshall already there—with a schooner wharf, warehouse, and hotel, and Wightman's store just inland on the wagon road east to Petaluma. Today's Marshall-Petaluma Road, this winding route was laid out in 1860, partly by local Jeremiah Blake, as one of the county's main arterials. (Photographs and caption courtesy of Brett Poirier.)

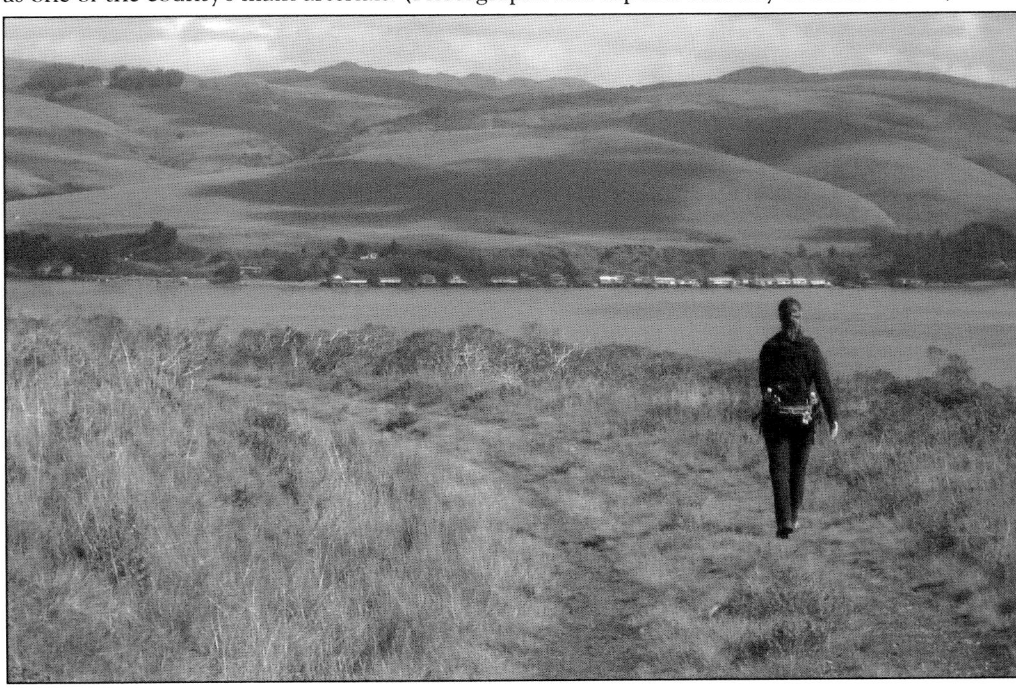

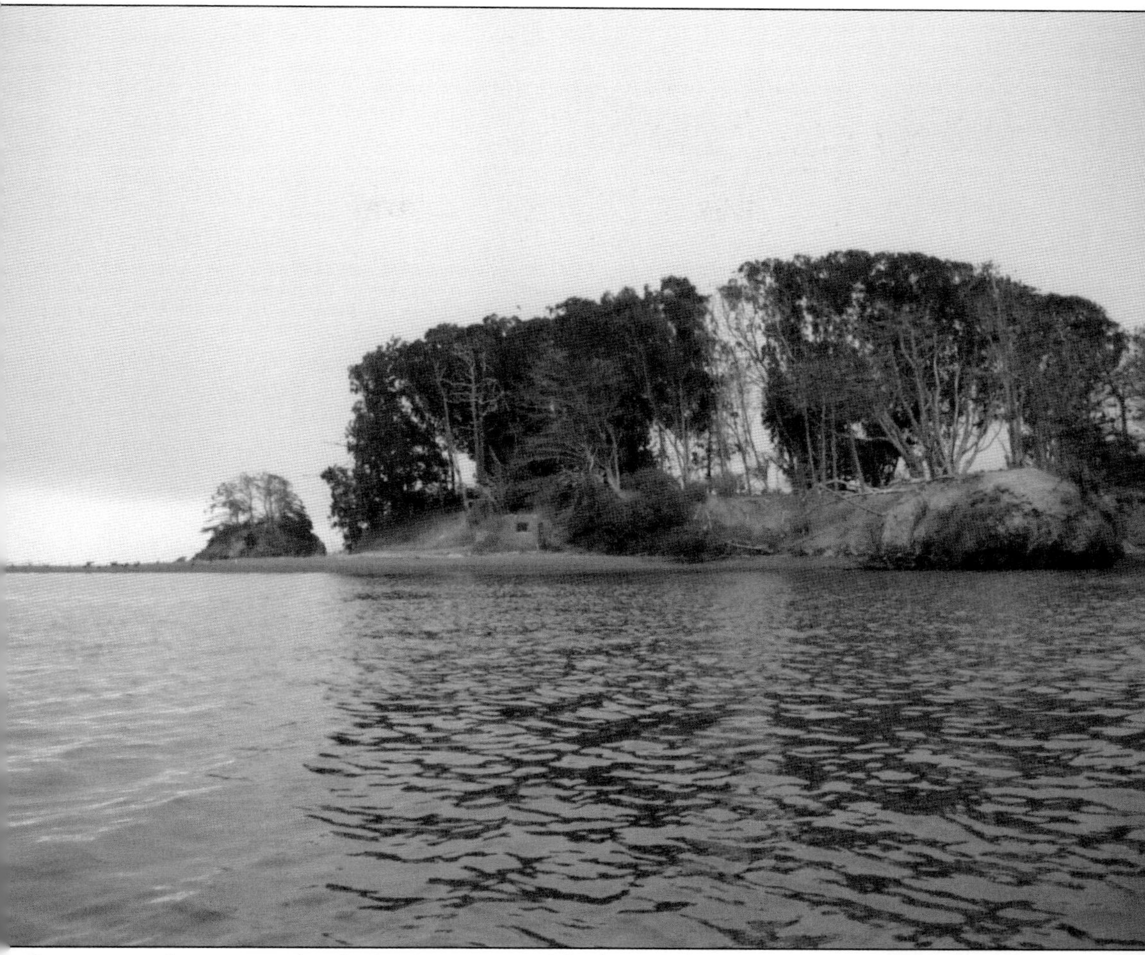

Once again, historiographer Jack Mason is cited for his scholarship regarding *Hog Island*: "By most accounts it got its name when a barge broke loose, depositing its cargo of porkers on the beach. President Rutherford B. Hayes patented it to its first owner, Christian F.T. Kuschert after the German immigrant had paid a few dollars for it at the general land office in San Francisco. A house stood on it for years, its water supply little more than a freak of nature: rainwater collected underground on a pan of hard rock. The Hulbe family called Hog Island home in the 1880s. . . . At least two Hulbe children, George and Martha, were born in the Hog Island house. The doctor who went over by rowboat to deliver George in 1884 was, I suspect, George W. Dutton of Tomales. The baby was named George, presumably for him." (Courtesy Brett Poirier.)

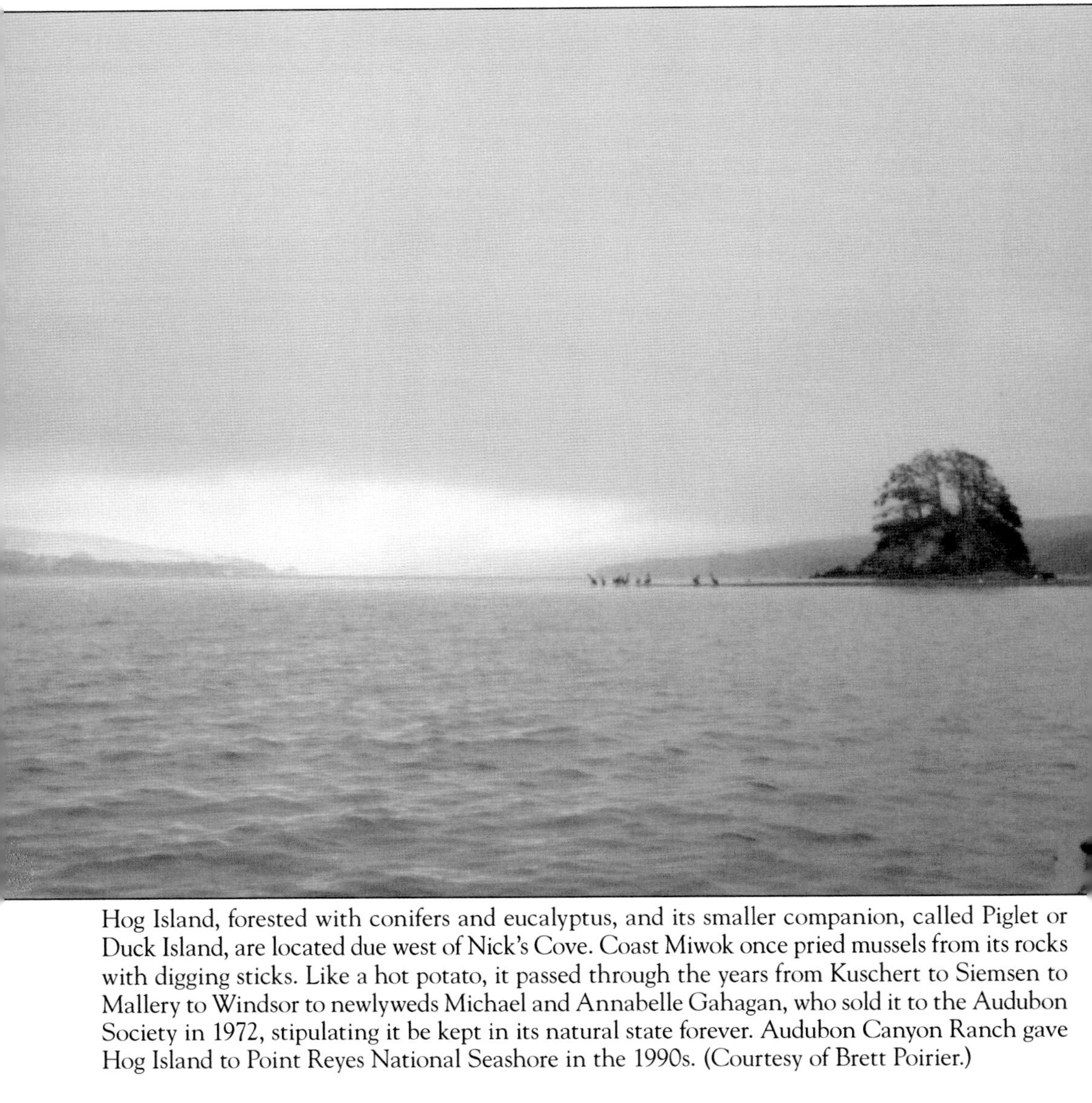

Hog Island, forested with conifers and eucalyptus, and its smaller companion, called Piglet or Duck Island, are located due west of Nick's Cove. Coast Miwok once pried mussels from its rocks with digging sticks. Like a hot potato, it passed through the years from Kuschert to Siemsen to Mallery to Windsor to newlyweds Michael and Annabelle Gahagan, who sold it to the Audubon Society in 1972, stipulating it be kept in its natural state forever. Audubon Canyon Ranch gave Hog Island to Point Reyes National Seashore in the 1990s. (Courtesy of Brett Poirier.)

Five

Tomales

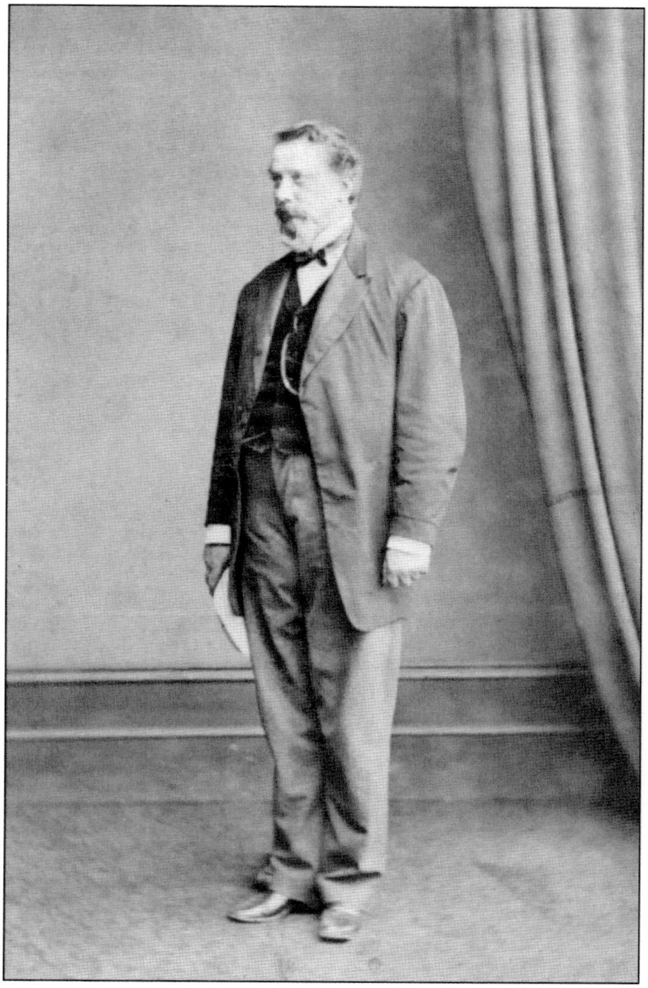

John Keys (pictured) and Warren Dutton could be called the Romulus and Remus of Tomales. Keys arrived in 1850, bought land, and became a successful farmer and businessman from the get-go. On September 1, 1852, Dutton located a claim adjoining that of Keys and commenced farming. Dutton proposed to Keys that they should jointly open a trading post, the latter to furnish $900 and the former to conduct the business. (Courtesy of the Tomales Regional History Center.)

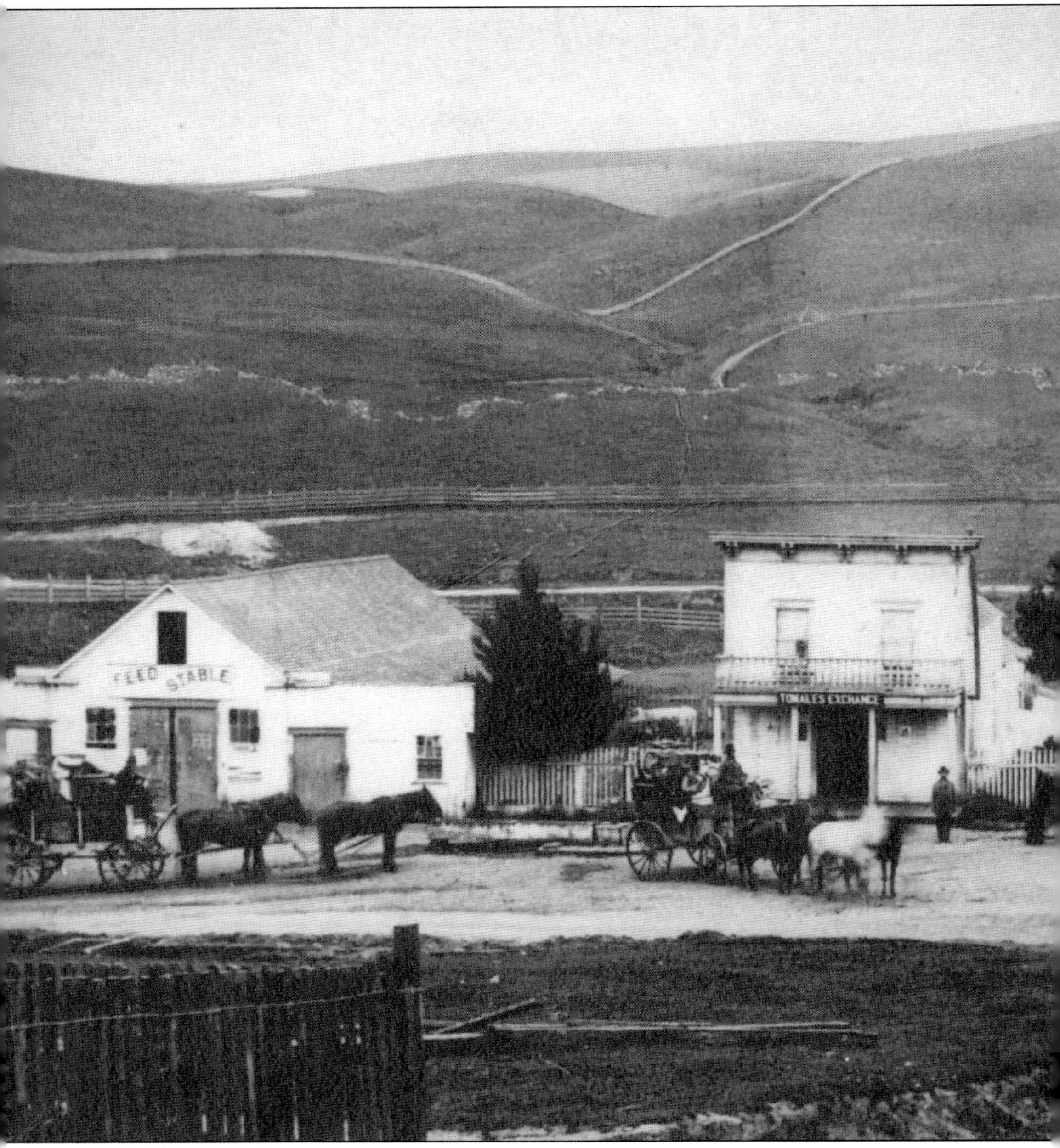

The arrangement met with the approval of both parties, and the plan was consummated with the first grocery store in Tomales Township opening in the spring of 1854 in the cedar-shake shanty erected by Keys years earlier. The businessmen had bachelor quarters therein with housekeeping undertaken by Alexander Stitt Marshall and his wife Fannie. Dutton kept shop while Keys took farm produce to San Francisco, bringing back saleable goods. For a round-trip to the city by boat,

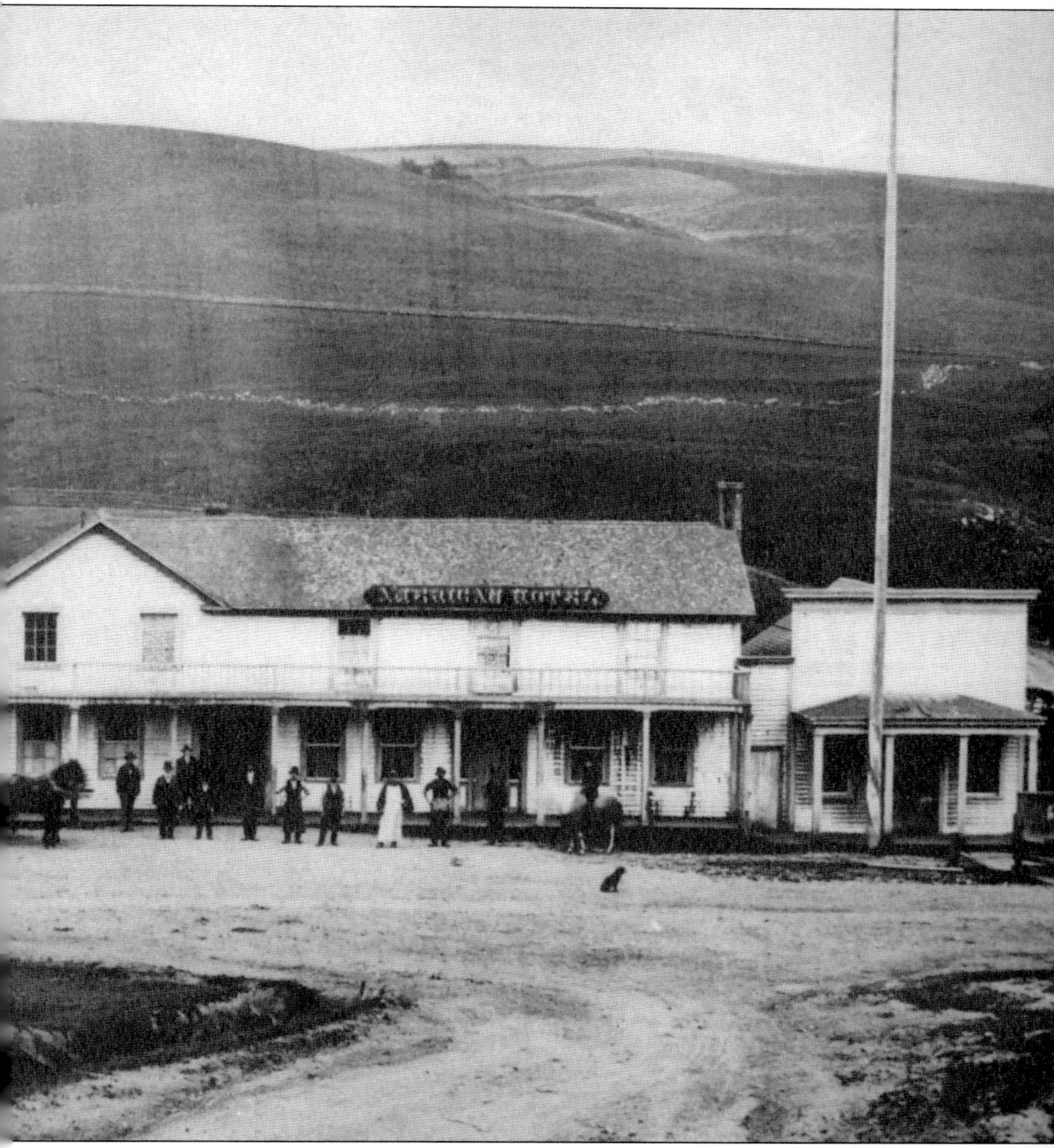

Keys charged $15. Their business arrangement collapsed in 1857. Henceforth, they divided Tomales between Keystown and the Embarcadero to the south and Dutton Town to the north. In this 1860–1861 photograph are the Tomales-Petaluma stagecoach to the left, the Tomales Exchange in the center, and the two-story American Hotel built by Keys. (Courtesy of Bessie Keys.)

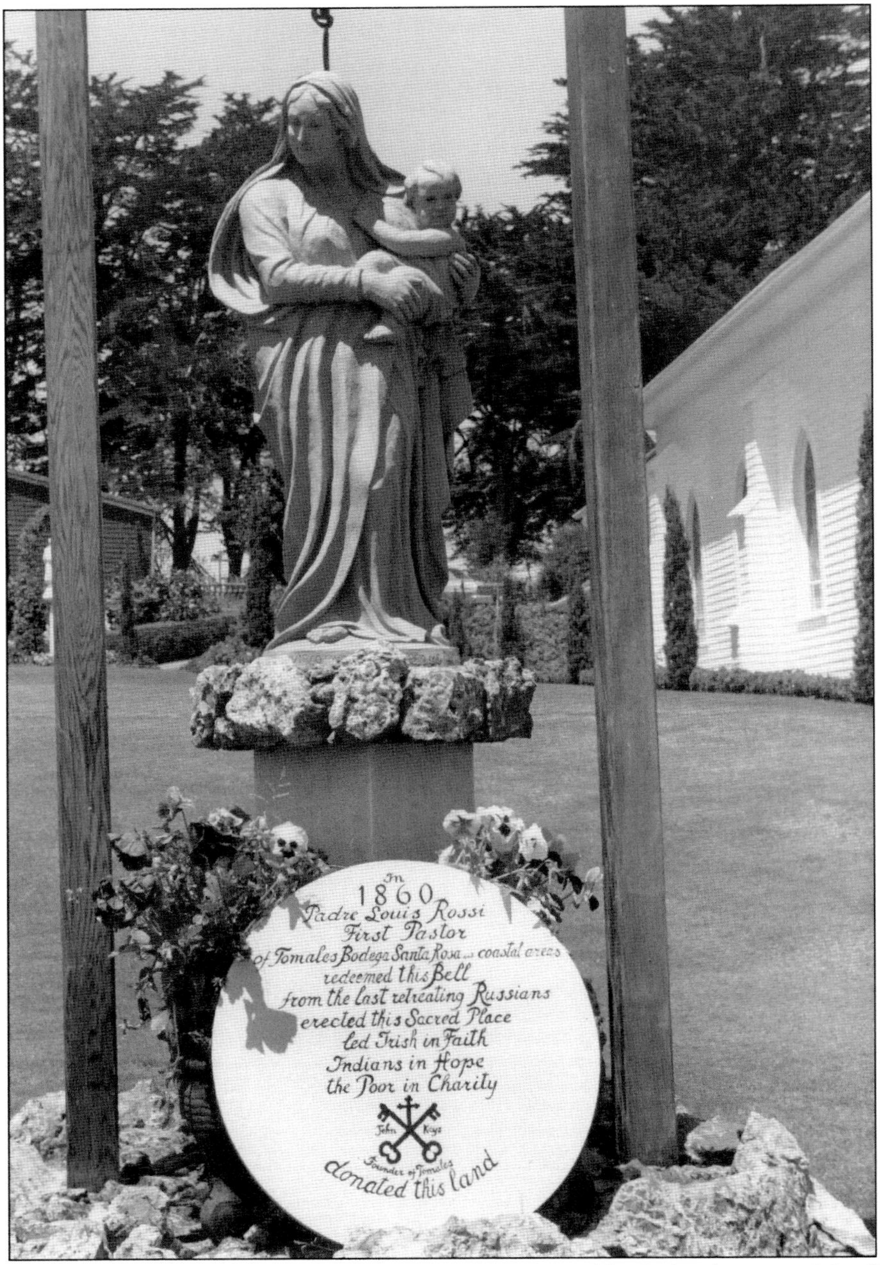

Jack Mason discovered that Tamales as a place name was cited by Padre Amoros of the Spanish Mission San Rafael when he baptized about 100 natives September 26, 1819. The name appears in the titles of three land grants, Punta de los Reyes or Canada de Tamales, March 17, 1836, and June 8, 1839; Tomales y Baulenes, March 18, 1836; and Bolsa de Tomales, June 12, 1846. There are also references to Tamal Indians in the baptismal records of Mission Dolores as early as 1901. Ethnographers vary in their interpretation of the word *tamal*; some define it as "bay;" another considers it the Miwok word for "west," so that the "Tamalenos" were coastal westerners. The plaque reads: "In 1860 Padre Louis Rossi First Pastor of Tomales Bodega Santa Rosa and coastal areas redeemed this Bell from the last retreating Russians erected this Sacred Place led Irish in Faith Indians in Hope the Poor in Charity John Keys Founder of Tomales donated this land."

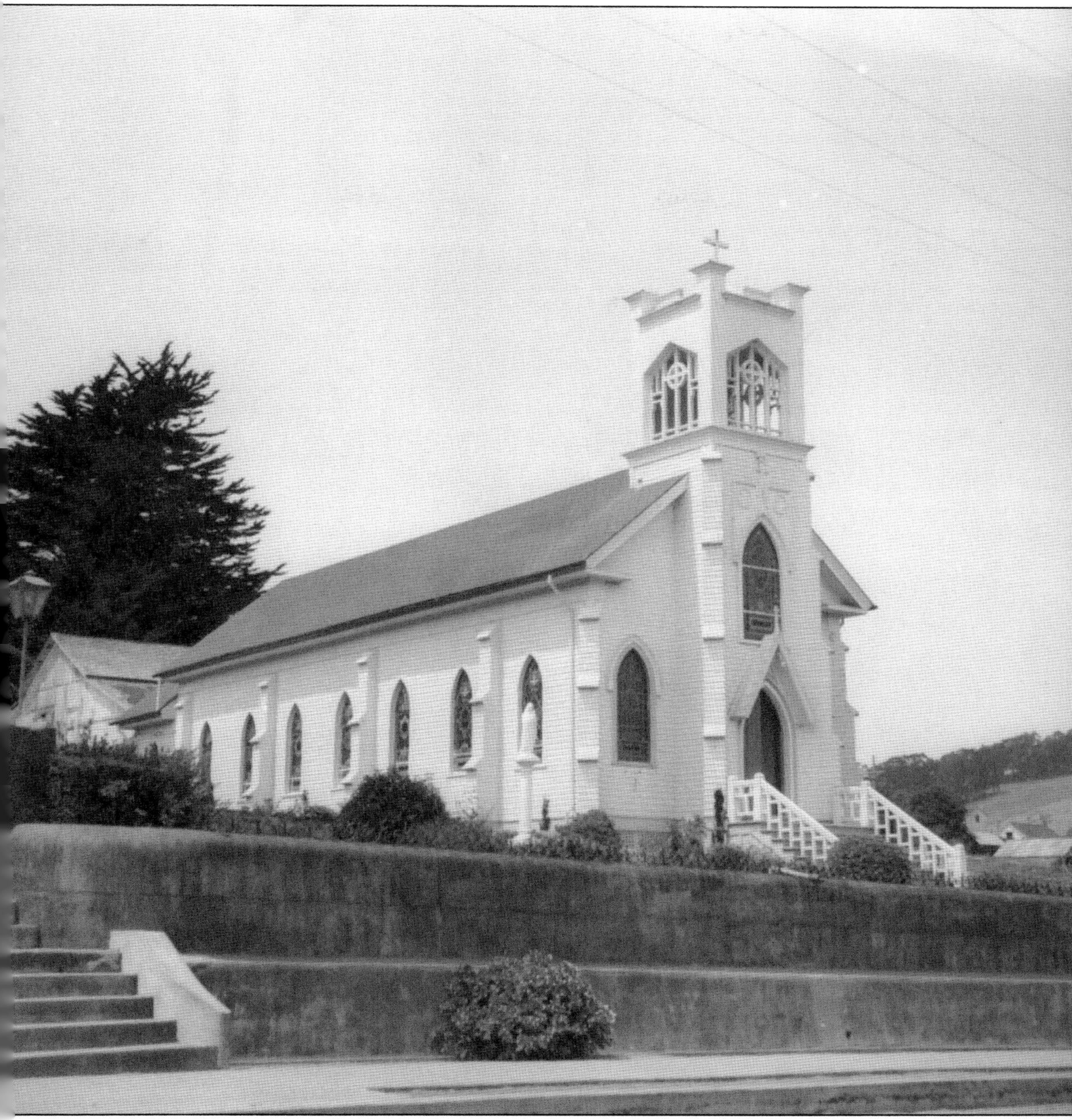

Born June 14, 1817, in Ferrara, Italy, to Italian Jewish parents, the future Father Rossi was christened Abramo. He was reared in the Jewish faith but converted to Catholicism in 1836, taking the name Luigi. He was the first resident priest assigned to a huge "churchless" territory of West Marin on March 8, 1860. He made his rounds on horseback, celebrating Mass on weekdays at the different homes or places of worship throughout his extensive parish. This extant Church of the Assumption with adjacent rectory was established March 8, 1860, built and completed in October 1860, and dedicated on Sunday, November 4, 1860, by Archbishop Alemany. Andrew Fisher and Peter Morrissey were contractors for the rectory, a four-room building costing $1,000. For 28 months, Father Rossi was a regular member of Jasper O'Farrell's household on the Annaly Farm in Freestone. His headquarters were in the original church water tower. In poor health, he retired to Europe in 1862 to write his memoir, *My Six Years in the USA*. He died in Paris September 9, 1871.

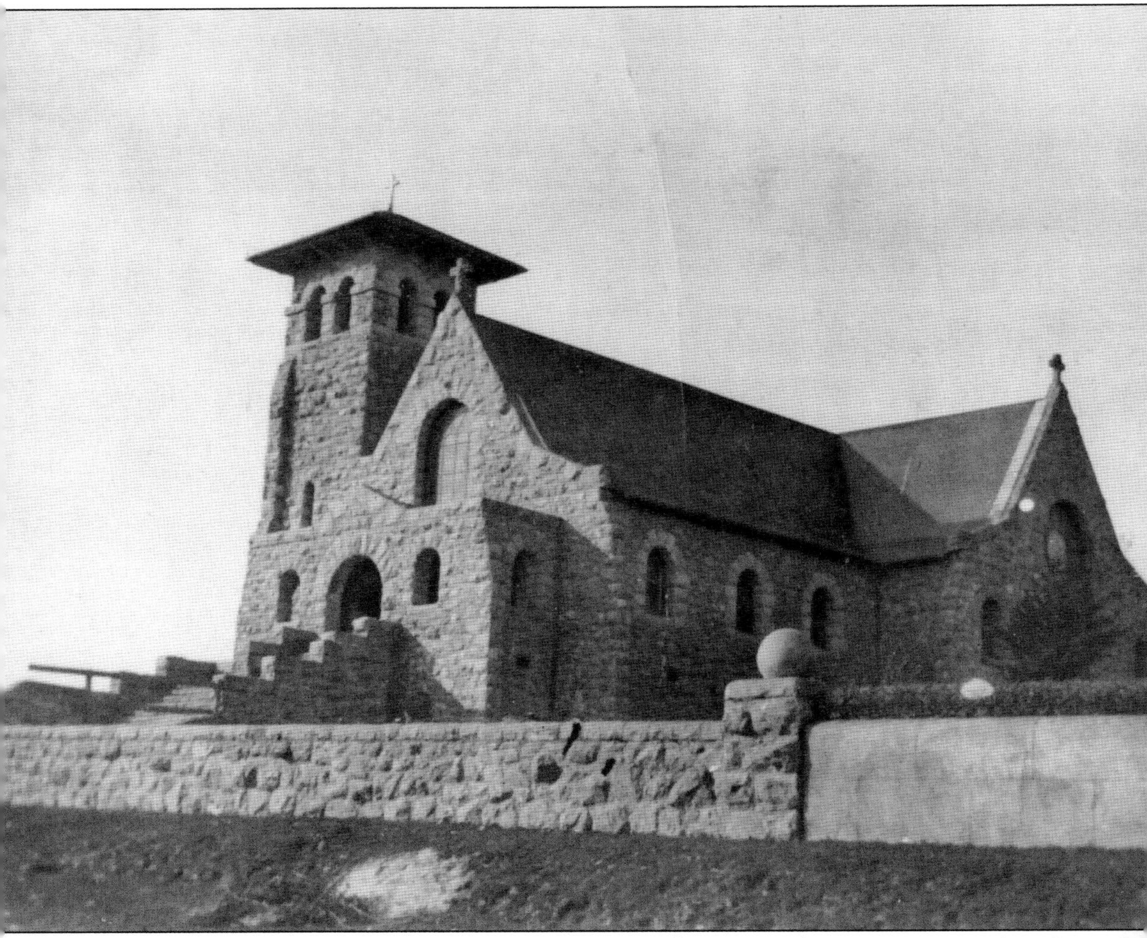

Ginny Mackenzie Magan is the curator of the Tomales Regional History Center; the editor of the quarterly bulletin published by and for the center; and the preparer of *Tomales: 1850–1957, Historic Resource Survey Report Vols. 1 and 2*, which includes 409 pages of the most comprehensive architectural historiography of the town she loves. Tomales is "her town," as *Our Town* was Thornton Wilder's. According to Magan: "The Catholic population continued to grow—partly due to the increasing number of Swiss and Italian immigrants in the area—and by the last years of the century the little wood frame church was becoming crowded. In 1897, ground was broken for a new Church of the Assumption, and the building completed three years later was dedicated in June 1900. The new church, designed by California pioneer architect Frank T. Shea, was a Richardsonian Romanesque building of local Rocky Canyon Ranch, Chileno Valley) blue and buff stone, surmounted by a red slate roof."

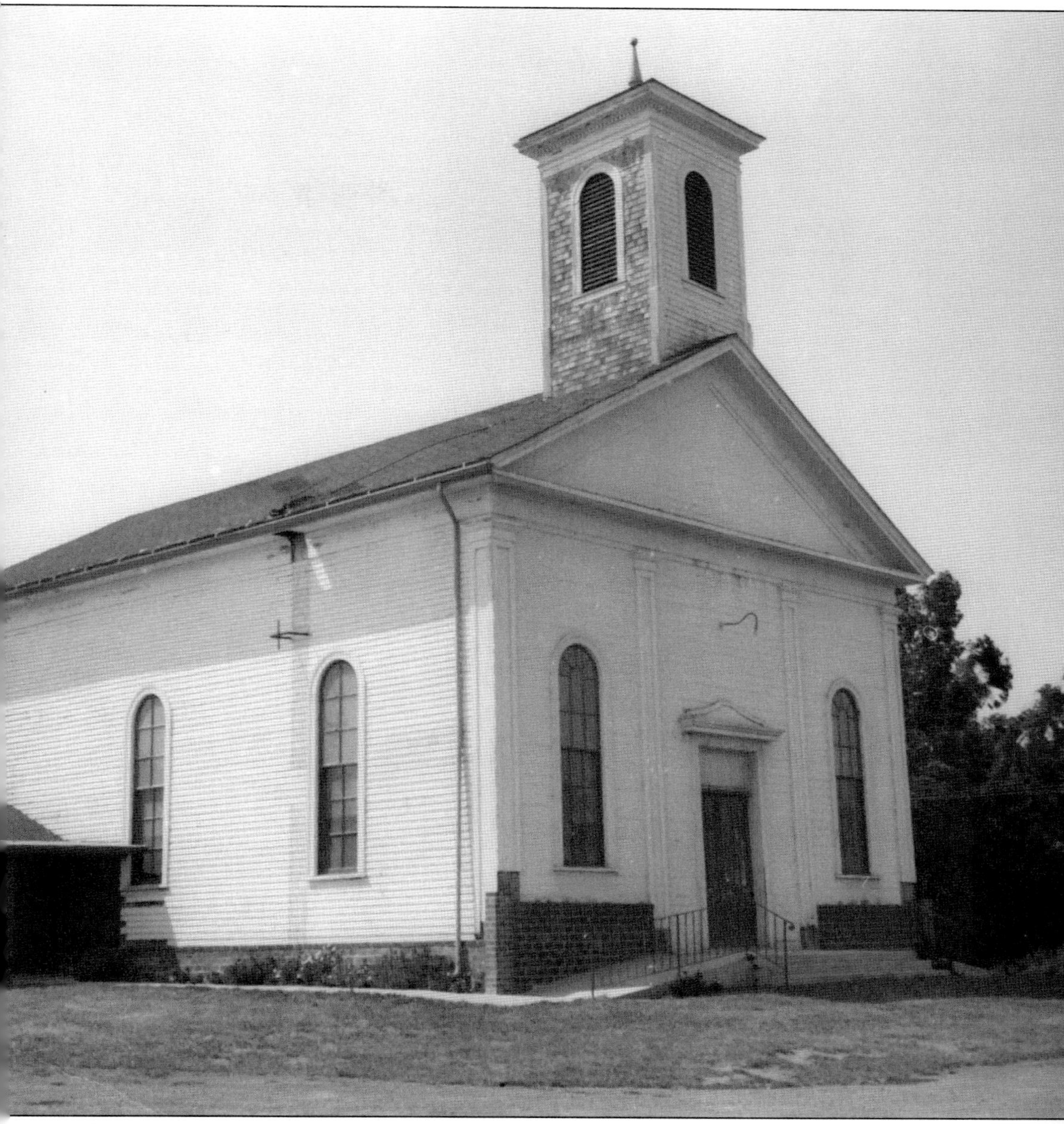

According to the *History of Marin County, California* (1880), Warren Dutton, Thomas McCune, G.W. Burbank, and Robert Bailey acted as trustees in charge of building a Presbyterian church, which was constructed during 1870 at a cost of $4,500. Unfortunately, the building took fire and was totally destroyed two days before the time appointed for its dedication. A second building was erected for the 19 members of the congregation upon the foundation of the former one and was completed in 1871 at a cost of $3,500. The first minister was Rev. C.M. Crawford, who arrived in September 1871; he was succeeded by Revs. H.R. Avery, Robert Scrimgeour, James White, and J.M. Dinsmore. A large and comfortable 10-room parsonage was built in 1872 at 27325 State Highway 1. A Sabbath school was created at the outset, under the direction of Arthur Patterson. Both church and parsonage stand today, though the parsonage is now privately owned. The First Presbyterian Church of Tomales, created initially under the care of the Presbytery of Benicia and Synod of the Pacific, was listed in the National Register of Historic Places in 1975.

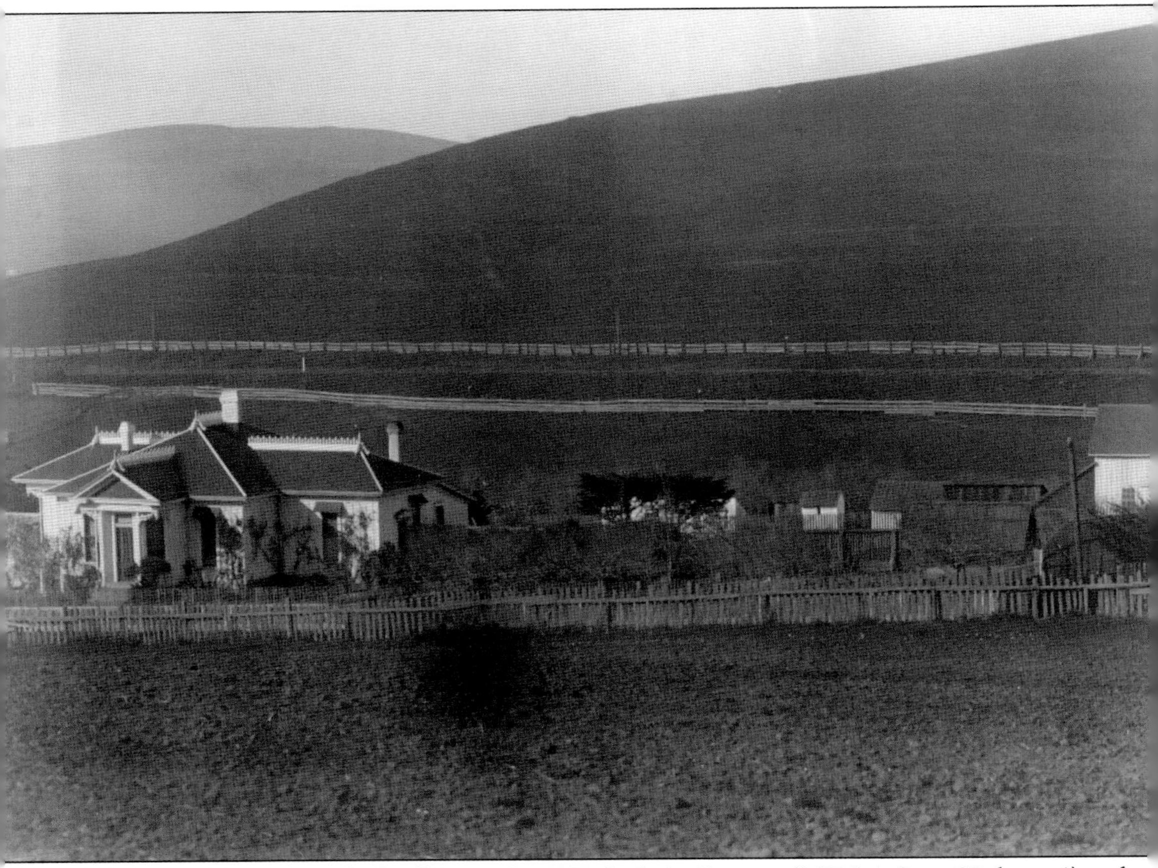

"Two Queen Anne style dwellings—the 1893 Catholic Rectory (26825-A State Highway 1) and the 1887–1888 Vanderbilt house (27600 State Highway 1) were the first two houses in Tomales built in a recognizable style," according to Ginny Magan. William Paton Vanderbilt (1831–1905) is listed in the 1870 census as a carpenter. Again according to Magan: "Probably the only board-and-batten house ever built in the town, the originally symmetrical facade is centered by a pedimented entry bay. The rhythmic repetition of trim (especially the brackets with pendants and windowed, cut-away corners) and hooded windows was an important design feature, and the rounded trim boards at the many outside corners a subtle and unusual detail. . . . Today is it is hidden behind a hedge and is perilously close to ruin."

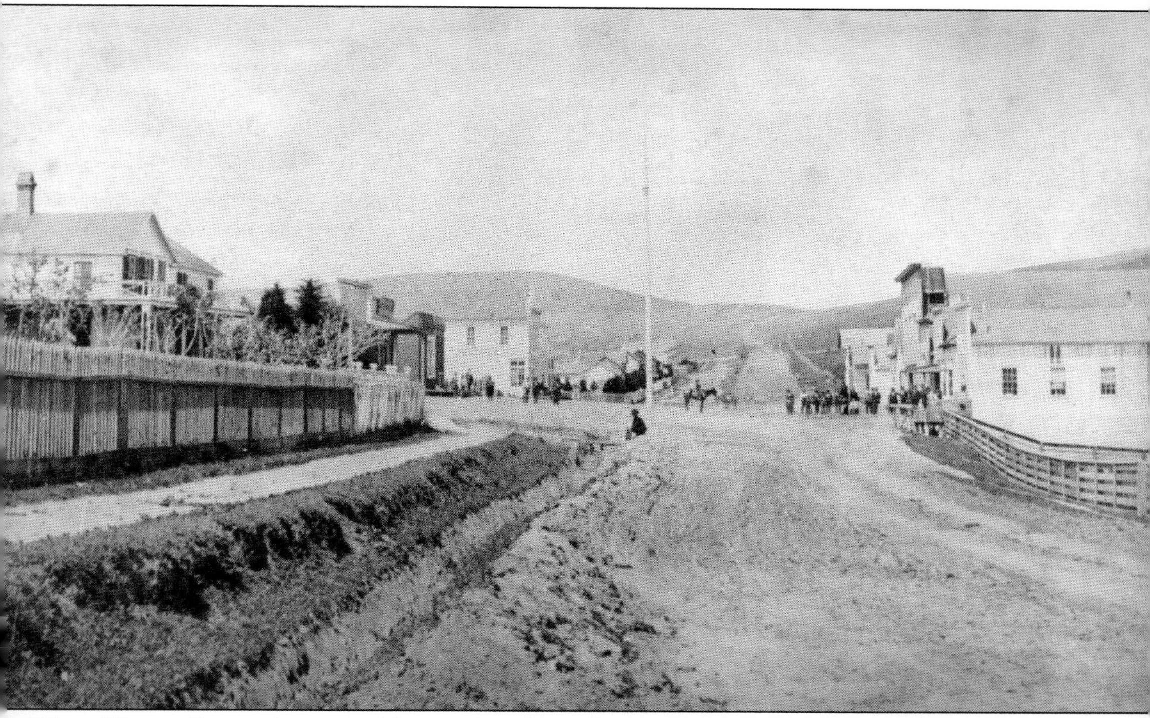

When Warren Dutton began building on his claim, the section shown in this 1878 photograph was known as Upper Town or Dutton's Town to distinguish it from the adjacent section known as Keys Town or Lower Town. This photograph shows the house (far left) erected for Dutton by William Davis in 1857 and later remodeled and enlarged to a 14-room structure, to which he brought his wife, the former Martha Holland of Boston. A year before this photograph was taken, a disastrous fire at 3:00 a.m. on August 17 destroyed the Metropolitan Hotel, the Bank of Tomales, a millinery store, watchmaker's building, and a drugstore. So rapid was the destruction that of the effects of the bank, only $300, unenclosed in the vaults, was saved. At a special meeting of the directors held on September 8, 1877, it was decided that a new edifice should be erected while the vault, which had done such good service in protecting its contents during the fire, was included in the new structure.

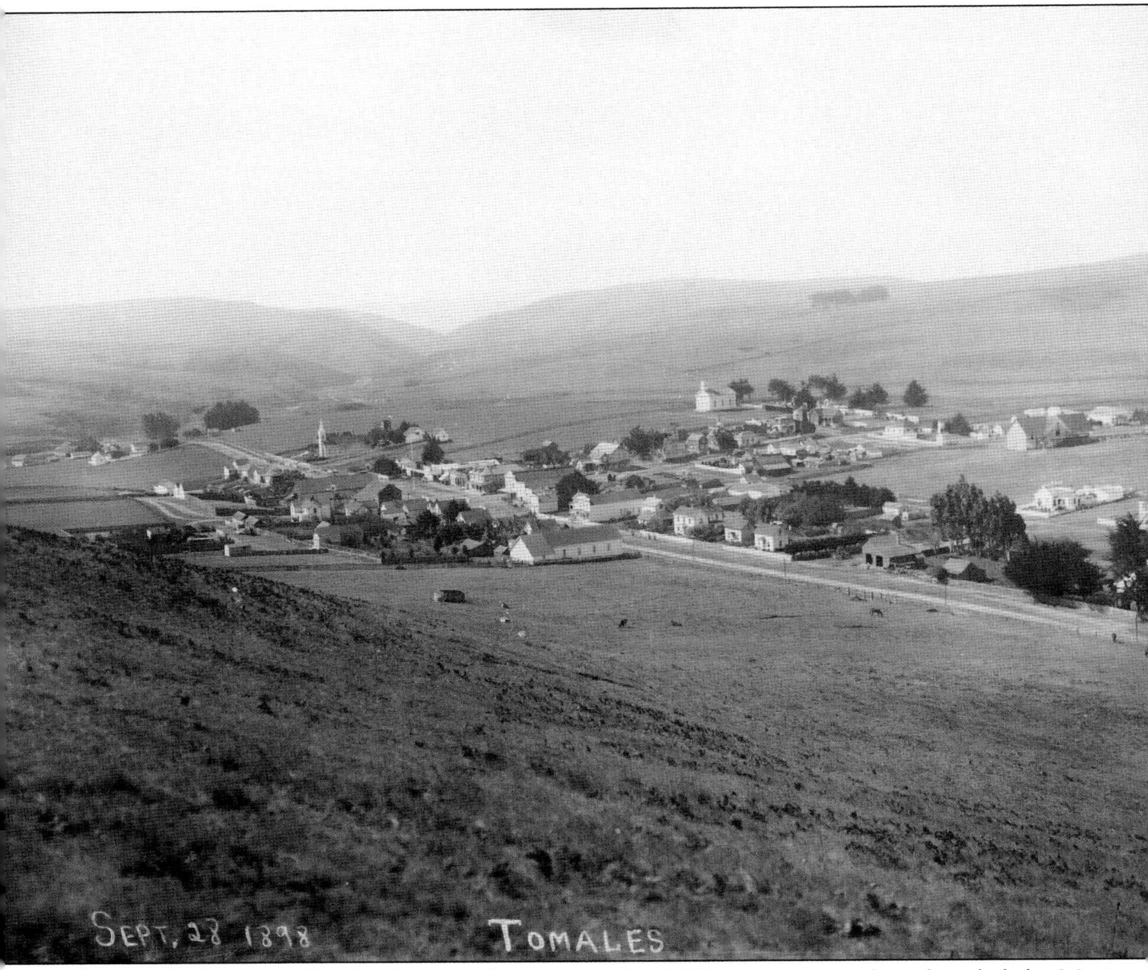

In 1935, Florence (Holland) Donnelly (October 16, 1892–June 10, 1969) co-founded the Marin County Historical Society with Belle Brown. In 1930, she had become the only reporter on the *San Rafael Independent*, now the *Marin Independent Journal*. The year Ella Frisbie Jorgensen took the photograph above was Florence Holland's second-grade year at school, and in a 1966 essay "A Child's Christmas in Early-Day Marin," she recalled her memories of 1898: "Several days before Christmas, my father, Frank Sargent Holland, my mother and I left our San Rafael home to travel by train to Tomales to spend the holidays with his parents, Mr. and Mrs. Franklin W. Holland (Julia Sargent). . . . The narrow gauge train wriggled across high trestles, around bends and through tunnels. . . . My grandmother stood at the front door of the white, two storey 14 room house previously owned by Warren Dutton . . . as we arrived all were smothered with kisses. I guess I received more than anyone because I was the first granddaughter."

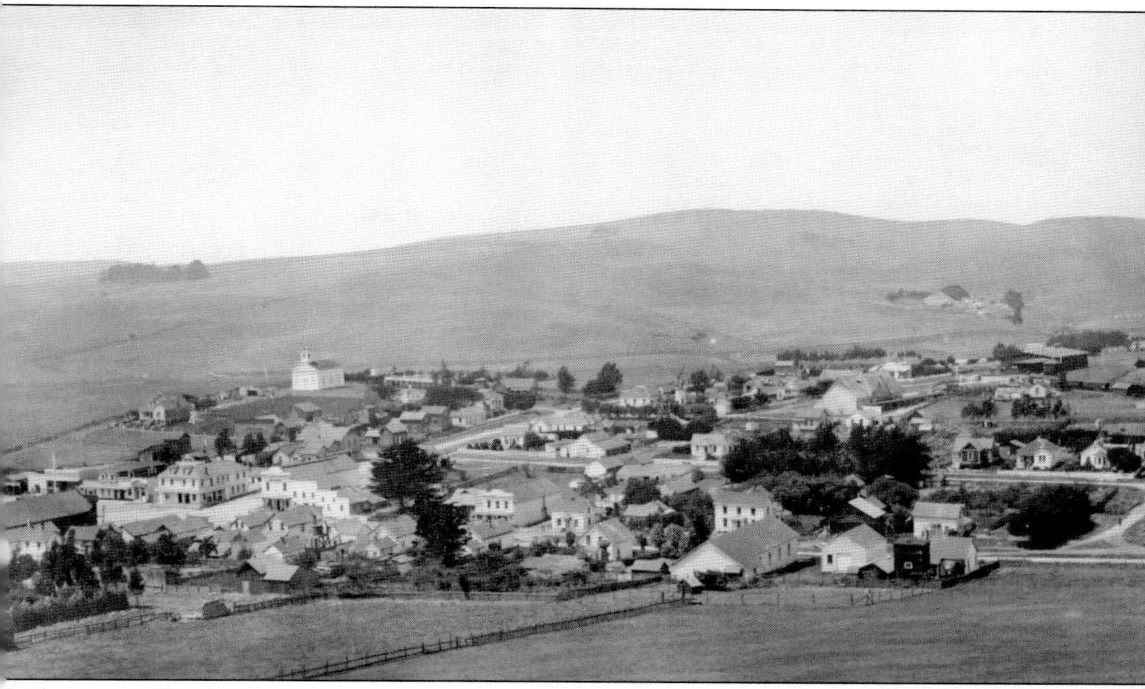

Florence Holland continued: "In winter, a dense gray fog hung over Tomales and the air was cold, so the warmth of grandmother's kitchen stove, fed with eucalyptus, was welcome. . . . Grandfather would test me on American history, of which, at that time I knew nothing. But he seemed pleased when I told him I had read the story of Little Nell. He loved to talk about Dickens and Shakespeare and could quote long passages from the works of the Great Bard. . . . When dinner was over we sat quietly. Grandfather would lean back in his chair, light a cigar . . . Grandmother did not approve of cigarettes and, evidently in deference to her wishes, my father did not light one, although he always smoked at home. . . . The fog had rolled over the hills from the ocean. It was dark outside. . . . Mother would be asked to play the piano and sing. She had studied for the opera and had a sweet soprano voice. She would play the old favorites, the Stephen Foster melodies, and all would join her in the choruses."

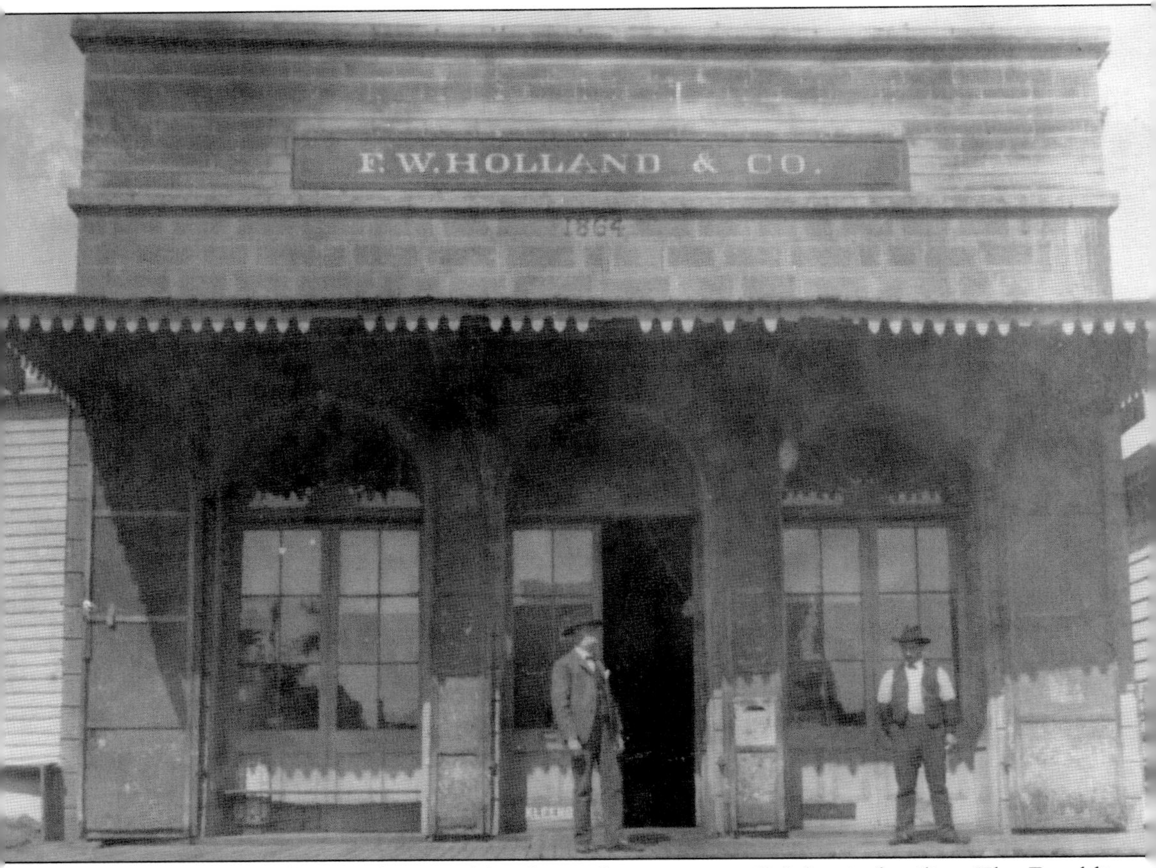

Florence Donnelly was the granddaughter of two pioneer California families. The Franklin Hollands could trace their ancestors to minutemen who fought in the Revolutionary War. The Hollands were married in Boston and spent their honeymoon traveling to California via the Isthmus of Panama, arriving in San Francisco in March 1866. Franklin went into business with his brother-in-law Warren Dutton, eventually buying out Dutton's interest in the business and Dutton's home. He also served the community as a school trustee and postmaster. In 1899, at the time of this photograph, with Franklin Holland at the front door of his establishment, the *Marin Journal* counted 300 people in Tomales; two hotels, the Plank and the United States; a public hall; a good school with teachers W.N. Taylor and D.B. Lawton; two doctors, Kurt Urban and A.C. Winn; and a number of stores, livery stables, and blacksmiths. The butchers were Ed Bean and L.C. Guldager.

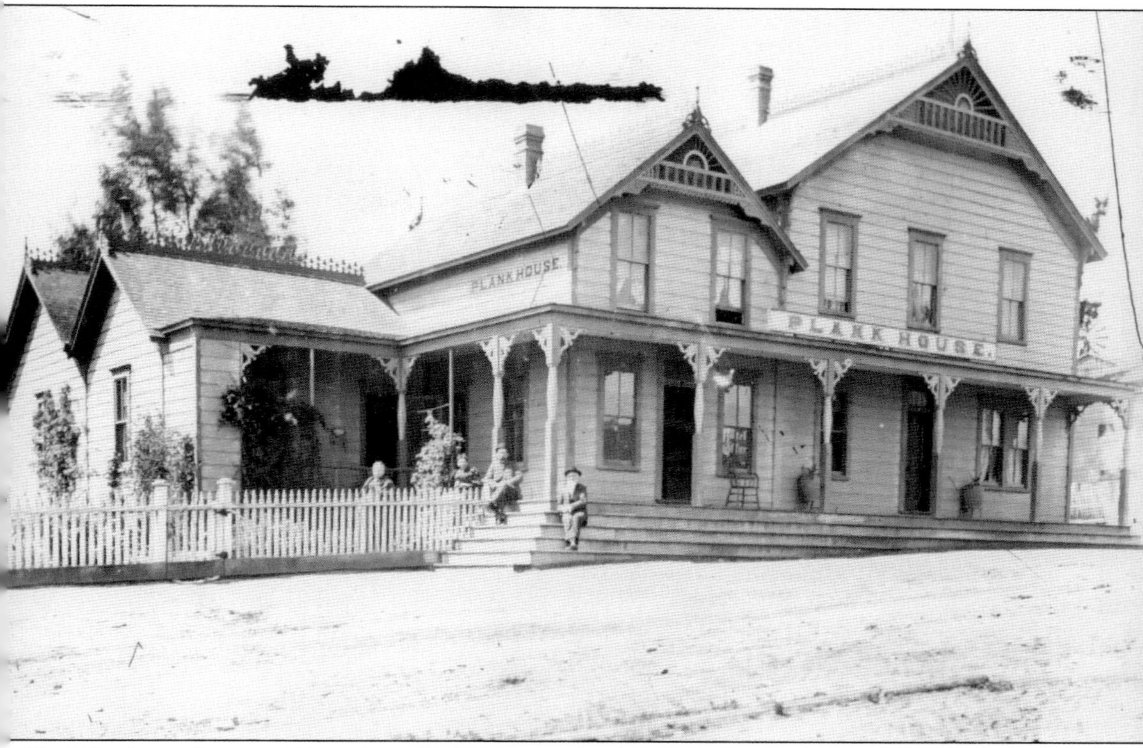

Fred Plank was born in 1834 in New York state, but his family immigrated to Wisconsin in 1848. The early death of his father compelled him to learn the daguerreotype business, which enabled him to support his mother. He married Betsey Ann Foster on December 29, 1859. Their only child, Fred, was born the following September. They crossed the plains in 1861, settling first at Knight's Ferry, Stanislaus County, and then moving on to Petaluma. According to Ables Bray Dickinson (1890–1958), they moved to Tomales Township by 1871. In this photograph of Fred (right) and brother John, both have long white beards. In November 1877, Fred took up residence in the village of Tomales where he opened the Plank House in November 1879. He had previously been the proprietor of the City Hotel in Petaluma for a year. In 1902, Fred passed away; his funeral services were held at the Presbyterian church. His remains were laid to rest beside many of his fellow pioneers. (Courtesy of Dan Brown.)

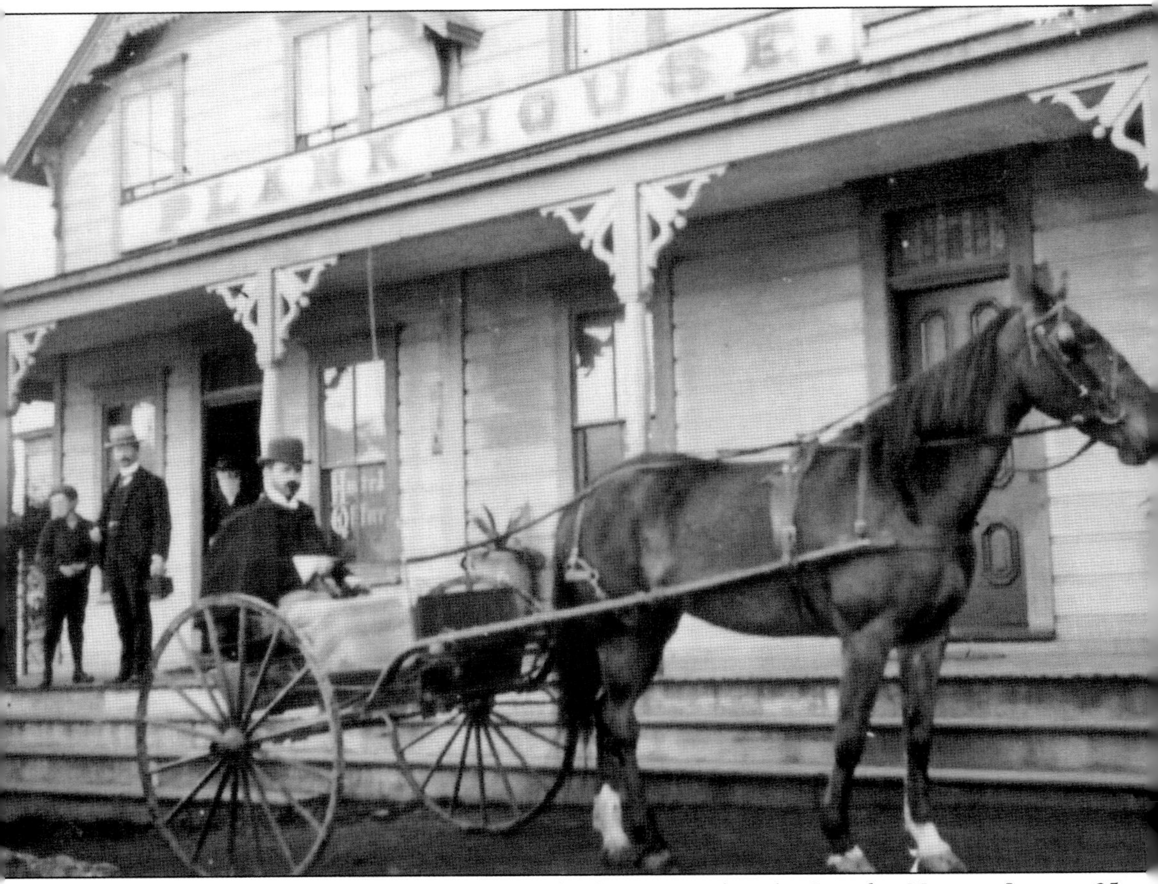

The obituary for Fred Plank, pictured in the door, printed in the *Sausalito News* on January 25, 1902, shows the sterling regard he was held in: "Mr. Plank was well known to all the people of Northern Marin as the proprietor of the Plank House. This house is in many respects noticeable, particularly as a California hotel. There is no bar in it and no intoxicating beverages were ever served or sold within its walls. Its custom was built up and maintained solely on the score of service, good accommodations, and an excellent table. The home-like surroundings, together with the courtesy, kindness, and geniality of the late host, and his family, commended the place to all. . . . He was jovial in disposition and enjoyed the association of the young. He was a leader in all the social sports of the town: entertainments and dances, church festivals, political meetings. He was foremost in feat of frolic and sage and serious in counsel. He leaves to mourn his death a widow, son Fred, two brothers and a sister." (Courtesy of Dan Brown.)

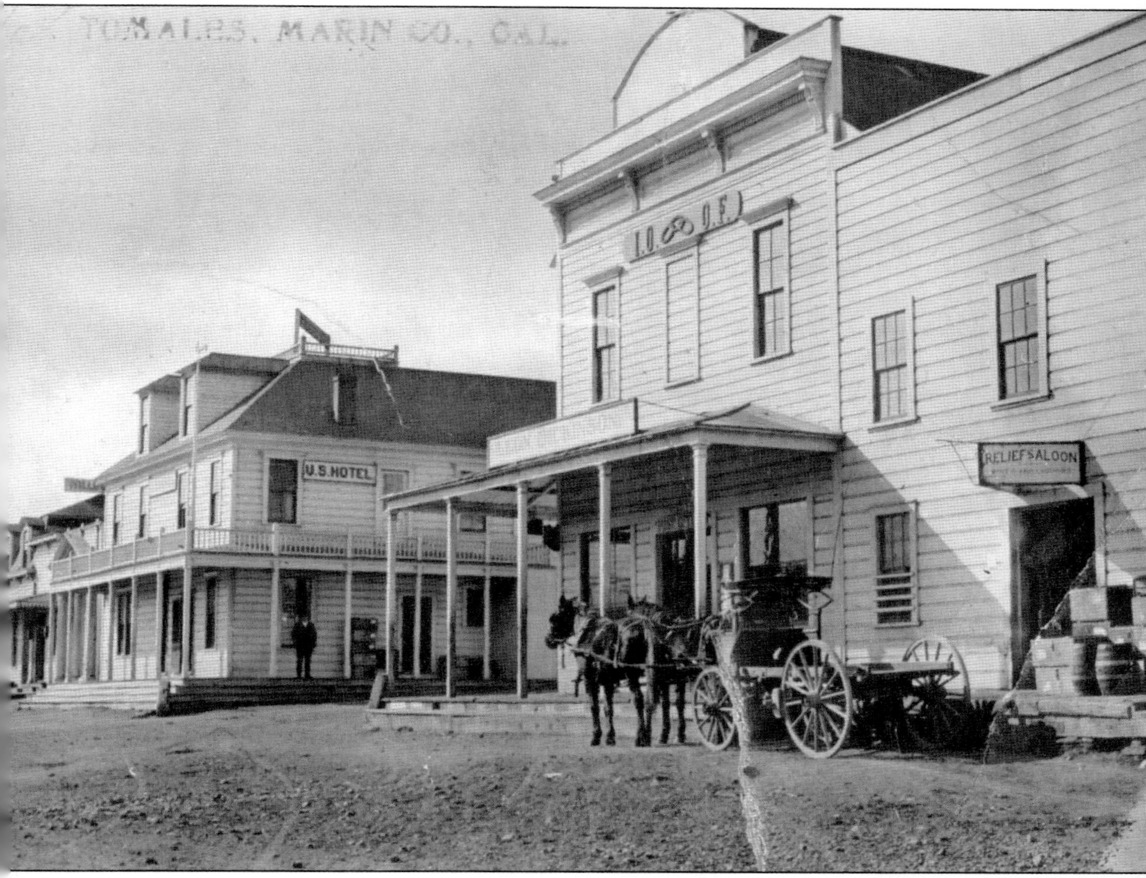

The foreground store building and post office opened in April 1875 as Kahn & Newburgh. Shortly thereafter, on July 1, Tomales Lodge No. 233 IOOF was instituted, the charter members being John Cook, Warren Dutton, William Vanderbilt, John Parker, A. Little, Thomas A. Johnson, and Thomas J. Ables. Ables had crossed the continent by wagon train in 1857. In the fall of 1858, he and his brother bought 200 acres in Tomales Township. His daughter Zilla, born in 1865, married Leon Dickinson in 1886. They purchased the store building at 27005 State Highway 1 and operated it until 1936, when son Bray became owner. Altogether, Dickinson's General Store (now Diekmann's) was operated by the Dickinson family for the first half of the 20th century. Zilla served as postmistress for 35 years, eventually to be replaced by Bray. As Postmaster Bray came in contact with almost everyone in the immediate vicinity of Tomales, the line of people waiting to buy stamps or pick up mail often came to a halt if someone had a story to tell.

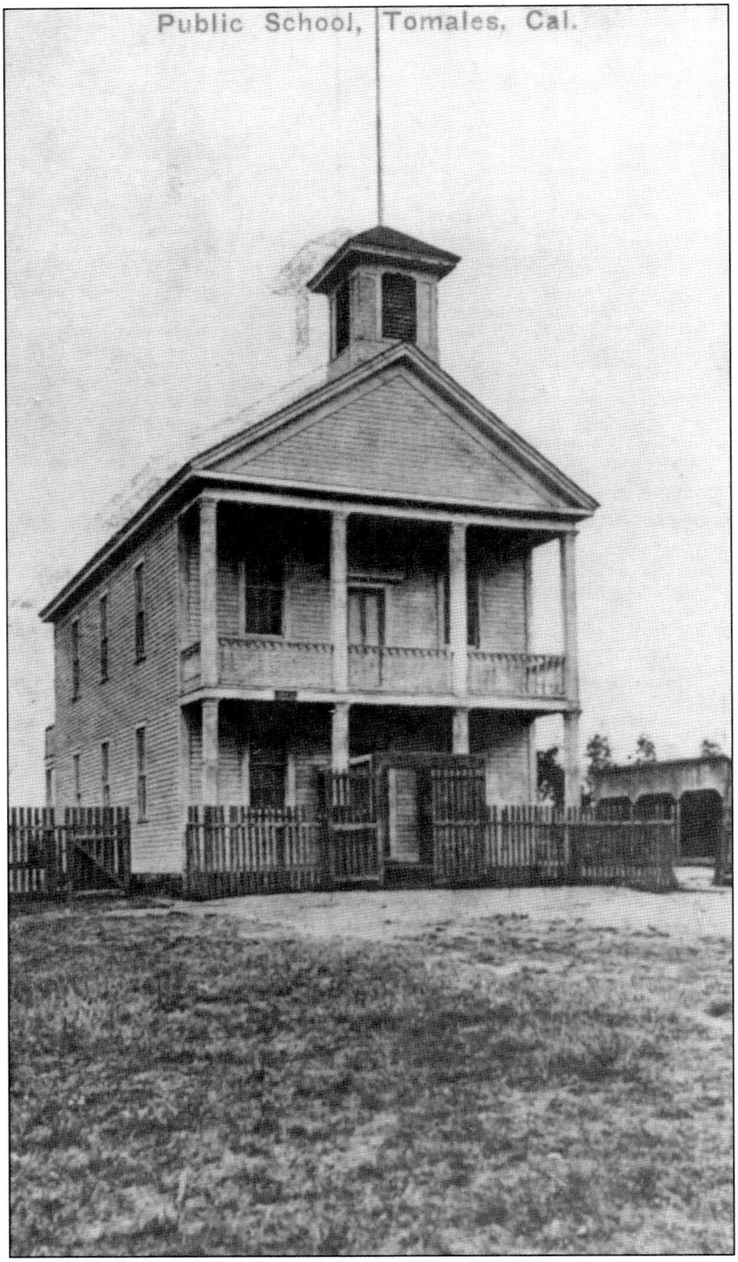

Thomas Ables served as the county's first school superintendent, bringing Marin schools into unification and establishing a coordinated teaching system. According to Ginny Magan: "In 1873 Tomales Grammar School's student body numbered 60; by 1875 it had increased to over a hundred, and that summer the building was jacked up and a primary room added below. The resulting two-story building was of simple Greek Revival style: three bays wide with a symmetrical facade and clapboard siding. A front, pedimented gable extended over the two-story verandah, onto which opened, on both levels, a centered entry door between windows. The second level of the verandah was completely enclosed by its balustrade—a stairway at the rear elevation provided access to the upper classroom. Surmounting the ridge at the facade was a hip-roofed belfry. The school bell was purchased and installed by early school trustee and local blacksmith Louis Guldager."

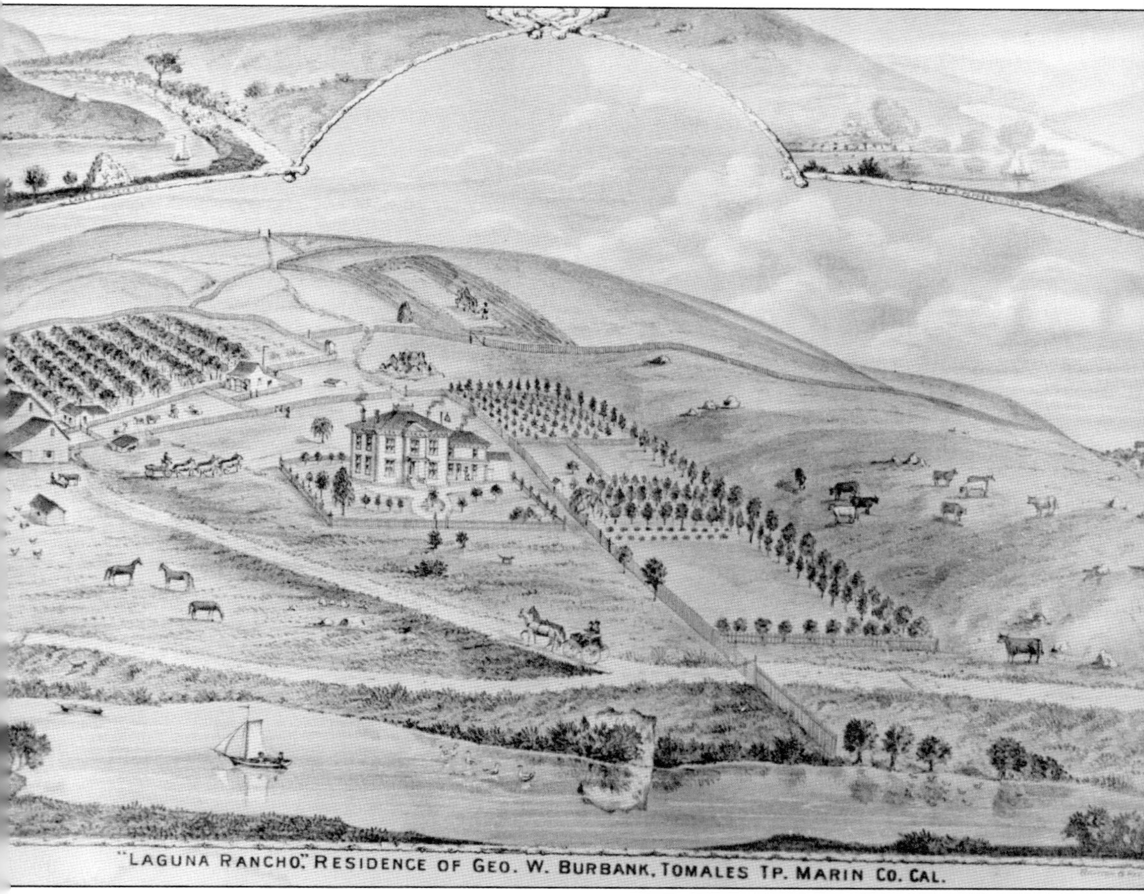

This lithograph by Britton and Rey shows the 325-acre Laguna Rancho residence of George Wilton Burbank (1829–1901), with a lake and buckeye grove in the top left and a lake and pepperwoods in the top right. Estero San Antonio is in the foreground. The land parcel was settled in 1855. As late as 2006, the ranch was still home to the Burbank family in the home he built in 1867. George and Apphie Blake were well known for their conservatory and flower garden, but it was younger brother Luther Burbank (1849–1926) who is better known today. His relationship with Warren Dutton (1823–1903) is a fascinating story, recounted by Ginny Magan in a 2008 *Bulletin* editorial and published by the Tomales Regional History Center. In March 1881, Dutton sent a rush order to Luther Burbank for 20,000 prune trees to be ready to plant that fall. By December 1, about 19,500 of the trees were ready for the planter; the others were furnished the next season. Dutton dutifully dubbed Burbank "the plant wizard."

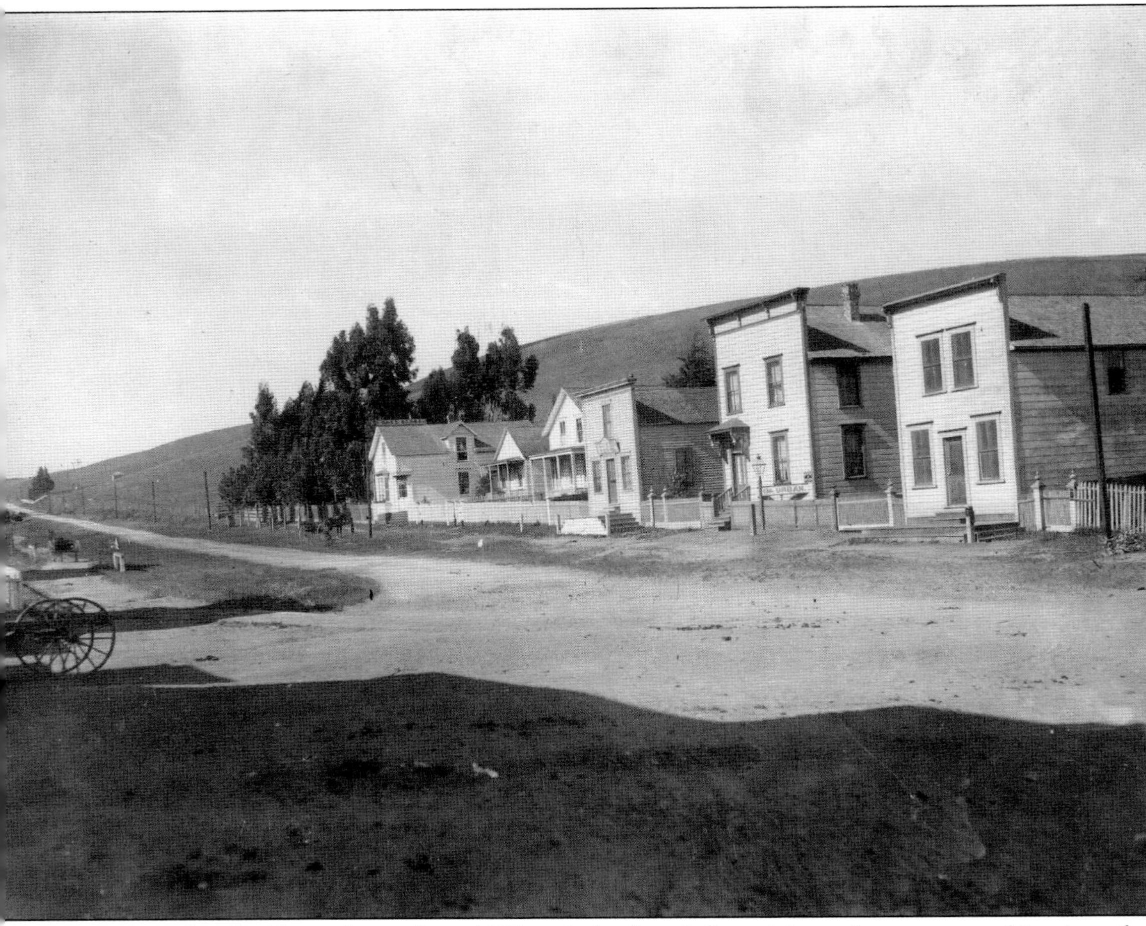

These four buildings dating from 1880 include, from left to right, a three-part combination of telephone office, physician's office, and dwelling; a bakery; and a combination physicians' offices and dwellings. Dr. Albert Clark Winn (1862–1909), seen earlier in front of the Plank House, and Dr. Kurt Urban were Tomales's primary physicians. According to Ginny Magan and Dr. Winn's granddaughter Bea Winn Glazier (1936–2002), Dr. Winn was born in Missouri in the middle of the Civil War, a conflict that drove his pacifist father, Willis, to Canada for the duration. Albert received his medical degree in 1883, the same year Willis died and his mother sold the family farm. Albert and his mother moved to Tomales, and his sister Annette followed later. She became the operator of the first Tomales telephone exchange. Albert and Tomales native Hattie Bassett (1876–1932) were married in 1903. Dr. Winn's medical bag, diploma, surgical instruments, and medical books are in the history center's collection and on exhibit in the museum.

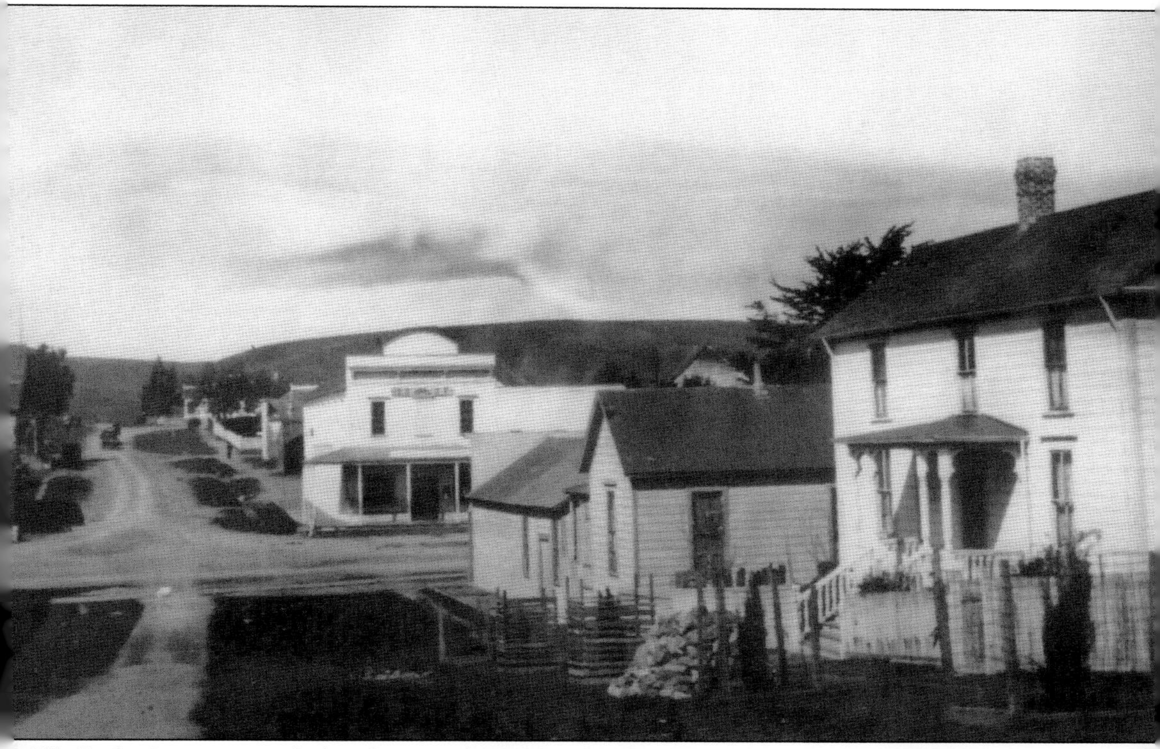

Ella Frisbie Jorgensen took this photograph in 1900 of 10 First Street (right) with its original porch. The view is to the west, across Maine Street (Highway 1) toward Dillon Beach Road. First Street is in the foreground. Ginny Magan has described the architecture as follows: "The Trainor House represents the last years of the Pioneer Era of Tomales's Residential Architecture, when a small number of two-story houses, slightly larger and more complex than their predecessors, were built in the village. The simplicity of style and ornament are characteristic of early Tomales architecture, and the individual typical components intact here include gable roof, shiplap siding, two-over-two window sash, boxed cornice with returns. The Trainor house conveys a perceptible sense of the typical domestic architecture of the period, and of its original self. . . . The first residents of the dwelling were Irish immigrants Sarah (1850–1935) and William (1852–1922) Trainor, who raised a large and active family here, and the house sheltered at least one subsequent generation of Trainors." (Courtesy of Dan Brown.)

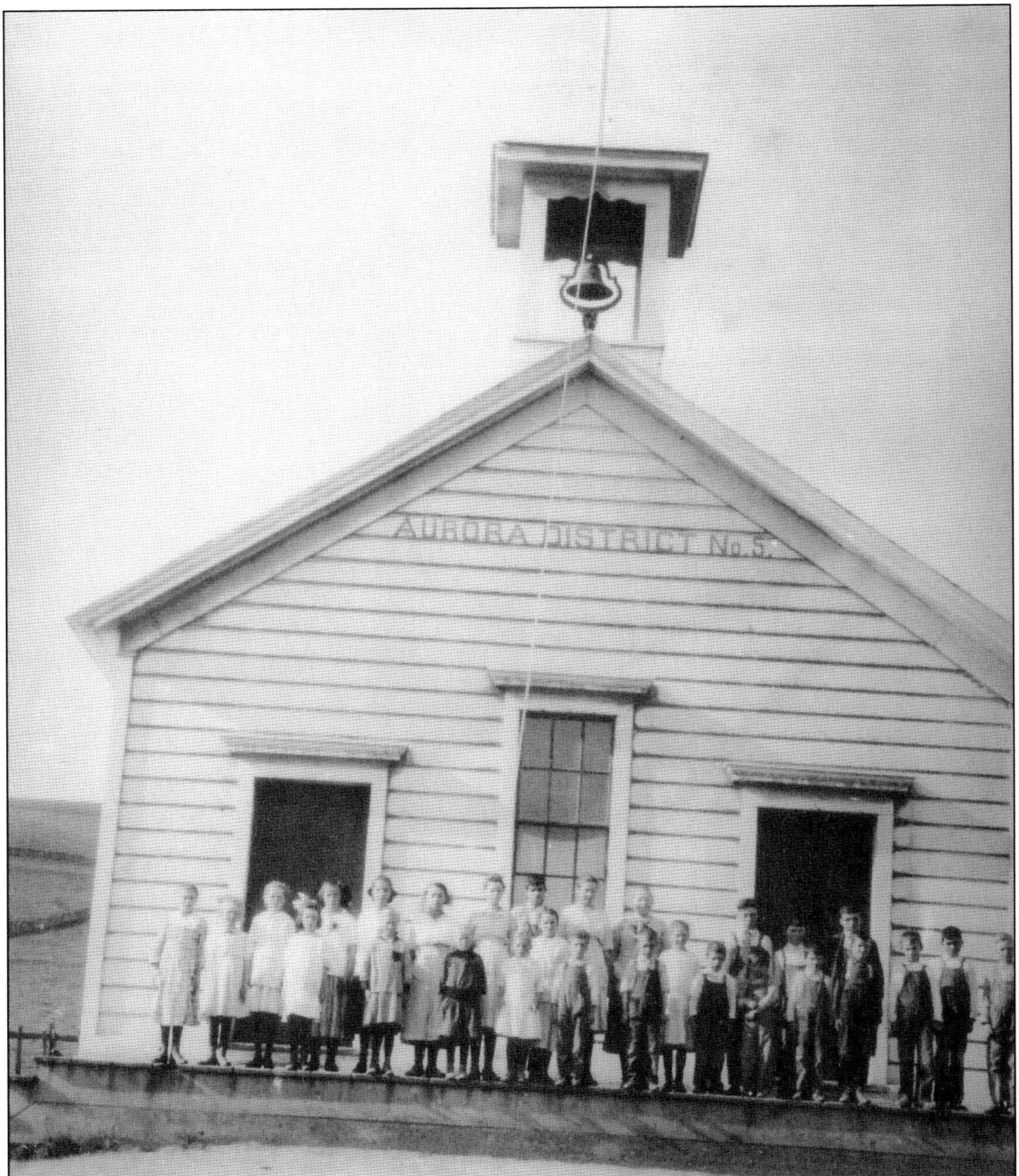

Tomales Township: A History, the Story of Bolsa de Tomales before the North Pacific Coast Railroad, by A. Bray Dickinson, edited with added material by Kathie Nuckols Lawson and Lois Randle Parks (1993), featuring the photograph collection of the Tomales History Center with over 100 photographs and maps, is an indispensable reference guide for the historian and curious reader alike. The members of the Tomales History Center are wholeheartedly to be congratulated for making this work available to the interested public. Dickinson corrects previous misinformation to write: "In 1857 the Chileno School District was the first to be established in what was then Tomales Township, and that Henry Ashley became the first schoolteacher for Tomales Town in 1866." Tomales School District No. 2 was created in 1858, but in 1862, the board of supervisors reformed Tomales School District No. 2 into the Aurora District. It was built on what is now Tomales-Petaluma Road in 1870. George W. Burbank deeded the land for the school with the proviso that no intoxicating liquor would ever be sold on the premises. (Courtesy of Dan Brown.)

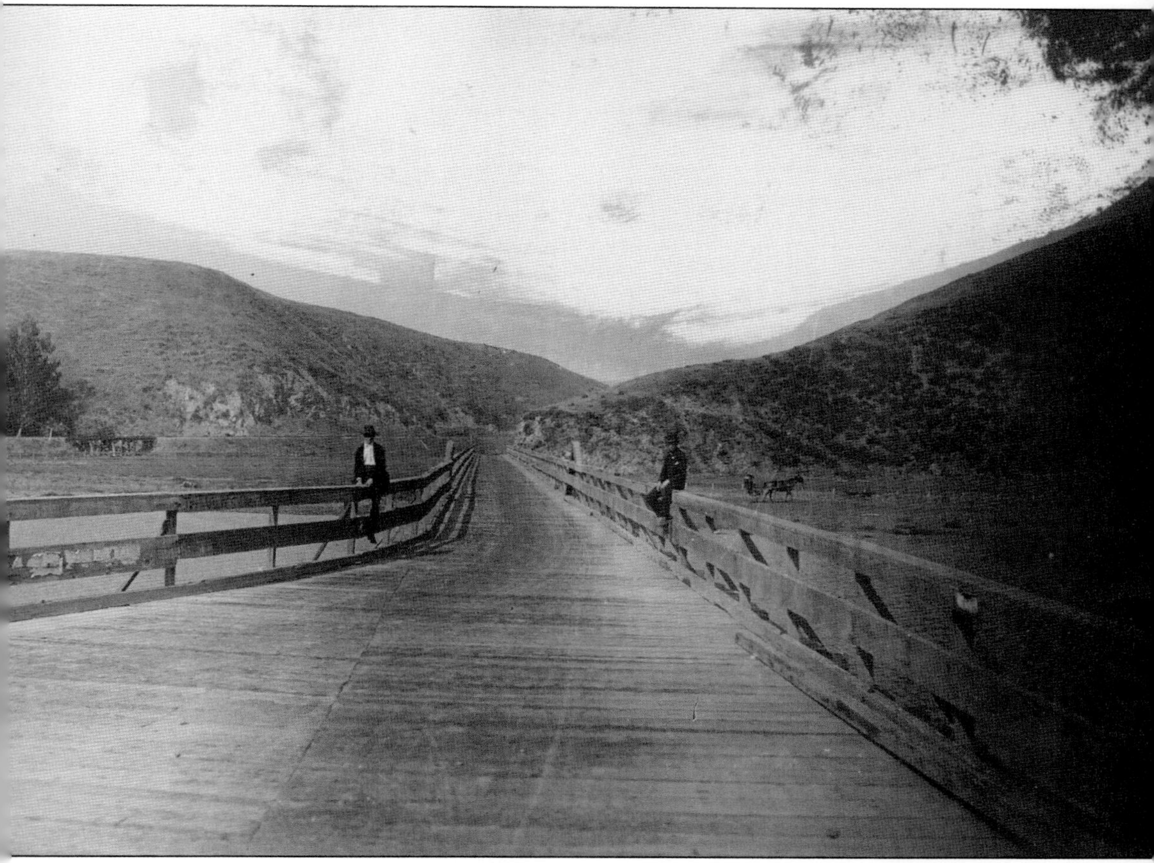

Walker Creek is named for Lewis W. Walker, who settled here in 1857. From the confluence of Arroyo Sausal and Salmon Creek, Walker Creek descends to the northwest, paralleling the Marshall-Petaluma Road as it curves westward. At the mouth of Verde Canyon, the creek crosses under the road and turns northwest, passing the mouth of Frink Canyon to a confluence with Chileno Creek. From there, it meanders westward, passing south of Tomales. It crosses under State Route 1 at milepost 44.45 and is immediately joined by Keys Creek, entering from the north. Walker Creek continues southward along the highway to enter Tomales Bay just east of Preston's Point. In the 19th century, Preston's Point joined Hamlet, Ocean Roar, and Marshall as shipping points for schooners picking up agricultural products from nearby farmers. R.J. Preston ran a store here as early as 1853. The Marshall brothers settled the Marshall Bros. Home Ranch on the north bank of Walker's Creek about three miles east and south of Tomales.

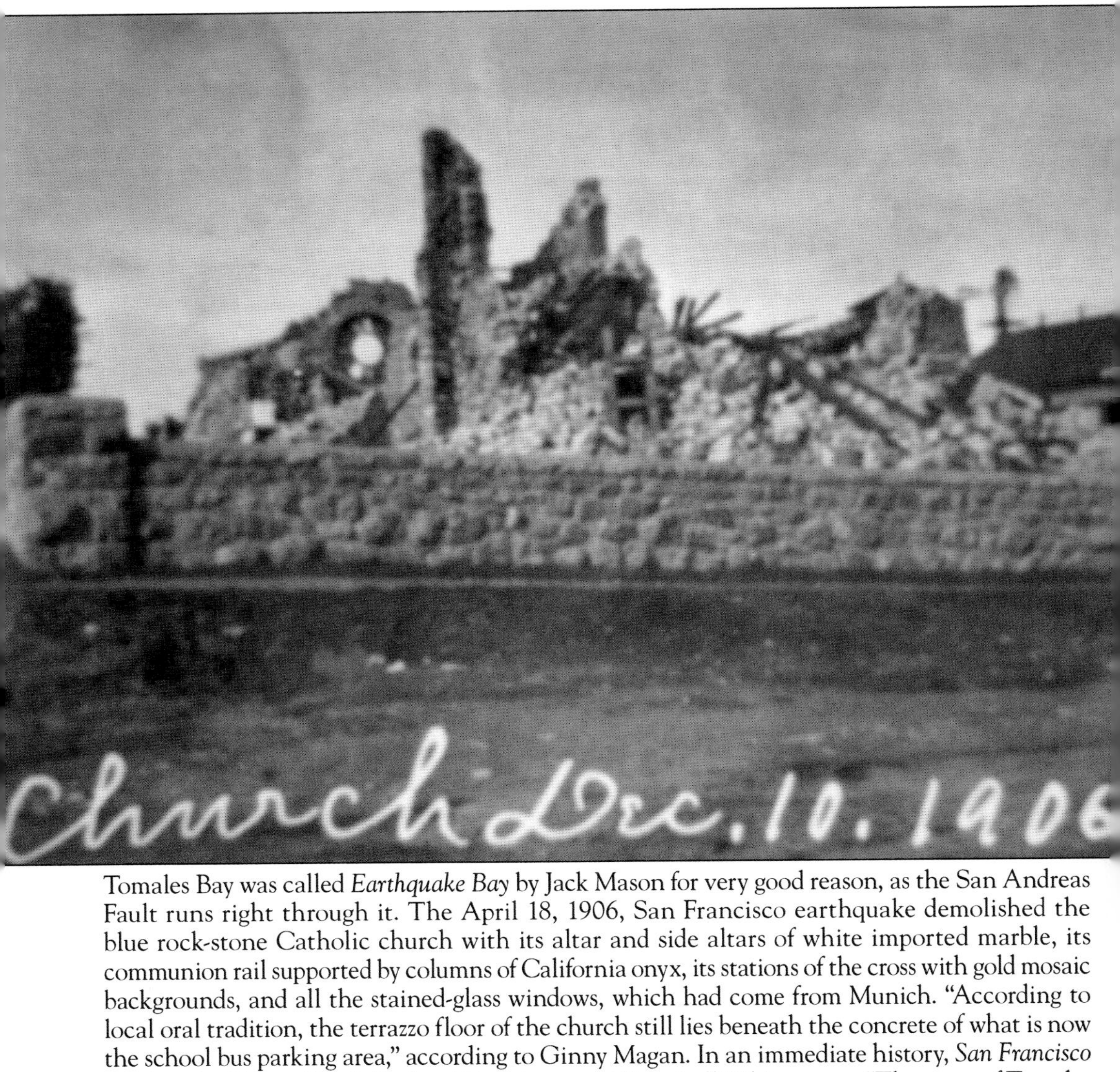

Tomales Bay was called *Earthquake Bay* by Jack Mason for very good reason, as the San Andreas Fault runs right through it. The April 18, 1906, San Francisco earthquake demolished the blue rock-stone Catholic church with its altar and side altars of white imported marble, its communion rail supported by columns of California onyx, its stations of the cross with gold mosaic backgrounds, and all the stained-glass windows, which had come from Munich. "According to local oral tradition, the terrazzo floor of the church still lies beneath the concrete of what is now the school bus parking area," according to Ginny Magan. In an immediate history, *San Francisco Earthquake Horror* (1906), Richard Linthicum and Trumbull White wrote, "The town of Tomales was converted into a pile of ruins. All of the large stores were thrown flat and many ranchos and barns went down."

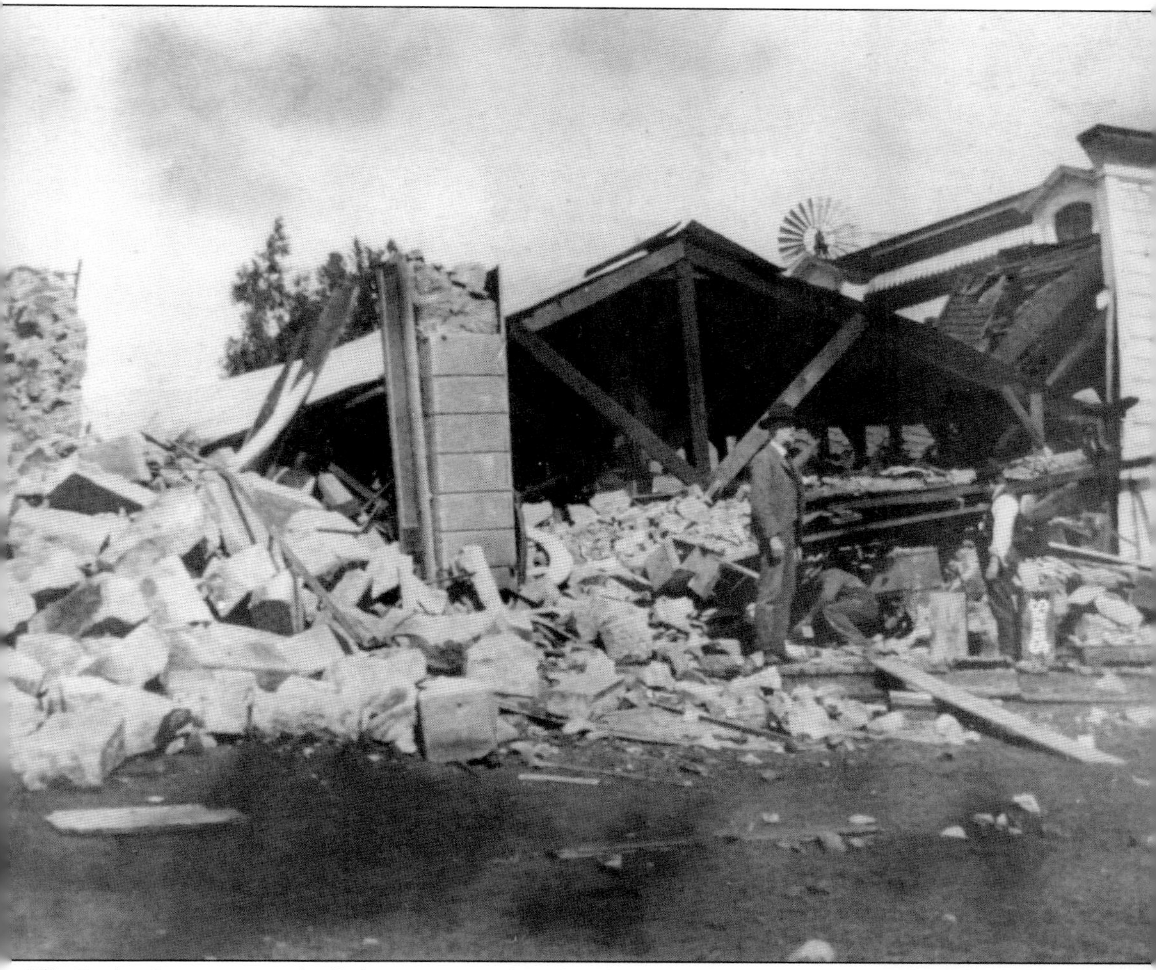

Ella Frisbie Jorgensen took all three post-earthquake photographs. Here, F.W. Holland stands to the right of center just as he stood proudly in an earlier pre-earthquake photograph, also taken by Jorgensen. Bray Dickinson printed this eyewitness account of George Fairbanks, whose father owned and ran the Tomales-Petaluma stagecoach in the 1870s: "The trees seemed to brush the ground as they swayed to and fro; the house appeared to spread out, then buckle up to a peak, much as one might press fingertips together and then move the palms back and forth. Immediately I looked toward town and church buildings had disappeared in a cloud of dust. Then I ran for the house to see what had happened to the folks. Soon a man came galloping down the road on horseback, shouting that the Cauzza children were buried in their home." Their tombstones included the following information: Anita, born July 8, 1887, died April 18, 1906; Peter, born January 30, 1884, died April 18, 1906; and Corina, born March 28, 1892, died August 27, 1908.

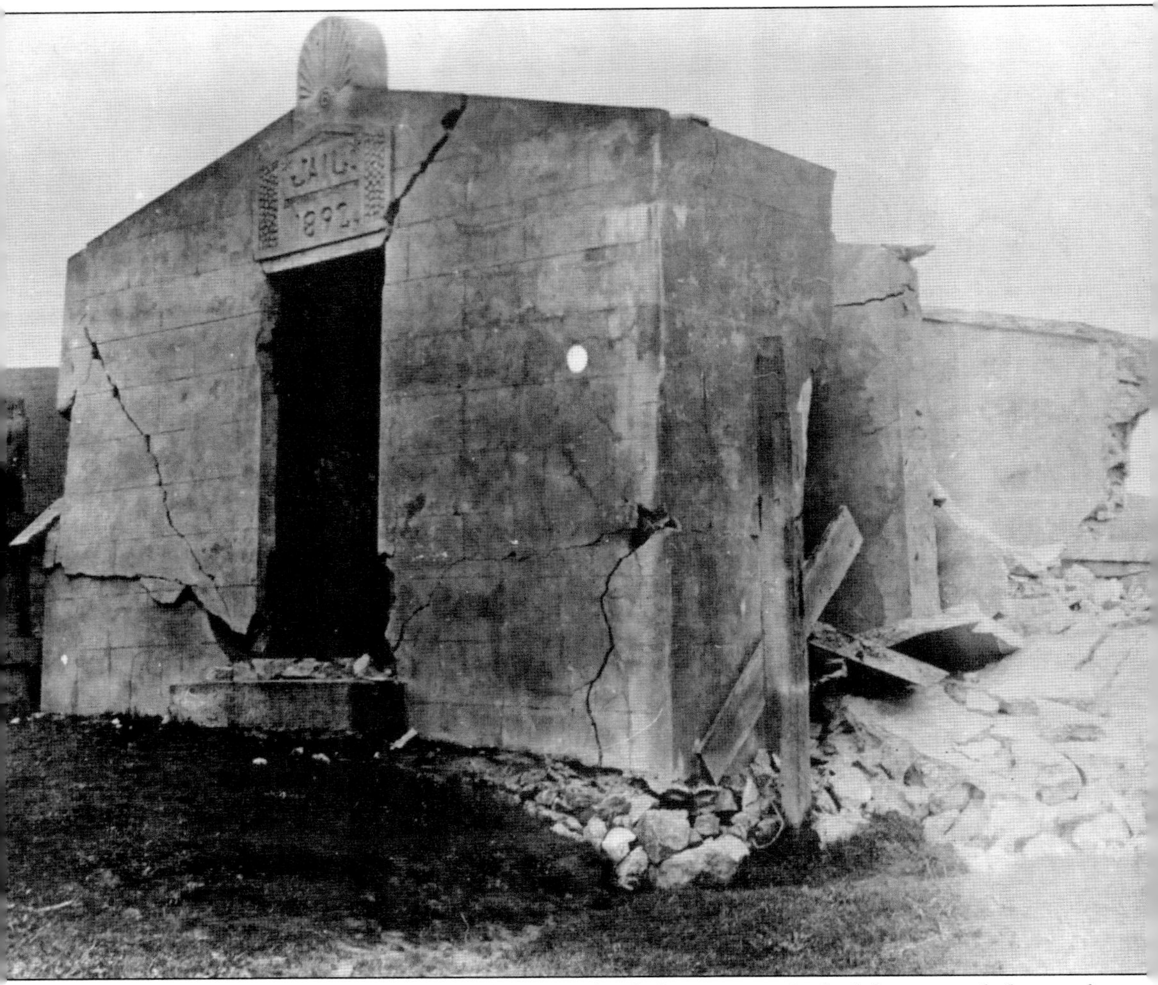

The best historiographers combine the research of a historian with the life stories of a biographer. Ginny Magan is one of the best, as exemplified, once again, in her investigation of "Judge's House and Jail Foundation," the former home of Judge Henry Darnell: "sitting empty and long abandoned in a field on the eastern edge of town . . . the property is in ruinous condition . . . on the same parcel, to the north of what is left of the dwelling, are the ruins of the old Tomales jail—part of its foundation, pieces of wall, and a section of a door jamb with parts of an iron hinge attached. The little jail appears to have been rectangular in plan, approximately 21 by 26 feet, of two or three small rooms, constructed with granite rocks heavily mortared together and over, with a stone pattern incised in the outer layer of cement." The jail was only 14 years old. Basing her conclusions on a 2003 interview with lifelong Tomales resident Bea NcCulla Phillips, Magan adds, "The title of 'judge' is thought to have been an unofficial one, possibly used because Darnell oversaw the jail in some way. It is said that a tall board fence once surrounded the property so that Judge Darnell, who was blind, would have a tactile awareness of the boundaries of his property. Another version is that the judge boarded himself up against intruders because he was blind."

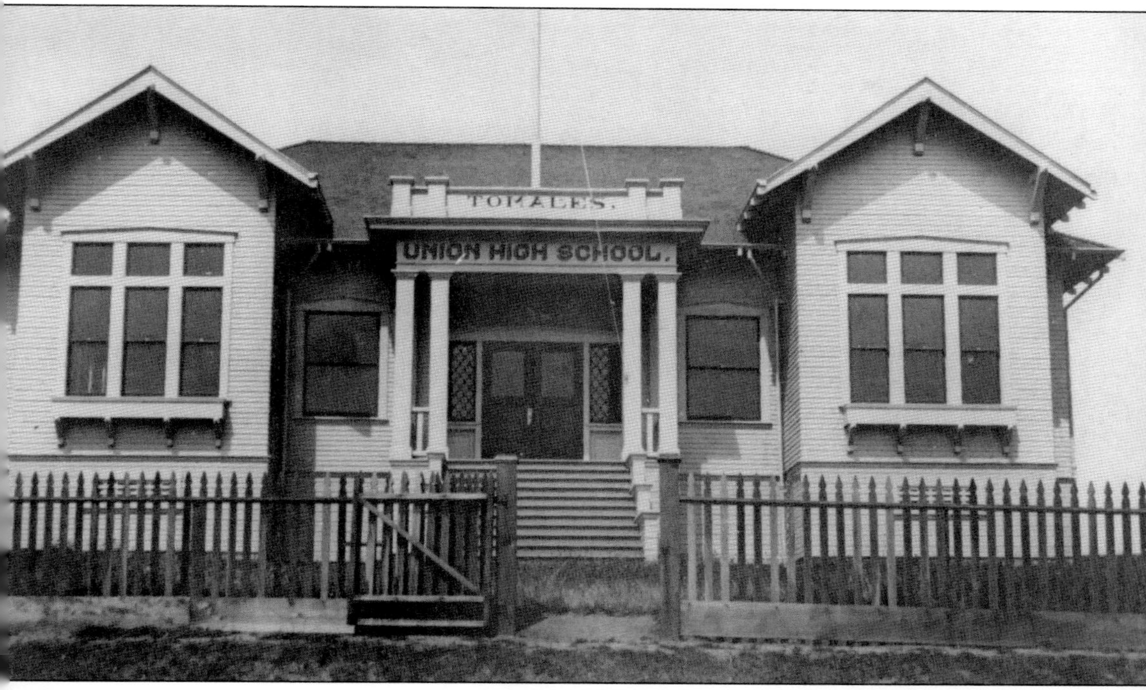

The population of Tomales was at 204 in the 2010 census, down six from the 2000 census, and 99 households comprise the total head count. The town's largest employer is the Tomales High School, which has a student body of approximately 190. Quoting from Ginny Magan, the story of the school's century-old beginning unfolds as follows: "For almost half a century after the establishment of the Tomales Grammar School there was no high school on the north coast between San Rafael and Point Arena. Only children whose families were willing and able to send them to board away from home received a secondary education. With the help and encouragement of former Tomales teacher, Supt. James Davidson, several residents circulated a petition to establish a local high school. A majority of Tomales citizens signed, an official election was held, and Tomales High School was established in 1912. . . . Tomales Union High School opened its doors on August 5, 1912, with a student body of twenty three and one teacher, I.M. Brazier." Ella Jorgensen took this photograph of the two-room school, whose architect remains unknown.

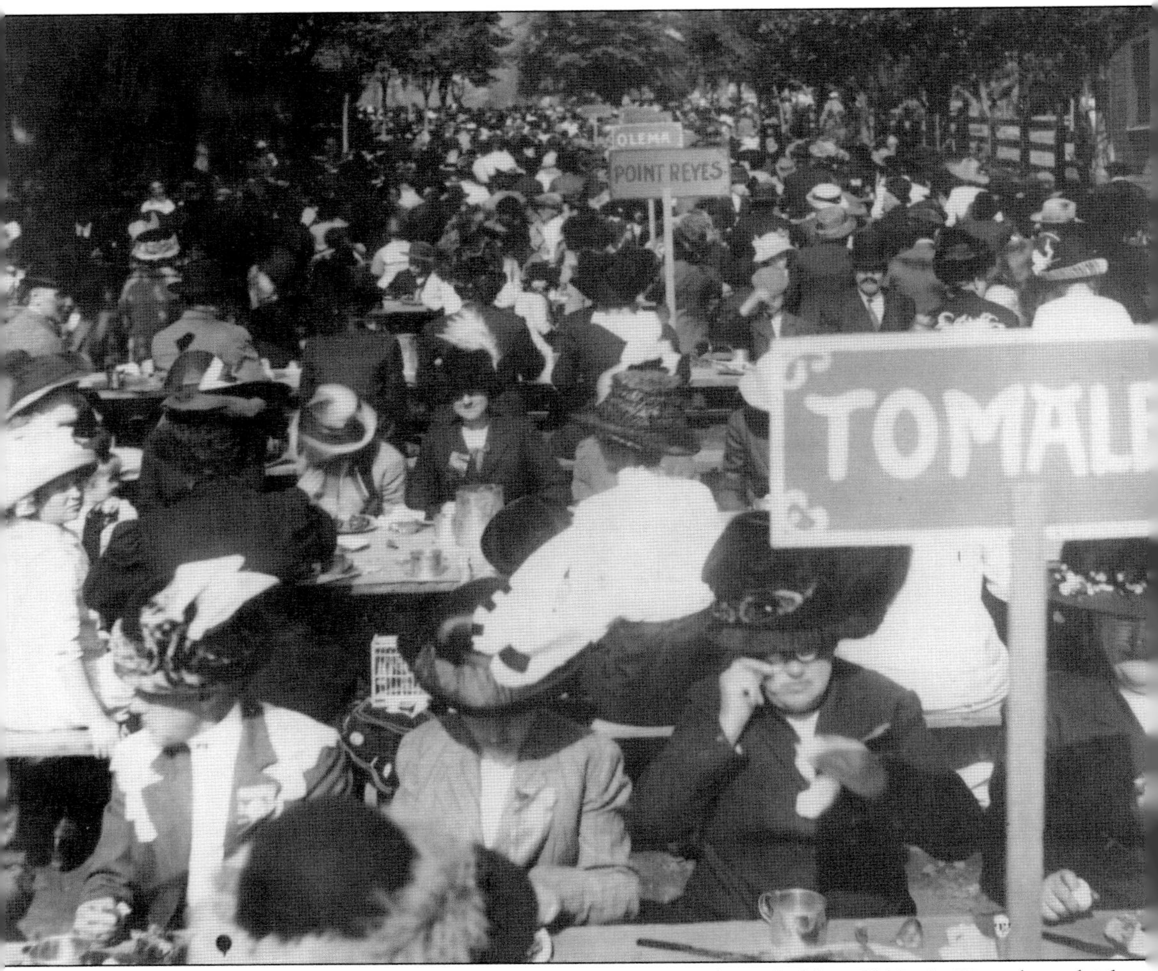

The first state election in which California women voted was held in 1912. At Tomales, which precinct included Dillon's Beach, Fallon, and parts of Valley Ford, of the 225 registered voters that year, 78 were women. Among these, Ginny Magan writes, the dominant occupation was housewife, though the women voters also included six teachers, three capitalists, a baker, a saloon keeper, a postmistress, and a telephone operator. Assembly speaker H.G. Cattell, who prepared the "Progressive Argument for Women's Suffrage, 1911," wrote, "Women who are in touch with public affairs are none the less womanly, but, on the contrary, they are better and more companionable wives, more interesting mothers, because they have a common interest with their sons." Woodrow Wilson won the national election that year, but women were unable to vote nationally. Not until the 19th Amendment gave women the right to vote nationwide in 1920 would voting equality exist.

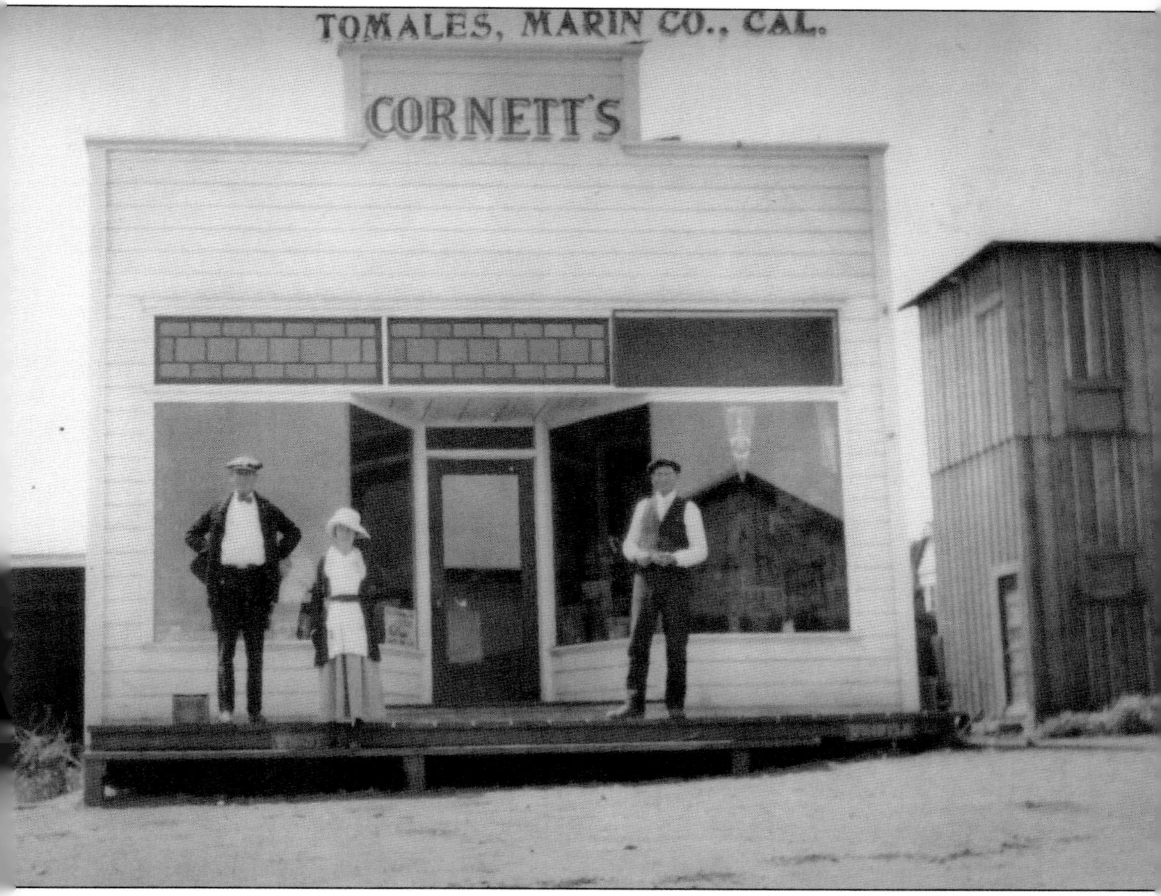

An early member of the Rural Merchant's Association, Thomas E. "Ed" Cornett and his brother Nat were partners in a popular general store in turn-of-the-century Tomales. When the Cornett Bros. Building burned in the 1920 fire, Ed erected this building on Dillon Beach Road almost immediately and continued the business. The building is extant, though much changed. The photograph was taken by Ella Frisbie Jorgensen. Ginny Magan fleshes out their biographies in this profile: "Sometime around 1890, three young Cornett brothers immigrated from Eastern Canada. Youngest brother Thomas, known as Ed, was still in his teens. In a few years, all three were well known Tomales Township merchants. Middle brother William T. Cornett became proprietor of the Fallon store in 1900 . . . and served as a Tomales High School Trustee. The oldest and the youngest Cornett brothers soon followed in William's footsteps, and opened Cornett Brothers & Company in Tomales in 1901. Nathaniel Wesley (Nat) Cornett and Thomas E. (Ed) Cornett were partners until Nat moved to Southern California. Ed continued to operate Cornett's Store until he sold the business in 1944." (Courtesy of Dan Brown.)

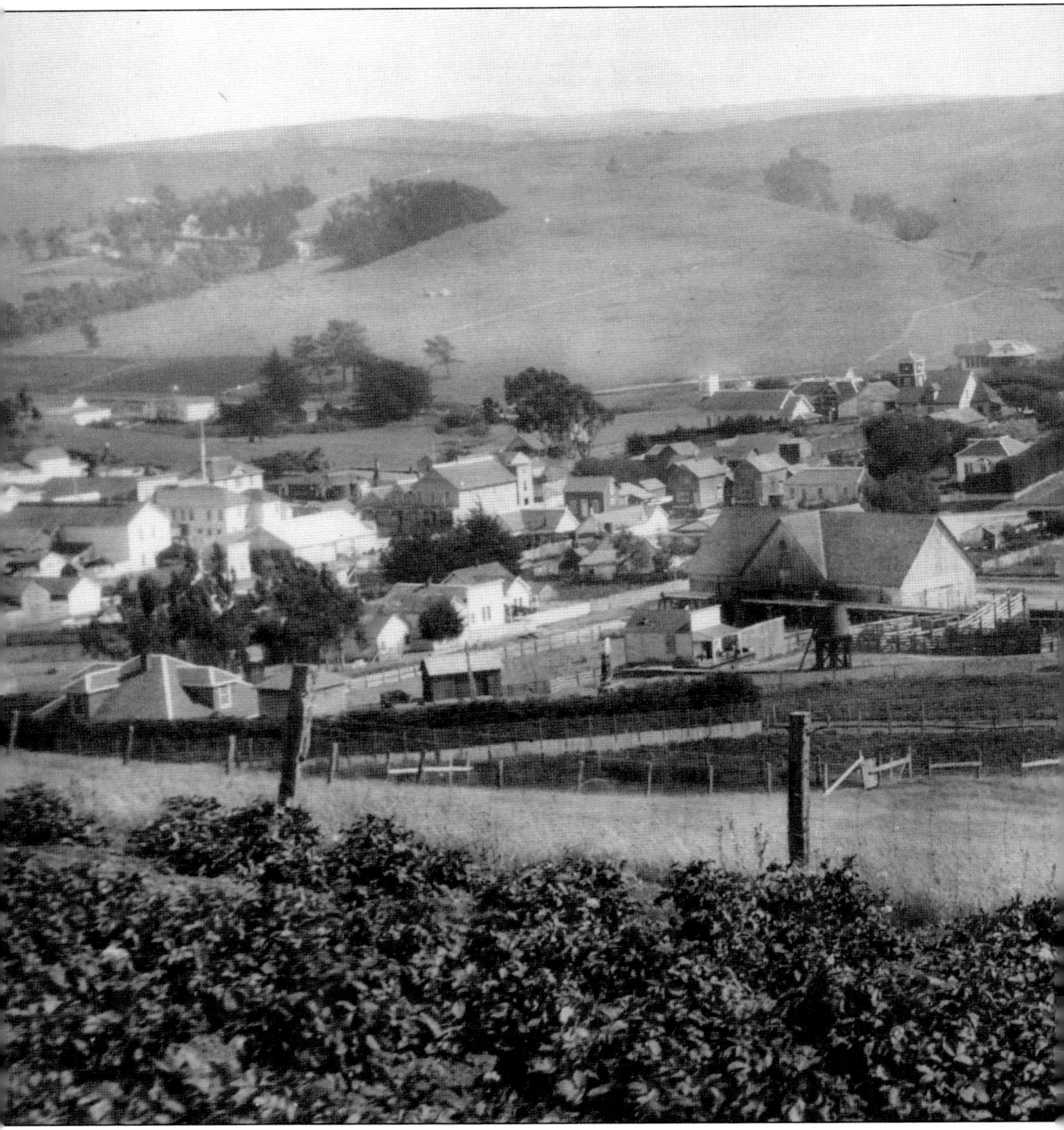

This 1915 photograph of Tomales from the collection of Roy Graves looks northeast with the narrow-gauge railroad in the foreground and the station and freight shed to the right. A. Bray Dickinson and his wife, Elaine, spent more than 10 years of research in order to get the complete story of the North Pacific Coast and its successors. *Narrow Gauge to the Redwoods*, featuring the photograph collection of Roy D. Graves, edited with added material by Ted Wurm and Alvin C. Graves, was published in 1967, nine years after the unexpected death of A. Bray Dickinson. In

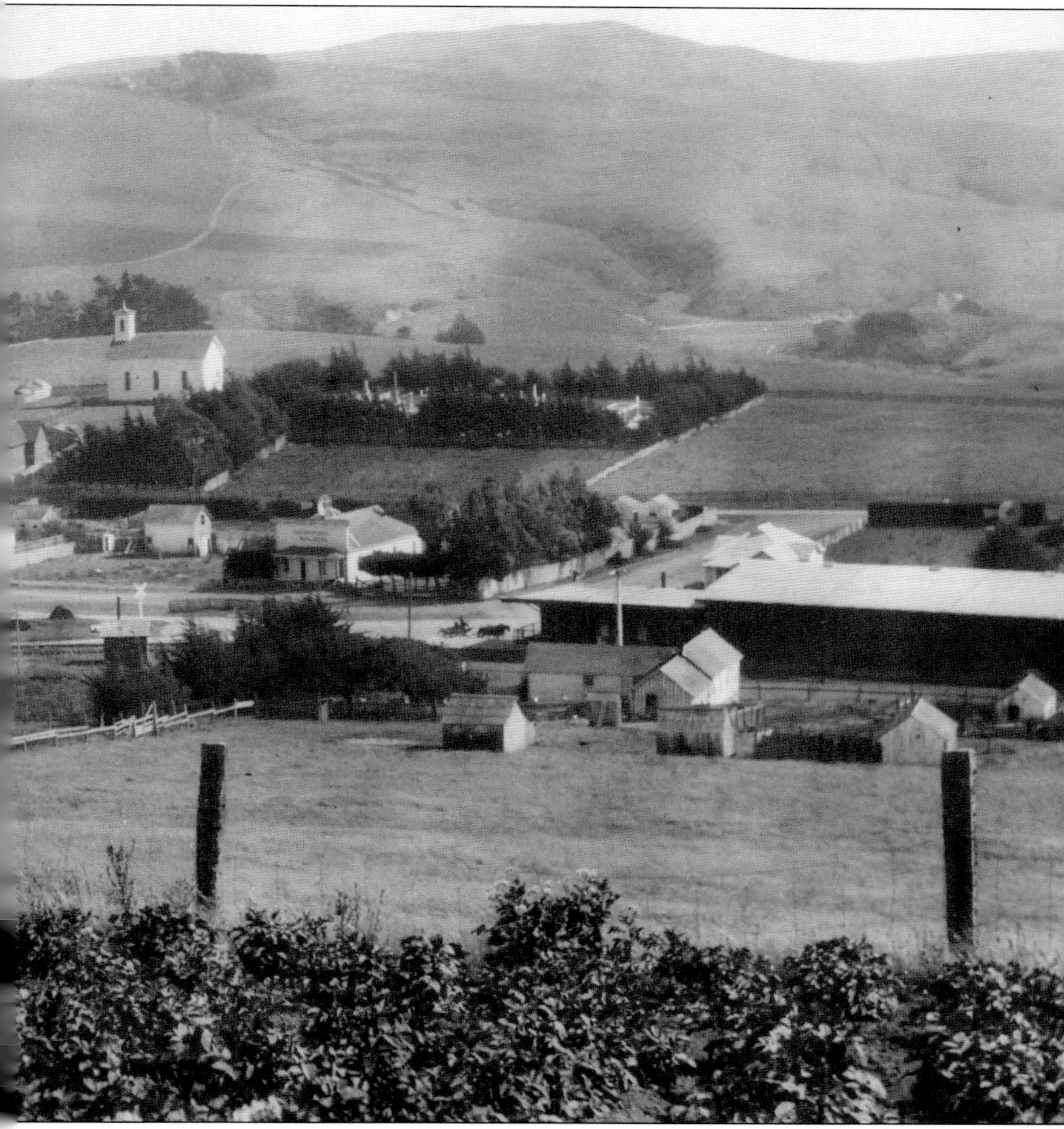

the 1870s, half of Marin County's population lived in and around Tomales and some of its richest businessmen, including Warren Dutton, owned large tracts at Tomales Bay. The narrow gauge was opened formally on Thursday, January 7, 1875, when 200 invited guests left San Francisco at 7:00 a.m. aboard the steamer *Petaluma*. Dickinson writes, "A train of two engines, two baggage cars, and six passenger coaches met the boat at Saucelito to carry the crowd over the entire length of the road. Nearly 100 additional passengers climbed aboard at San Rafael."

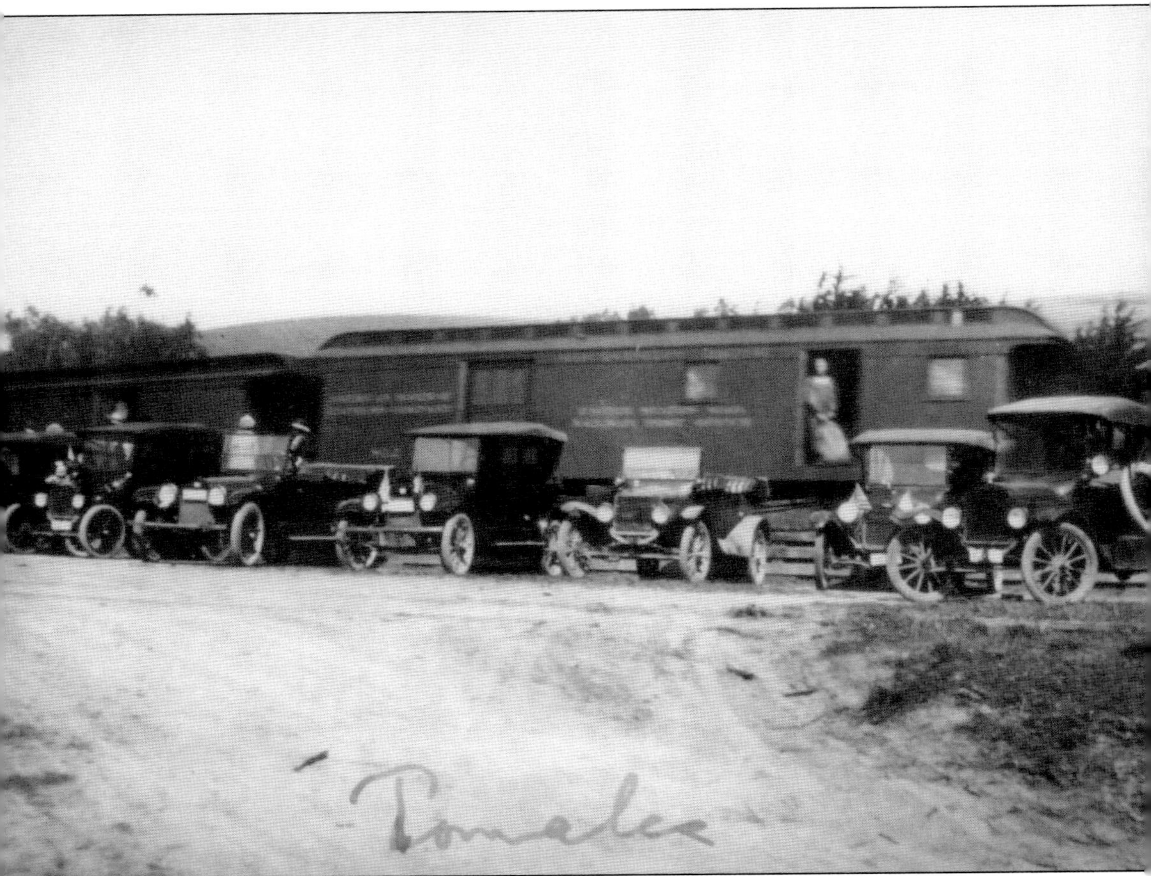

Dickinson continues: "When the train reached Tomales, people lined the hill tops, flags were flying, and the whole region had the appearance of a festival time. Jubilant greetings and handshaking marked the arrival of the cars 54 miles out from Saucelito at what was then the northern terminus of the railroad and would be for the next 18 months. Warren Dutton, a 49er turned farmer who was the town's leading citizen, made a speech of welcome; then the doors of the warehouse were thrown open to reveal tables stretching the entire length of the building loaded down with turkeys, chickens, lambs, pigs, beef and a profusion of pastries." Dutton had anticipated this day a year earlier when he erected this 70-by-300-foot warehouse. Through the entire length of the warehouse was a sunken railroad track, with the floor being level to the railroad car so that goods could be loaded with ease. The warehouse helped to avoid all the drawbacks of inclement weather. Dutton later sold the building to the railroad company for a considerable profit. (Courtesy of Dan Brown.)

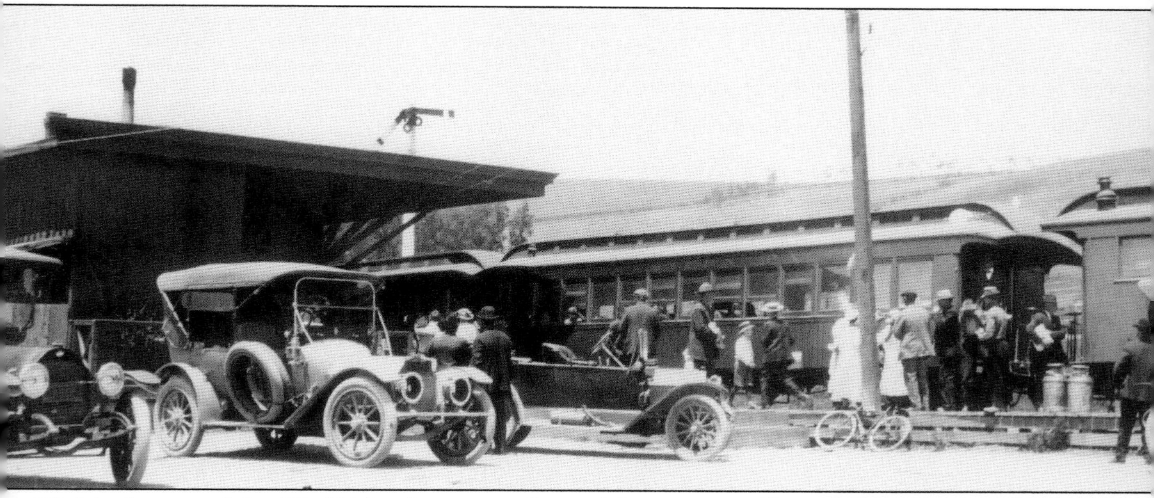

Of this photograph by Ella Frisbie Jorgensen, Ginny Magan writes: "Into the 20th century the narrow gauge railroad vitalized the Shoreline area villages, bringing them into maturity. At the Tomales depot, carts and a bicycle wait while passengers and those meeting them stand next to milk cans on the platform." It is not as though Tomales lacked modernity. Its pioneers were savvy businessmen who had forced the railroad to come to them, and they were going to take full advantage. These businessmen were knowledgeable on the political front as well. In 1853, as well as 1854, John Keys was elected to the Marin County Board of Supervisors. Warren Dutton became county assessor in 1854 and, in the 1870s, was still a member of the California State Board of Equalization. In the 1864 presidential election, Tomales voted 192 for Lincoln and 85 for McClennan. Though narrow gauge was eventually superseded, Tomales still prospered in the early 20th century from the popular "Triangle Trip" one-day 150-mile excursion from Sausalito to Monte Rio to Fulton and back to Sausalito on the Northwestern Pacific Railroad.

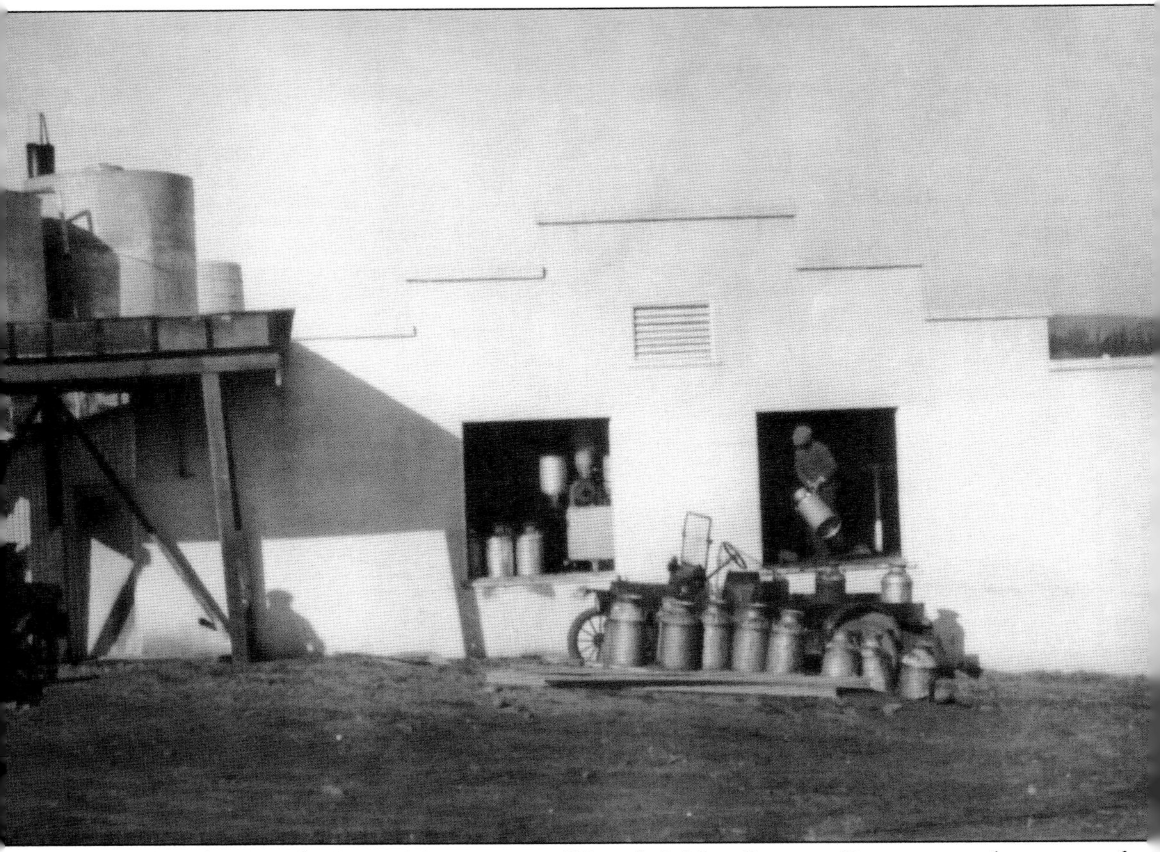

Of this photograph, Ginny Magan writes, "Tomales's New Sonoma Creamery, at the corner of John and First Streets, was built in 1924, and included state-of-the-art sterilizers and stainless steel tanks. Here, milk cans are being unloaded while empty cans wait for pick up." She continues, "Representing the Railroad and Automobile Era—the second phase of Tomales's Economic Development—the old creamery building was an extension of the thriving dairy industry of Western Marin and Sonoma Counties. . . . Operated by Giovanni Peluso and Serafino Iacono its primary products were 'Tomales Jack' and Romanello, both dry, Italian-style grating cheeses. In its heyday (1924–1960), the cheese factory employed ten men and for years was the largest employer in Tomales, using the product of 54 dairies as far away as Bodega, Sebastopol, Valley Ford and Two Rock as well as local Tomales ranches." (Courtesy of Dan Brown.)

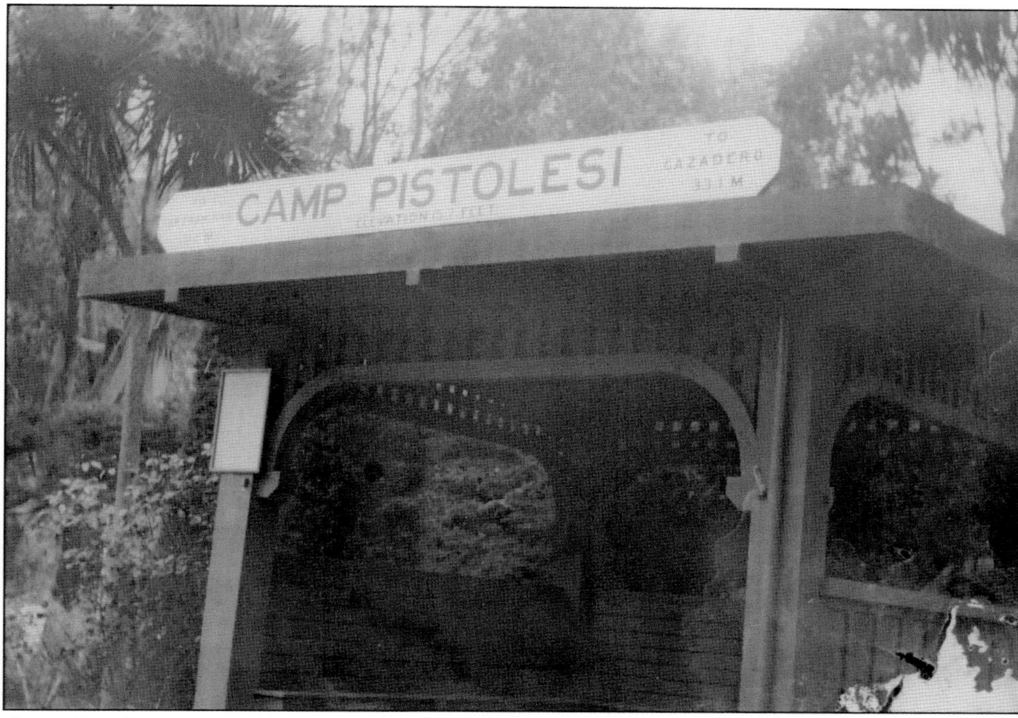

Camp Pistolesi was a resort just south of Tomales, established on Keys Creek where Walker Creek feeds into Keys Estuary. Located 51.2 miles from San Francisco and 33.1 miles from Cazadero with an elevation of 15.7 feet, it was developed by Sausalito lawyer Frank V. Pistolesi in 1902. The area below Tomales was once known as Coy's Tract. In new hands, the resort was renamed Camp Tomales, and in 1928, it advertised, "Groceries for sale, hunting, bathing on a fine sand beach (Keys Creek), little neck clams, abalones and a large dancing pavilion." There were small board-and-batten cabins quite close to the railroad tracks. Unfortunately, a train struck a deaf man here while he walked obliviously on the track.

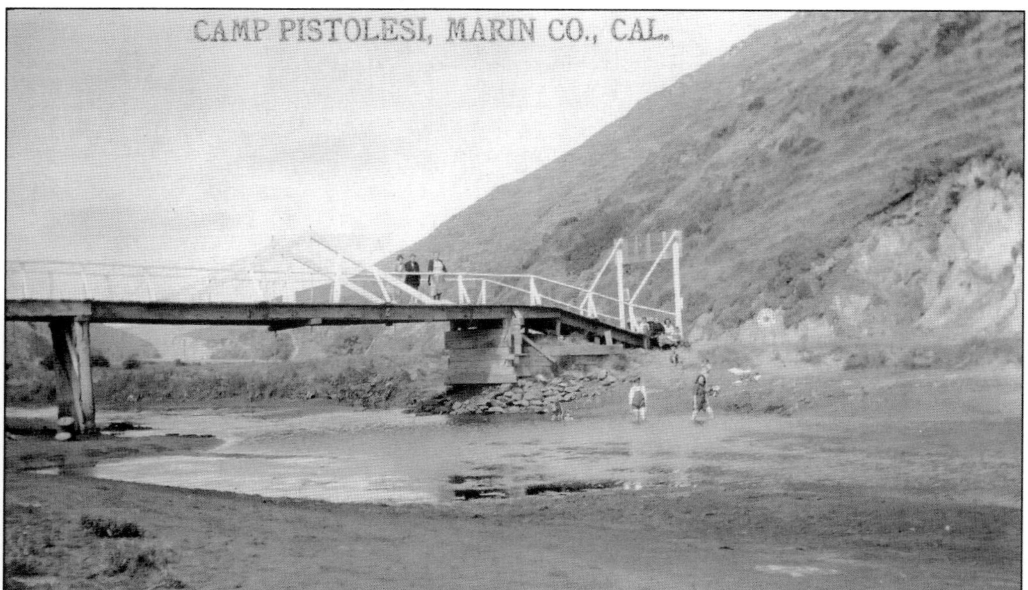

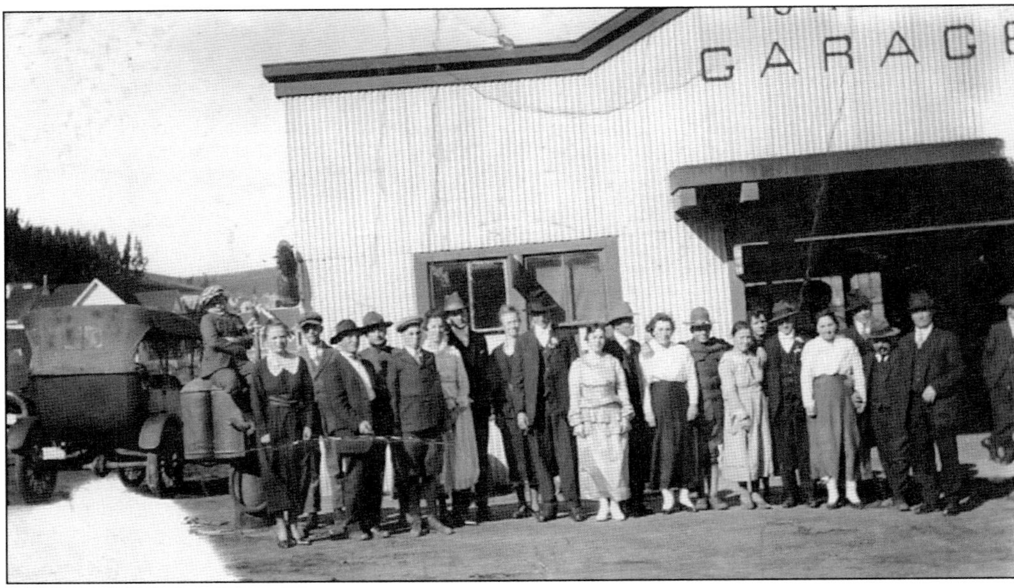

Today, California has more Swiss than any other state. From Ticino, the Italian-speaking canton of Switzerland, the first Ticinese came in the 1850s, attracted first by gold and then by dairying opportunities. Dickinson mentions that Giacondo Cerini's house was moved to its present location and enlarged in 1879. The Tomales Garage and Machine Shop at 98 Dillon Beach Road, owned in 1915 by Swiss immigrant Isadore Cerini (1883–1982) and his short-term partner Gene Pedrani, was the first business in town with a primary purpose to serve the emerging automobile industry. Ginny Magan came by this information through a 1998 interview with Eleanor Conroy, granddaughter of Isadore Cerini.

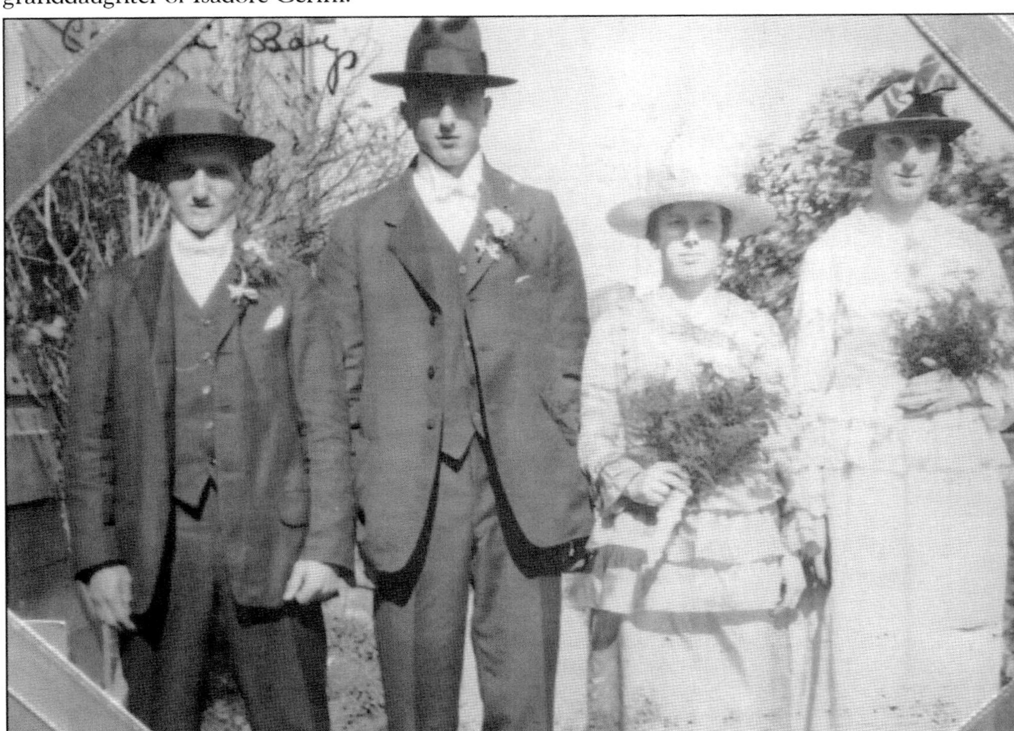

Ed Conti, who later built Isadore and Martha Cerini's family home at 125 Valley Avenue, as well as the William Tell house at 26955 State Highway 1, constructed the Tomales Garage and Machine Shop. Isadore and Martha Cerini's sons Roy and Theo took over the business in the late 1940s. Roy and his wife, Maxine, continued its operation until 1985. Silvio Piezzi, the uncle who sponsored his Cerini nephews Isadore, Giacondo, Sylvio, Romeo, Giovanni, and Arcangelo to come to America, created the Piezzi Garage at 27000 State Highway 1 in 1919. Arcangelo (August 4, 1896–August 14, 1940) and Mary (née Pacheco) Cerini (August 14, 1899–September 11, 1989) are pictured here; they were married (right) on February 17, 1919. True to his Ticinese background, Arcangelo became a dairy farmer and, with Mary, raised three sons and two daughters. Sadly, Arcangelo died on his wife's birthday.

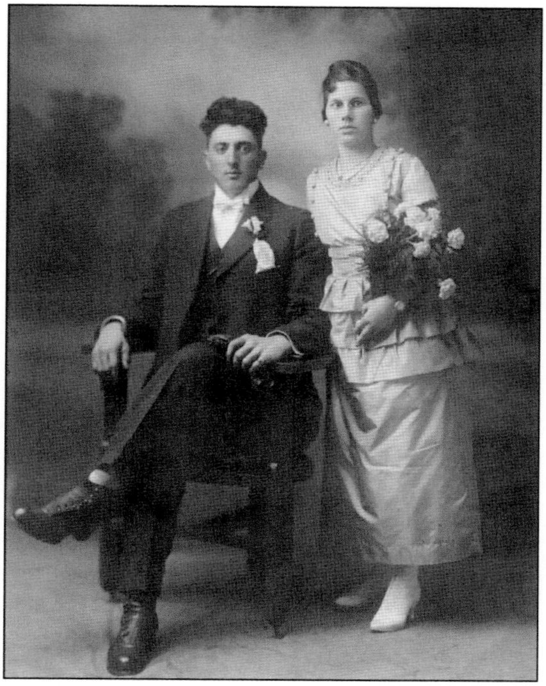

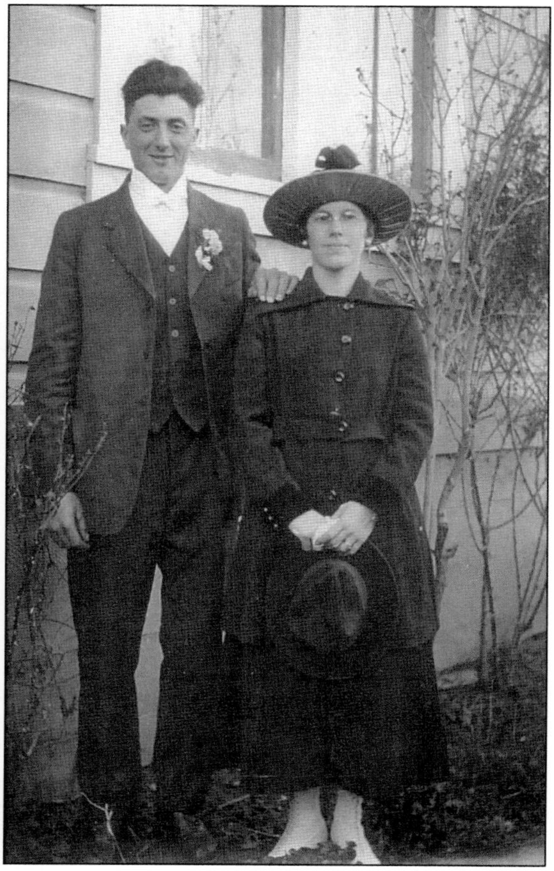

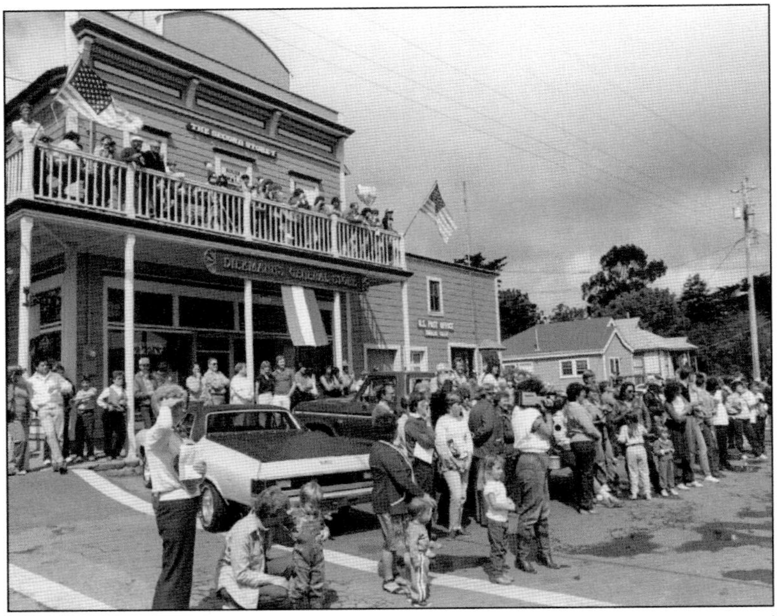

These two photographs showcase a recent Tomales Italian Club Parade, a century-old tradition. Ginny Magan noted: "The Italian Catholic Federation, apparently based on religion as well as nationality, started a Tomales branch around the turn of the 20th century; the group was to share the IOOF meeting hall above Leon Dickinson's general store. Its inaugural meeting was so well attended Mr. Dickinson became fearful that the second-story hall's floor would collapse, and the meetings were thereafter held at the town hall." Today, Diekmann's General Store has replaced Leon Dickinson's Store, the Second Storey has replaced the IOOF sign, and the post office has taken the place of A. Kahn's original Relief Saloon. Bordessa's Saloon, 280 Dillon Beach Road, named after Dave Bordessa (1875–1936), an Italian who immigrated at 14, was another gathering place for the parade around 1920. In the foreground below is the Anecleto Mazzucchi family composed of 41 relatives. Mother Venezia Mazzucchi was the Italian Club queen in 1921. (Both courtesy of Silsby Pelissero.)

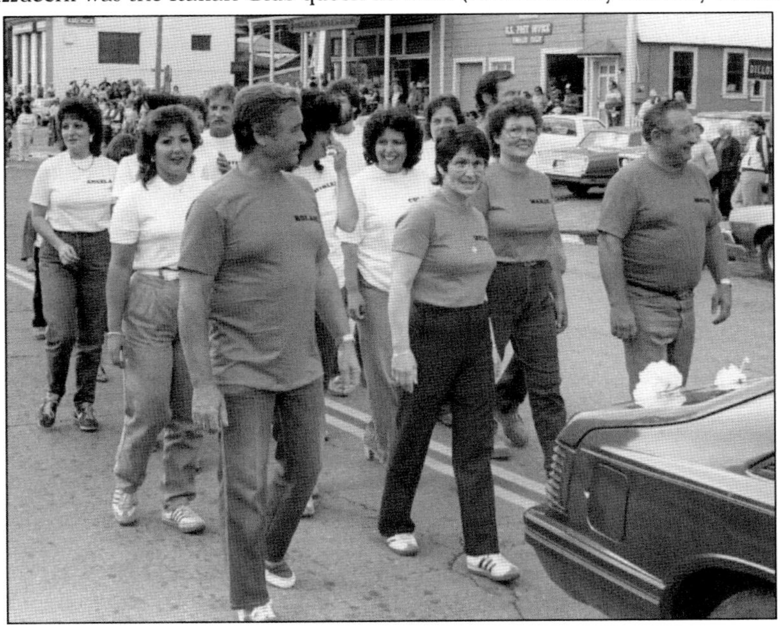

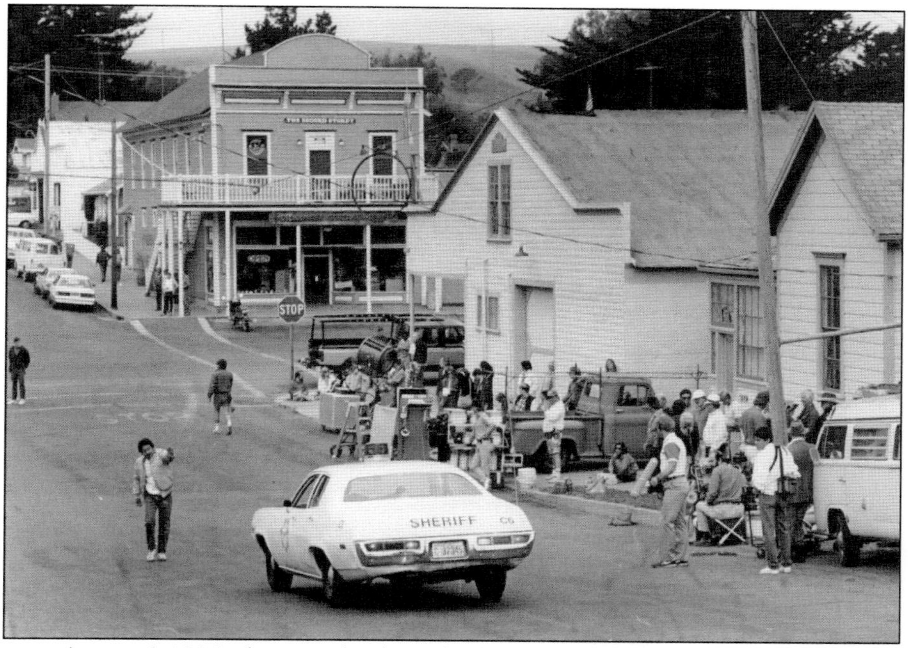

These two August 6, 1986, photographs show the filming of *Wild Fire*, starring Linda Fiorentino and Steven Bauer, directed by Zalman King. Parts of the movie *Village of the Damned* (1995), *Scream* (1996), and the opening shots of *Mumford* (1999) were filmed in Tomales. Film critic Rachel Dovey gave this review of *Mumford*: "The 1999 film *Mumford* begins with an old-timey shot of Tomales and the voiced-over line: 'I got out of the truck in this two-bit town.' But though the idyllic, fictional town of the movie's title is actually a mashup of nearly every Sonoma County city, the West Marin hamlet is not among them. Instead, Tomales forms the backdrop to a minor character's twisted fantasies, filled with obliging landladies, their even more obliging teenage daughters and nurses who know tricks 'they did not teach in nursing school.' " (Courtesy of M. Little.)

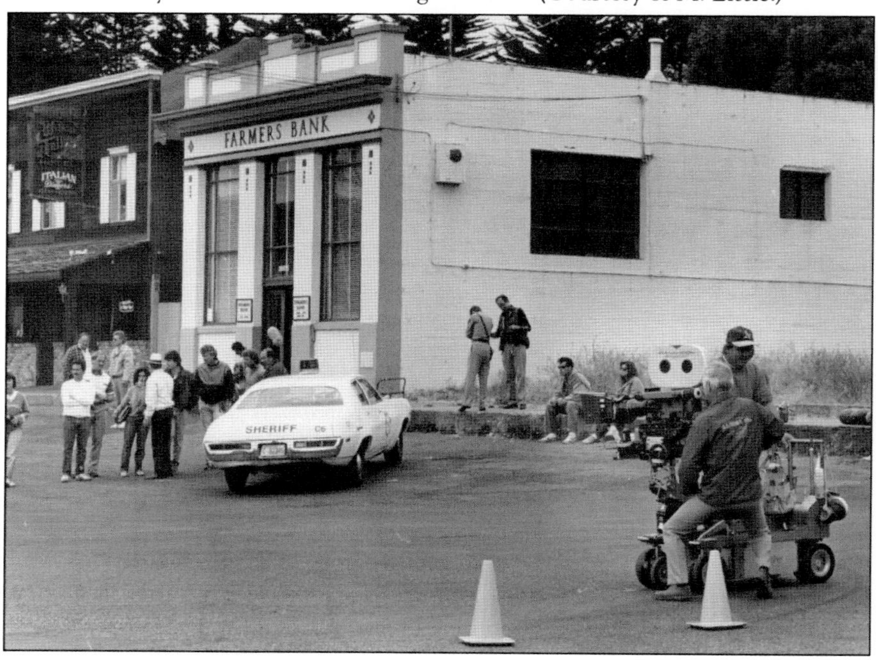

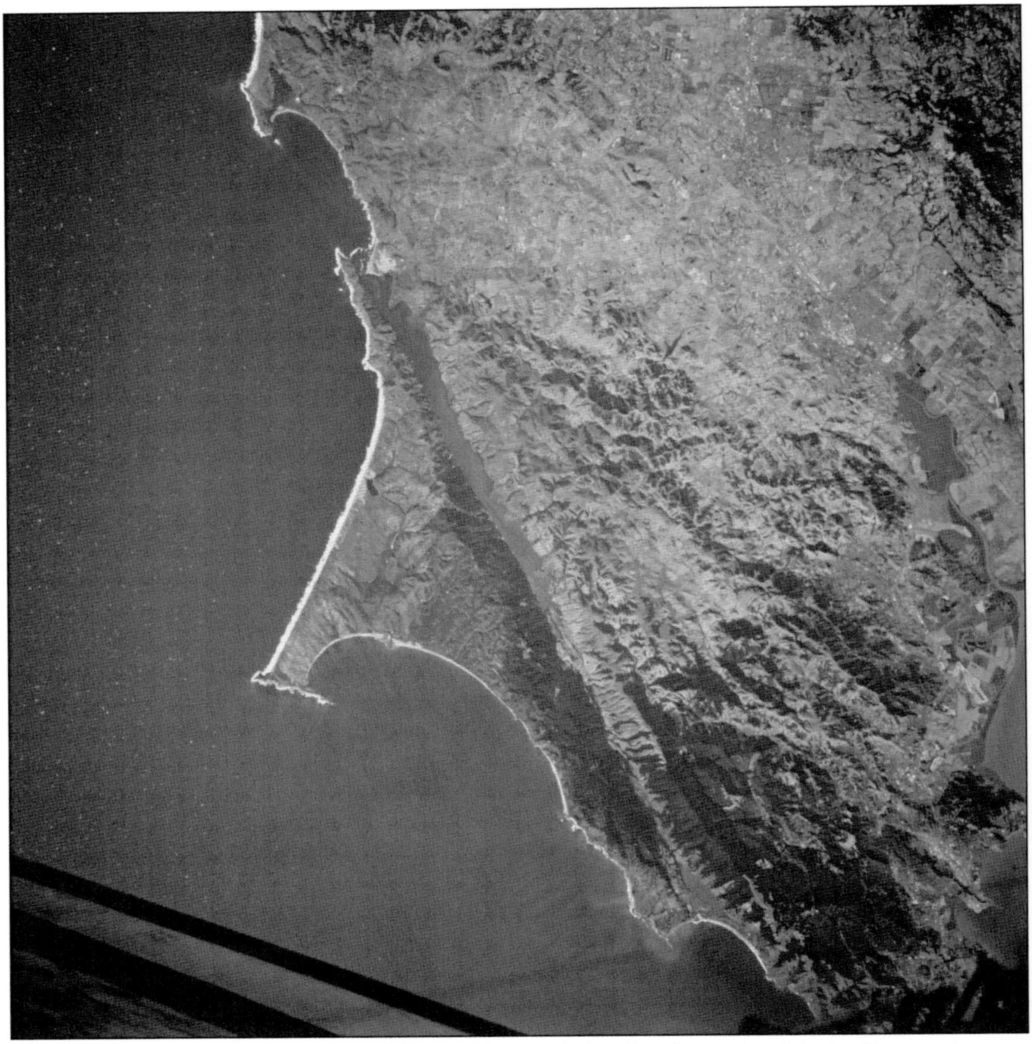

This image was taken from aboard Space Shuttle *Columbia*. For other Marin County images, please read the following Arcadia books: *Fairfax* by William Sagar, *Early Mill Valley* by Claudine Chalmers, *Mill Valley* by Suki Hill, *Hamilton Field* by Novato History Guild, *San Anselmo* by Judy Coy, *Early San Rafael* by the Marin History Museum, *Marin County* by Branwell Fanning, *Marin Headlands* by Dorothy Gibson, *Maritime Marin* by Branwell Fanning, *Modern San Rafael: 1940–2000* by the Marin History Museum, *Nicasio* by Anne M. Papina, *Houseboats of Sausalito* by Phil Frank, *Sausalito* by the Sausalito Historical Society, *Angel Island* by Branwell Fanning, *Tiburon and Belvedere* by Branwell Fanning, *The Tiburon Peninsula* by Branwell Fanning, *Bolinas and Stinson Beach* by the Bolinas Museum, and especially *Point Reyes Peninsula: Olema, Point Reyes Station, and Inverness* by Carola DeRooy and Dewey Livingston, the companion volume to *Tomales Bay*. (Courtesy of Image Science and Analysis Laboratory, NASA-Johnson Space Center. "The Gateway to Astronaut Photography of Earth.")

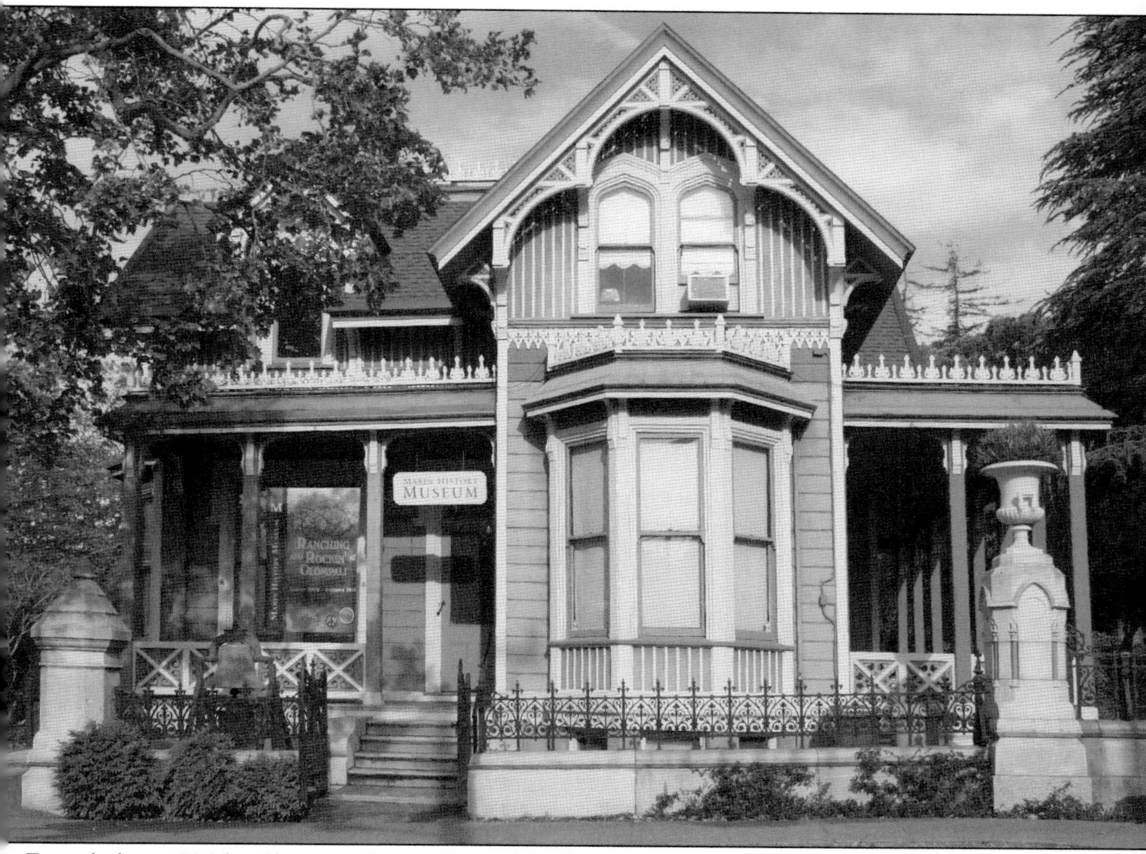

Founded in 1935 by Florence Donnelly and Belle Brown, the Marin History Museum is a multicampus, nonprofit museum, which celebrates Marin County's history through exhibitions, programs, and collections. Since 1959, the museum has been located in the Boyd Gate House, which is listed in the US Department of the Interior's National Register of Historic Places. The Boyd Gate House is open Tuesdays through Saturdays from 11:00 a.m. to 4:00 p.m. and until 8:00 p.m. on Thursdays. The museum cares for over 20,000 artifacts and 200,000 photographic images in its Research Center, located in Novato. These materials are available to the public, and researchers are encouraged to explore their family roots and local history. Like us on Facebook, follow us on Twitter, and visit our website: www.marinhistory.org.

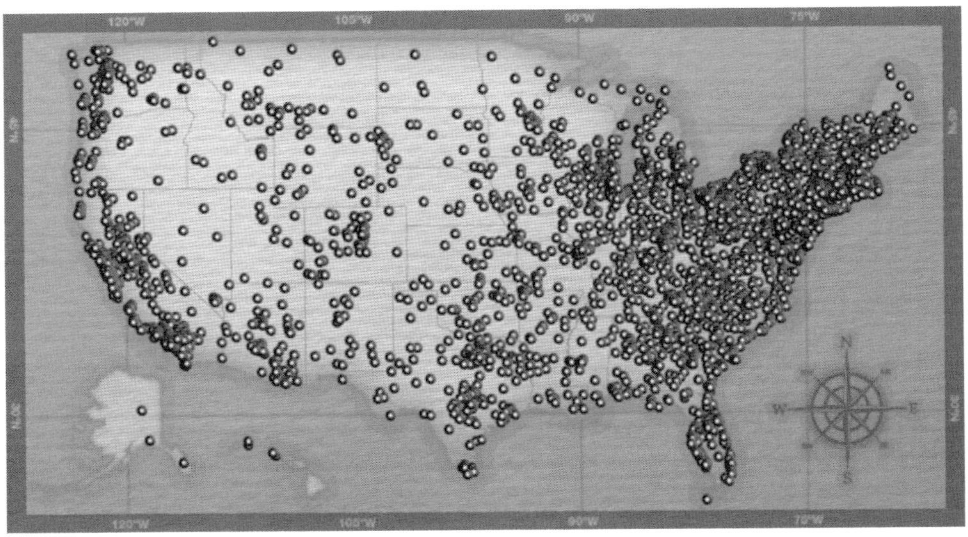

Consistent with our mission to preserve history on a local level, this book was printed in South Carolina on American-made paper and manufactured entirely in the United States. Products carrying the accredited Forest Stewardship Council (FSC) label are printed on 100 percent FSC-certified paper.

MADE IN THE USA